CW00720035

Shooting to Kill

This book is dedicated to the memory of over
3500 untimely deaths during the "Troubles"

Shooting to Kill
Filmmaking and the "Troubles" in Northern Ireland

Brian McIlroy

FLICKS
BOOKS

A CIP catalogue record for this book is available from the British Library.

ISBN 0 948911 52 2 (Hb)
ISBN 0 948911 53 0 (Pb)

First published in 1998 by

Flicks Books
29 Bradford Road
Trowbridge
Wiltshire BA14 9AN
England
tel +44 1225 767728
fax +44 1225 760418

© Brian McIlroy, 1998

All rights reserved. No part of this publication may be reproduced, stored in a retrieval system or transmitted in any form or by any means: electronic, electrostatic, magnetic tape, mechanical, photocopying, recording or otherwise, without prior permission in writing from the publishers.

Printed and bound in Great Britain by Bookcraft (Bath) Ltd.

Contents

Acknowledgments

This book has been researched with the help of a grant from the Social Sciences and Humanities Research Council of Canada. A wide variety of people have given intellectual, moral and practical support for this project. I would like to thank Donald Harman Akenson, Arthur Aughey, Terence Black, Jennifer Cornell, Wheeler Winston Dixon, Lynn Doyle, John Wilson Foster, Lester Friedman, Joan Harcourt and the reviewers for the Aid to Scholarly Publications Programme, Cheryl Herr, Kathleen McCracken, James MacKillop, Eve Shamash and Justin Wyatt. I also owe a debt of gratitude to Gillian Coward and Phyllis McKay of the Film and Sound Resource Unit at the University of Ulster at Coleraine; the staff of the Northern Ireland Political Collection at the Linen Hall Library, Belfast; Liam Wylie and Sunniva O'Flynn at the Irish Film Archive at the Film Institute of Ireland in Dublin; Christine Chisholm at the Northern Ireland Film Council; Janet Moat and Tessa Forbes at the British Film Institute's Reference Library and Special Collections; Ekta Nadeau of the A/V Services in the Faculty of Arts at the University of British Columbia; and staff members Gail Oelkers, Richard Payment and Craig Volker in the Film Program in the Department of Theatre, Film and Creative Writing at the University of British Columbia. I would also like to thank Bernice O'Donoghue and Grainne McAleer of the Film Institute of Ireland for inviting me to the "Imagining Ireland" Conference in Dublin in October 1993, where some of the ideas in this book were first postulated. Every writer owes gratitude to editors of journals and books for publishing earlier versions of essays, and I am no exception. An early version of chapter 1 was published as "When the Ulster Protestant and Unionist Looks: Spectatorship in (Northern) Irish Cinema", *Irish University Review* 26: 1 (spring/summer 1996): 143-154. Thanks are due to editor Christopher Murray. An embryonic version of what has turned out to be this book was published as "The Repression of Communities: Visual Representations of Northern Ireland during the Thatcher Years", in Lester Friedman (ed), *Fires Were Started: British Cinema and Thatcherism* (Minneapolis: University of Minnesota Press, 1993): 92-108.

For illustrations, I would like to thank Stephen Burke, Anne Crilly, Paul Donovan, Jacqueline Etheridge at the BFI Stills, Posters and Designs, Louise Faulkner-Corbett and Julia Aldhamland at Channel 4, First Run Icarus Films, David Fox, Margo Harkin, David Hyndman, Bobbie Mitchell of the BBC Photographic Library, James Mitchell, Aletta and Matthew Stevens, and Justin Wyatt.

Preface

The Northern Irish raise special problems when British national identity is being discussed, and since I could not hope to do justice to these problems I shall simply set them to one side. (David Miller)[1]

Taking into account the equivalent proportion of victims to population, Northern Ireland's death toll...would translate into about 500,000 deaths for the US or approximately ten times the American death toll in Vietnam. (Paul Power)[2]

The subject of this book has a personal interest for me which goes far beyond the academic. My formative years in Northern Ireland in the 1970s coincided with the worst of the "Troubles". Growing up in Belfast at that time was a wonderful experience from a historical, political and ethnographical point of view, but it frequently resembled a dark theatre of the absurd and sometimes a veritable theatre of cruelty. As the quotations above signify, the political and historical disagreements were so deeply felt and the violence so pervasive that it affected all kinds of social activity. I count myself fortunate not to have been physically scarred; I would, however, suggest that everyone living in Northern Ireland has been affected by the conflict in important psychological ways.

In talking to other people who grew up in Northern Ireland, I have discovered that my own experiences were quite normal or surprisingly quiet. The perception of violence is always relative. My normal experiences included the IRA killing of a former friend in a premature bomb explosion; the IRA bombing of another friend's house in our street, and the severe wounding of his father; the rather bizarre experience of going into a city to school every day while bombs were exploding (I remember one bomb explosion smashed a fair number of windows during a Latin class, lifting our desks slightly off the ground); the fear that periodically gripped everyone at the sight of marauding gangs – on one occasion, a few of us, chased by a Protestant gang who were convinced (wrongly) that we were Catholics, escaped only by entering the Linen Hall

Library in Belfast (thank goodness one of us had a membership, our pursuers had none!); the invasion of our own property by a gang who were running from the British Army; the intimidation of a Catholic friend's family who subsequently moved to the Republic of Ireland in mysterious circumstances; and the anonymous threats made against our Protestant neighbours who felt forced to move away.

One of the fascinations of living in Belfast was that one could on occasion compare what one saw on the streets with the evening news. My generation became media-literate very quickly, even though media studies in the 1970s did not exist for us at secondary school level. We knew at school that there was an unresolved question being contested daily – the gunfire we heard while studying First World War poetry has always stuck in my mind as a near-perfect merging of form and content – and that we would have to confront it some day. Too often, we were simply just trying to keep out of harm's way.

Nevertheless, I recall attending Current Affairs and Debating Society meetings to hear and question political figures such as William Craig, Gerry Fitt, Brian Faulkner and Enoch Powell; being frogmarched by our teacher-poet Frank Ormsby to go to hear poetry readings by John Hewitt; learning from teacher Tom Bartlett that history is a noble, if contentious, discipline; enjoying the Film Society for its programme of films which suggested that the world was a much larger place than our own experiences would allow. Even the entrance to my school, rather portentously named The Royal Belfast Academical Institution ("Inst"), was a conflicted space. A statue of Henry Cooke, the 19th-century Presbyterian preacher who opposed the liberal educational values that my school espoused, stood with his disapproving back facing the school gates. In the inimitable way of Dissenter culture, we had been truly shunned by the statue, known locally as the "black man". This intellectual and historical rejection did not worry us at the time; we had Protestant and Catholic teachers, although few Catholic students, due to the Roman Catholic Church's hold over Catholic education. We played rugby and cricket, although we did try our hand at shinty and handball, sports not associated specifically with British culture. We had an English principal who assiduously avoided controversy and remained unflappable through bomb scares. At one parents' evening, the sound of an enormous bomb explosion shook the hall in which we had all assembled, only for the principal to drily remark, "If you go in the direction of the bomb, you'll find some refreshments". Black humour, a northern Irish trait, saw us through some very dark days.

This background in literature, history, film and personal experience has in large measure led to this book, an examination of how the euphemistically named "Troubles" have been represented in narrative and documentary film and video, and television drama. At a time of increasing residential, social and work segregation of Catholics and Protestants in Northern Ireland, and yet also at a time of complicated framework proposals and forums for peace, British and Irish filmmakers and videographers have an important part to play in the reflection upon and mediation among the various participants. It is time to take stock of these roles, and this inventory and analysis represent the modest aim of this book.

Notes

[1]   David Miller, *On Nationality* (Oxford: Clarendon Press, 1995): 173n25.

[2]   Paul Power, *Irish Literary Supplement* 12: 2 (autumn 1993): 31.

Introduction

The visitors' book was still in the dining room so I went in, ready to sign my name. The couple from Omagh had each signed, giving their full names and address. When it came to nationality, they had both signed themselves British. I had always known that Protestants in the North considered themselves British, but when I saw it there in fresh biro it came as a shock. They were from Omagh, they talked with Omagh accents. How could they be British? (Colm Tóibín)[1]

The purpose of this book is to establish in what ways Irish and British films, television dramas and videos have represented the Northern Ireland conflict.[2] It argues that the prevailing visualisation of the "Troubles" in drama and documentary, particularly in the 1980s and 1990s, is dominated by Irish nationalist and republican ideology. It also posits several subtheses: that this tendency can be traced back to such classic films as Carol Reed's *Odd Man Out* (1946); that video is the form most favoured for radical opinions; that British television drama locks itself into a "soft" nationalist position; and that the Protestant community is constantly elided by both British and Irish filmmakers and videographers who prefer to accept the anti-imperialist view of Northern Ireland's existence. This latter point, the limited – or lack of – treatment of the Protestant community, is a recurrent theme throughout my analysis.[3]

Screening Northern Ireland during the "Troubles" has always been a difficult geographical and national question. To begin with, throughout the worst of the disturbances, production companies could not film on location (mostly due to high insurance). Secondly, northern Irish people rarely had the opportunity to use film to represent themselves and their conflict. Thirdly, most television dramas and documentaries commissioned and broadcast from Northern Ireland which deal with the "Troubles" tended to be obsessed with liberal balance, thereby risking misrepresentation of the key ideological splits in the community at large. Fourthly, too often the northern Irish cities and countryside became an opaque background to standard genres, often the revenge tragedy or thriller.

1

Despite these handicaps and economic determinants, films, television dramas and videos written or directed by Irish people have slowly begun to dominate perceptions of the northern conflict. From mainstream films to independent film and video workshops in Belfast and Derry, to specific filmmakers and videographers, Irish people, together with some English, have played a major role in reconfiguring the "simplistic" representations of Northern Ireland by English and North American news media. Implicit within this body of mainly Irish films and videos is an attempt to frame the "Troubles" into a more overtly historical, political and feminist "struggle". While this movement is welcome generally, as it shows an independence from "mainland" Britain's "imperial" perception of the violence, it still can become captive of an equally powerful yet emotionally stunted rhetoric: that of Irish nationalism in full poetic flight, with its exclusionist tendencies to emphasise "blood and belonging".[4] In other words, a paradigm shift has occurred in public consciousness from the "inexplicable Troubles" of the 1970s to the "overdetermined Struggle" of the 1980s and 1990s. This book concentrates on the latter period, and, as the text develops, I move from consideration of narrative fiction to documentary.

The methodology employed in this book – cultural materialism – is introduced in the first two chapters. In "Cultural and critical contexts", I survey and define the borders of the northern Irish conflict. This necessitates definitions of Irish nationalism, republicanism, unionism and loyalism, as well as a discussion of cultural Irish nationalism and Protestant cultural production. In this chapter I also explain how feminist film theory and spectatorship theory lead to my argument that a form of political spectatorship needs to be adopted to appreciate the visual material relating to the "Troubles". To illustrate briefly the spectatorship and masquerades of the Ulster Protestant and unionist evident throughout this book, I discuss a number of short films and videos that make such an approach enabling and instructive.

In chapter 2, "Historical and political contexts", I chronicle the major events in Irish and northern Irish history that are frequently taken for granted in the films, television dramas and videos that I analyse elsewhere in the book. I also raise the thorny issue of revisionism in Irish history, which has spilled over into culture and politics. In this connection, I explain Tom Nairn's notion of the anti-imperialist myth, a political structure of understanding which I believe has had a dominant impact on cultural production in and about Ireland.

One of the best-known films set in Northern Ireland is the subject of chapter 3. In "The Rorschach test: anti-imperialism in Carol Reed's *Odd Man Out*", I illustrate by textual and contextual means how Nairn's twin myths of "atavism" and "anti-imperialism"[5] inform this classic work of British cinema. Contrary to previous criticism, I argue that the anti-imperialist myth is at the base of the film's structure. Chapter 4, "Troubled fictions: contemporary Irish film", focuses on features directed by Irish filmmakers Neil Jordan (*Angel*, 1982; *The Crying Game*, 1992); Pat O'Connor (*Cal*, 1984); Jim Sheridan (*In the Name of the Father*, 1993; *The Boxer*, 1997), Joe Comerford (*High Boot Benny*, 1993) and Terry George (*Some Mother's Son*, 1996), and reveals how each work marginalises the Protestant and unionist position.

Equally marginalised in these films are the aspirations of women, the topic of chapter 5, "Irish herstories; or what feminism thinks of republicanism". Here I consider four Irish films – Pat Murphy and John Davies' *Maeve* (1981), Margo Harkin's *Hush-A-Bye Baby* (1989), Orla Walsh's *The Visit* (1992) and Stephen Burke's *After '68* (1994) – that raise often-unexplored women's issues in relation to the "Troubles". These films argue that feminism may often coincide with republicanism, but at important junctures they must part company.

Chapter 6, "The elephant at the kitchen sink: British social realists", profiles the work on Northern Ireland by Englishmen Alan Clarke, Ken Loach and Mike Leigh. Each has his own distinctive style, but the soft and sometimes hard nationalist positions of these filmmakers readily come to the fore when their productions are even lightly scrutinised. Chapter 7, "'I want out of this bloody country': British television drama", interrogates selected BBC Northern Ireland (BBC-NI) and other British television dramas which dwell on the "Troubles". Here, I argue that a soft nationalist position is strongly present in their conception and execution.

In turning mainly to the consideration of the documentary over the next four chapters, I have inevitably been selective. The major decision has been to focus on independently-made documentaries, those not emerging from an established television station. Although these independents must sell their concept and completed programme to one of these very stations (since theatrical release is unusual), I believe that these productions bring us closer to ground-level politics. This explains why I have focused on local documentary productions. Chapter 8, "Gorillas without lipstick: the documentaries of Northern Visions", examines one of the leading independent video houses in Belfast and discusses six of their programmes, while chapter 9, "The feminist historical and political documentary reconsidered: Anne Crilly's *Mother Ireland*", looks at Derry Film and Video Workshop's major documentary and its ramifications. By way of comparison, chapter 10, "Unacceptable levels: losses and games", explores the work of British and European-funded feature docudrama and documentary films, such as John Davies' *Acceptable Levels* (1984) and Marcel Ophüls' *A Sense of Loss* (1972), and argues that there are surprising similarities with the home-grown product. In the films and videos discussed in these three chapters, the general sympathy is directed towards nationalist and republican political positions.

Chapter 11, "'We'll fight and no surrender': Protestant visions", considers Thaddeus O'Sullivan's fictional narrative, *Nothing Personal* (1995), and documentary films and videos by Protestants John T Davis and Desmond Bell. These unusual Protestant visual representations are particularly critical of the majority community's unionist and loyalist traditions. That few sympathetic treatments of Protestantism (and unionism) exist is reinforced by this critique from within their natural community. The book concludes with some reflections on the role that narrative and documentary films can play in the debate over Northern Ireland.

Undeniably, the British media, by which I mean chiefly the television news media, have been guilty of oversimplification, and have often followed the government's desire to emphasise its various policies, such as "Ulsterisation" (the attempt to put the Royal Ulster Constabulary [RUC] presence front and centre over the Army) and "criminalisation" (the labelling of the IRA as wealthy godfathers, evil men, and so on). As the British media, including BBC-NI and Ulster Television (UTV) in the province, endeavoured to broadcast to a divided community, razor-sharp investigative reporting often went missing. To report and to make programmes on Northern Ireland involve the producer and director in a series of complicated moves, including self-censorship. For that reason, much television news is decontextualised, in much the same way that the snapshot by the freelance photographer of a rioter in the middle of a street disturbance (which the national newspapers in England invariably use with a short and misleading caption) is decontextualised. One expects more from films, television dramas and videos (all of which eventually end up on television). They have the opportunity to provide this framework, to contribute to the debate in a more productive way than the news. As a work of criticism, rather than history or theory, this book explores how many of these films negotiate or avoid that context.

Notes

[1] Colm Tóibín, *Bad Blood: A Walk Along The Irish Border* (London: Vintage, 1994): 93.

[2] I have deliberately set to one side North American depictions or use of the "Troubles", as they tend slavishly to follow standard generic forms, often using Northern Ireland as a convenient metaphor for unmotivated violence. A good example of this is Phillip Noyce's *Patriot Games* (1992), which revolves around a CIA agent fending off an avenging IRA man. In chapter 10, I do look at several European-funded films. It is also unnecessary for my purpose here to discuss each and every one of the films which belong to the corpus relevant to my theme. For example, I do not discuss Kieron Walsh's *Bossanova Blues* (1991), which uses the violence in the North to wrap up its mainly southern Irish tale; Peter Smith's *No Surrender* (1985), which looks humorously at the two

communities transplanted in England; Tony Luraschi's *The Outsider* (1979), which focuses on an American recruit for the IRA; Milad Bessada's *A Quiet Day in Belfast* (1973), which depicts the outrages of the early 1970s bombings and shootings all too graphically; Karl Francis' *Boy Soldier* (1986), which dwells on the trials and tribulations of a Welsh soldier who has killed an Irish Catholic civilian; John MacKenzie's *The Long Good Friday* (1979), which seems to portray the IRA as an invincible force; Mike Hodges' *A Prayer For the Dying* (1987), a rather embarrassing vehicle for Mickey Rourke to play an IRA terrorist with a conscience; Bill Miskelly and Marie Jones' *The End of the World Man* (1985), a light-hearted children's film which highlights the ecological battles in the North; Don Sharp's *Hennessy* (1975), which stars Rod Steiger as a crazed IRA man intent on blowing up the Westminster Parliament after his wife and child are killed in a Belfast street riot; George Schaefer's *Children in the Crossfire* (1985), a feel-good American television movie which sought to focus on children from the "Troubles" brought to California to mix together in peaceful surroundings; Richard Spence's *You, Me and Marley* (1992), which draws on the problem of punishment shootings and teenage joyriding in nationalist/republican areas; Michael Whyte's *The Railway Station Man* (1992), which recounts the tale of a RUC widow trying to restart her life in the Republic of Ireland, only to lose her son to further political violence; Ceri Sherlock's *Branwen* (1995), which tries to link Welsh and Irish nationalism. For a discussion of some of these films, see my *World Cinema 4: Ireland* (Trowbridge: Flicks Books, 1989): 59-88; my "The Repression of Communities: Visual Representations of Northern Ireland during the Thatcher Years", in Lester Friedman (ed), *Fires Were Started: British Cinema and Thatcherism* (Minneapolis: University of Minnesota Press, 1993): 92-108; and my "Liminal Lives: Irish Emigrant and Immigrant Films", in Robin Burns and Michael Kenneally (eds), *The Irish Overseas in Fact and Imagination* (Amsterdam: Rodopi Press, forthcoming, 1999).

[3]   I have chosen not to dwell on Edward Bennett's *Ascendancy* (1982) in the text proper, even though it is a film that technically puts Ulster Unionism front and centre. However, as the film concentrates on the War of Independence period of 1920 in the North, it technically falls outside my analysis of the Northern Ireland state and cultural production. In addition, Bennett's film somewhat too enthusiastically equates unionism with sectarianism, militarism and violence to bear much scrutiny. The main female character, who is a partially paralysed upper-class Protestant who wanders around in shock for most of the film, leaves little to the imagination.

[4]   Michael Ignatieff, *Blood and Belonging: Journeys into the New Nationalism* (London: Vintage, 1994).

[5]   Tom Nairn, *The Break-Up of Britain: Crisis and Neo-Nationalism*, second expanded edition (London: Verso, 1981): 222.

5

1

Cultural and critical contexts

[T]here are many ways of being Irish, and I suppose that
Protestant Unionist is one of them. (Neil Jordan)[1]

Unionists are not reluctant nationalists, waiting to be enticed
or persuaded into a united Ireland by the generosity of
Dublin. (The Cadogan Group)[2]

Culture is a sort of theater where various political and
ideological causes engage one another. (Edward Said)[3]

In the late-1980s, I wrote a short book on Irish cinema history which
was intended merely to urge an awareness of the possibilities and
ramifications of an Irish visual culture, consideration of which had,
to some extent, been neglected.[4] Since then, we have seen a virtual
explosion in interest in Irish film, both creative and academic in
focus.[5] This interest parallels exciting developments in fine arts,
popular music, literature and theatre. With the Irish Film Centre
and Film Institute in Dublin, including an archive and library, the
Northern Ireland Film Council, various publications such as the
magazine *Film Ireland*; the Liam O'Leary Film Archives in the
National Library, the Irish Film Board, and the numerous home-
grown production companies, Ireland now demands a much more
sophisticated approach to film culture and film's relationship to
society at large.

The debate has moved on, but perhaps it is currently fiercer. The
infrastructure or base, although needing consolidation, is in place.
What seems now to be an important question is whether the
superstructure – in particular, the films on Northern Ireland, short
or long, documentary or narrative fiction, made by Irish and non-
Irish people – is geared to advance in a constructive way the
necessity of dialogue within Northern Ireland today and among
Northern Ireland's communities, the Republic of Ireland and Great
Britain.

The preceding paragraph contains within it a number of
assumptions which need to be elaborated. The most problematic for

many observers is that film, culture and politics are intertwined in Ireland in such a way that no artefact can easily escape into art for art's sake. Indeed, one Dublin production company conscious of this stricture actually advertised its forthcoming film by referring to what it is *not* about – namely, "the IRA, 'the land,' or drugs".[6] Nearly all the productions I discuss dwell on permutations of the first two topics. The relationship between culture and politics has always been a fascinating one in Ireland, and this book is an addition to that body of literature.

Another assumption is that films, television dramas and videos (the core of the material I analyse here) can affect people's views on their social and political status, and also affect those not living in Northern Ireland but who have an indirect influence over policy there: the voting populations of Great Britain, the Republic of Ireland and the United States. Films do become part of political and national discussion. We have only to look at the hostile British reaction to the release of Neil Jordan's *Michael Collins* (1996) and Terry George's *Some Mother's Son* to realise that films on Irish history are not viewed as simple entertainments.[7]

Whether or not we will see the disappearance of violence from the Northern Ireland political scene, a series of questions will remain. One of these is to what extent the forces of Irish nationalism and republicanism have pushed their way to the centre of attention through sustained and strategic cultural interventions. Unquestionably, the republican movement in Ulster has sparked a remarkable rise of interest in the Irish language, history, music, dance and the visual arts. The Foyle Film Festival and the West Belfast Film Festival are part of this trend. In the 1980s and 1990s, the Field Day project (discussed below) and the success of Seamus Heaney in gaining the Nobel Prize for Literature have underscored the general sympathy towards Irish nationalism.[8]

With culture and politics uppermost in his mind, David Butler has written that in Northern Ireland "every signifier is spoken for".[9] In Irish film and video, I would argue that some signifiers have maintained supremacy over others quite effortlessly. And it is the nationalist and republican signifiers and *signifieds* that are dominant and in need of re-examination.[10] By the same token, I would argue that the dearth of articulate civilian Protestant unionist voices in film is indicative of a beleaguered community which is only slowly becoming aware of the necessity to get its message out. The work of the unionist Cadogan Group in Belfast, with its pamphlet publications such as *Northern Limits*, is possibly a sign of change to come which may begin to have cultural implications.[11] The Cadogan Group is a separate development from the government-sponsored Northern Ireland Community Relations Council. This latter body was established in 1988 to "encourage a tolerance of diversity amongst the communities in Northern Ireland". It has organised conferences on "Varieties of Irishness" (1989), "Varieties of

Britishness" (1990) and "Varieties of Scottishness" (1996); some of these proceedings have been published.[12] The Cultural Traditions Group is a tributary of the Council; it awards money to projects that explore cultural diversity under the working assumption that what is needed is parity of esteem between the two communities. The conferences and the theory underlying this government project reflect the influence of revisionist Irish historians whose views I discuss in the following chapter.[13]

But before one can proceed far in any debate on Northern Ireland, some definitions and clarifications are required. The terms "Catholic" and "Protestant", "nationalism" and "republicanism", and "unionism" and "loyalism" resemble incendiary devices which have to be defused carefully. Although it is true that Protestant nationalists and Catholic unionists exist, the vast majority of Protestants believe in the union of Great Britain and Northern Ireland, while the vast majority of Catholics believe in the unification of Ireland.[14] In Northern Ireland, and in this book, when the terms "Protestant" and "Catholic" are used, they refer beyond religious affiliation to include cultural, historical and political resonances.

Irish nationalism has a long pedigree over many hundreds of years, stretching back to Anglo-Norman conquest and settlement in the 12th century. The nationalists subscribe to the belief in a "one-nation" theory: that the geographical limits of the island of Ireland encompass a nation which has been prevented by British imperialism from achieving its natural development and destiny. Some difficulty arises when we contrast nationalism with republicanism. Both share a wish for the eventual unification of Ireland. Whereas Irish nationalists will gladly wait until demographics or circumstances in Northern Ireland finally push the province towards the South, numerous Irish republicans believe that only violence against the British state will achieve their goal. It is also assumed that, while nationalists may have conservative views, republicans prefer a Socialist, if not a Marxist, analysis of how society should operate. Evidence at the ballot-box would seem to suggest, if we take the Social Democratic and Labour Party (SDLP) as nationalist and Sinn Féin as republican, that, within the Catholic population, social class significantly determines voter preference. Sinn Féin is strong in working-class areas, and the SDLP is strong in middle-class areas.

The divide between the SDLP and Sinn Féin is broadly equivalent on the Protestant side. People who vote for the Ulster Unionist Party (UUP) tend to be conservative and middle-class; those who vote for the Democratic Unionist Party (DUP) are more likely to believe in the essential link between unionism and the Protestant religion, particularly with Ian Paisley, the Moderator of his own Free Presbyterian Church, as the leader of the DUP. Paisley's Party has further benefitted from the Protestant working-class unemployed vote, as have the two fringe unionist parties, the Ulster Democratic Party (UDP) and the Progressive Unionist Party (PUP), who have ties to paramilitary organisations. Liberal middle-class Protestant and Catholic voters, who are more flexible unionists, tend to vote for the Alliance Party and the new UK Unionist Party. The relative strength of all these parties may be gleaned from the outcome of the May 1996 elections in the province, which helped to provide the 30 delegates from the top ten parties to the Northern Ireland Peace Forum:[15]

Ulster Unionist Party	181 829 (24.4%)
Social Democratic and Labour Party	159 985 (21.5%)
Democratic Unionist Party	141 393 (19.0%)
Sinn Féin	116 377 (15.6%)
Alliance Party	49 176 (6.6%)
UK Unionist Party	36 393 (4.9%)
Progressive Unionist Party	26 082 (3.5%)
Ulster Democratic Party	15 815 (2.1%)
Northern Ireland Women's Coalition	12 154 (1.6%)
Labour Party	6119 (0.8%)

Unionism as a political philosophy argues for the continuance of Northern Ireland within the United Kingdom. Full integration into the British political system never occurred in Northern Ireland because it had its own devolved assembly at Stormont, and the Conservative, Labour and Liberal parties were reluctant to organise there. The national question therefore dominated public debate, sometimes invisibly, and led to an immense range of opinion within the old Nationalist Party of Northern Ireland (which was replaced by the SDLP in 1970) and the governing UUP (1921-72). Commonly, two people with extremely opposed right-wing and left-wing views could find themselves voting for the same Party. In fact, part of the genius of the UUP's hegemony during the Stormont years was fending off Right/Left politics.

There are many varied strains in unionism. Some vote unionist because they fear incorporation into a state which is currently 93% Catholic and only 5% Protestant, and whose first legal divorce did not occur until January 1997. Despite the modernisation of the southern state in terms of business opportunities and social issues – in particular, family planning – memories are long. Unionists point to what they see as the decimation of the Protestant community in the Republic of Ireland, due mainly to the Roman Catholic Church's requirement or pressure that children of mixed marriages be brought up as Catholic; to the 1937 Constitution which gave a special position to the Roman Catholic Church; and to articles 2 and 3 of this Constitution which claimed jurisdiction over Northern Ireland without any mention of Protestant consent.

Others vote unionist because they see themselves as British first

9

and Irish second. They belong to a culture that plays cricket and rugby, not hurley and Gaelic football; that watches British television, not Irish television; that values secular individualism perhaps more than community values; that plays a larger role in world affairs than their southern neighbour, one which stayed neutral in the fight against Fascism, and whose Prime Minister Éamon De Valera offered condolences in person at the German Embassy in Dublin once Hitler was known to be dead.[16]

Still others vote unionist because there are sound economic reasons to do so. In general, the standard of living is higher in Northern Ireland than in the Republic of Ireland, although this difference may now be exaggerated. Nevertheless, the prospect of the Republic of Ireland having to pick up the subvention that Northern Ireland receives from the British Treasury, and the subsequent financial and economic chaos it would cause have undoubtedly cautioned would-be nationalists, and confirmed the vote of wavering unionists.

There are also those unionist voters who sincerely believe that the unionist cause is intellectually superior to the nationalist one. These voters like the concept of a federal arrangement, as it is in keeping with all the historical and economic ties with Britain. In this vein, the UK has allowed southern Irish citizens to work and live in its territory without being regarded as alien subjects. Unionism to these people is not intrinsically sectarian; it is a means by which citizens can be treated equally under the law within a primarily secular state. These unionists argue that the fault of the Stormont regime was that it made the mistake of thinking that unionism could only survive by sectarian methods. The faults of the past do not need to be repeated.

Much confusion has arisen between the terms "unionism" and "loyalism". In the common stereotypical imagination, loyalists are young, often unemployed and undereducated working-class men who belong to marching bands and paramilitary organisations such as the Ulster Defence Association (UDA) and the Ulster Volunteer Force (UVF). While there is some truth to this stereotype, it belittles the intellectual basis behind the manifestation. Loyalists are loyal both to the British Crown (not to a particular British government or political party) and to the Protestant religion which the Crown represents. The Queen is the Defender of the (Protestant) Faith, and it is both significant and controversial that Prince Charles, the heir to the throne, has floated the idea that the monarchy should become the Defender of *Faiths* in the 21st century. Just as there are many more nationalists than republicans among Catholics, many more unionists than loyalists exist among Protestants.

Loyalists, however, are not nationalists of the British kind (a two-nation theory which tries to explain the conflict as a struggle between Irish and British nationalism);[17] they give *conditional* allegiance to Great Britain as long as their Protestant religion and civil freedoms are supported and protected. This allegiance is based, therefore, on a contractual arrangement, perhaps Lockean in origin, and possibly for some resembling a covenant.[18] One can see how this desire overlaps with mainstream unionist political voters discussed earlier. This conditionality has also led Irish nationalists and republicans to believe that the unionists can be persuaded into a united Ireland. To some observers, this is a fundamental error in political judgment. That an ethnic community does not mobilise itself as a nation does not mean it is weak or lacking in resolve. An unplanned British Army departure from Northern Ireland could well lead to civil war and a partition of Northern Ireland into a small Protestant state surrounded by a larger Catholic one. It is not a hopeful or desirable scenario, but it could happen.

What cultural historians have noticed is that nationalism has always been able to attract articulate Protestants to its cause – Wolfe Tone, Henry Joy McCracken, Robert Emmet, Charles Stewart Parnell, Douglas Hyde, W B Yeats, Roger Casement, to name only a few; and, more recently, three of the six Field Day directors were born Protestant (Tom Paulin, Stephen Rea and David Hammond). The same cannot be said about Catholics rallying vocally to the unionist cause, but, given the real threat in the past, and certainly in the present, to life and limb for doing do, this situation is hardly surprising.

That the intellectuals among the Protestant unionist community have not developed cohesive arguments in the way in which intellectuals favouring nationalism have done is not proof of the apparent weakness of the unionist case.[19] It speaks far more about the diffusion of Northern Ireland Protestantism, the range of unionist thought, and the ability of Protestants, more than Catholics, to feel more at home within the British orbit.[20]

Irish cultural nationalism, like nationalism itself, has had its significant moments. Indubitably, the Gaelic Revival and Literary Renaissance between 1890 and 1930 are key. How, one may ask, can Douglas Hyde's *Beside the Fire: A Collection of Gaelic Folk Stories* (1890) be considered alongside James Joyce's *Ulysses* (1922)? The truth is that a distinction must be made between the Gaelic Revival and the Literary Renaissance.[21] Whereas the latter saw an exceptional outpouring of original Irish writing in English, the former was freighted with more political overtones. The interest in reviving Celtic myths and stories (such as in the early poetry of Yeats) was in part due to the need to solidify a pure Irish identity to counterbalance the dominance of British culture on the island of Ireland. Put simply, if the Irish were to govern themselves, they would have to have a distinctive culture to give that rule moral legitimacy. This approach had its fair share of difficulties. Firstly, the assumption that literature can be subordinated to politics is debatable and reductive; secondly, the tendency to extrapolate from this bygone literature can lead to strange exclusionism. For example, the argument was too well made that the only Irish worth talking about were those with a rural Catholic peasant background.

The Renaissance writers, such as Synge, O'Casey, Joyce and even Yeats mostly broke from this easy alliance between their cultural products and the national issue. Not insignificantly, apart from Joyce, these writers were Anglo-Irish Protestants who were fundamentally ill at ease with any movement that inserted religious values with political aspirations. The riots over the production of Synge's *The Playboy of the Western World* (1907) at the Abbey Theatre in Dublin were just as much about the inadequacy of the rural Catholic peasant image in national self-esteem as about lewd language and insinuation. Synge's play is of critical interest because there are many possible symptomatic readings. The symbolism of the believed killing of Old Mahon, the dominating father, is ambivalent, as it may refer to British colonialism or to native Irish nationalism. It marks a possibility of departure from convention and from "Irishness".

The play's riotous reception has provoked many commentators, including Conor Cruise O'Brien in his *States of Ireland* (1972), who rather ironically provides a structuralist analysis of six groups who viewed the play. O'Brien notes that, while the majority of protesting audience-members perceived the production as a demeaning comedy of Irish-speaking peasants, there were "counter-demonstrators" waving Union Jacks, men from Trinity College, Dublin, who would have likely been Ulster Protestants.[22] What this shows is that art can often be a forum for probing political tensions in society. In 1907, the Abbey Theatre was establishing itself as a "national" theatre, and, for that reason alone, close attention was focused upon it. The play was brought to the screen in 1962 by an Ulster Protestant, Brian Desmond Hurst, who clearly enjoyed pointing out the inconsistencies in the myth of the peaceful rural Catholic peasant life.

In more recent years, the cultural activities of Field Day have attracted immense critical attention, and the group has been linked controversially with a nationalist ideology. Field Day was set up in 1980 by Brian Friel and Stephen Rea initially to produce the former's play, *Translations* (1980). Gradually, a collective was formed with Seamus Deane, Seamus Heaney, Tom Paulin and David Hammond joining to form a board of six directors. Their goal was to revisit and reimagine Irish history and culture in an effort to push beyond the nationalist/unionist binary opposition. These were laudable aims – so laudable, in fact, that they are approvingly mentioned at length in the afterword of Edward Said's 1994 edition of *Orientalism*.[23] As it turned out, the plays, pamphlets and anthology associated with the collective provoked intense debate within Ireland.[24] The unfortunate aspect of the group was that it contained individuals hugely sympathetic to nationalism and republicanism, but lukewarm at best to unionism or even Protestant cultural experience.[25] For example, two plays depicting the Protestant experience were rejected by the six directors of Field Day. David Rudkin's *The Saxon Shore* (1986) was to appear in 1983 but was deemed inappropriate, while the more well-known *Observe the Sons of Ulster Marching Towards the Somme* (1985) by Frank McGuinness was offered but turned down. Clearly, to most Protestant and unionist observers, the northern Irish Protestants were being written out of cultural history by an organisation that claimed inclusiveness. Later, the anthology editors, particularly Seamus Deane, were rightly criticised for excluding key women writers from their anthology.[26]

Never explicitly stated, but almost implied, was Field Day's assumption that Protestant cultural production was somehow neither plentiful nor appropriate. As a generalisation – although one which should be constantly tested – the relationship between Protestantism and culture has been a troubled one. The Calvinist influence on Northern Ireland's Protestants of all stripes has made notions of culture difficult to flourish. Indeed, it has been adumbrated that Protestantism fears culture because it will invariably pull the unsuspecting Ulsterman or Ulsterwoman into the nationalist orbit, a place where culture is celebrated.[27] The rhetoric here relies upon the assumption that, following Tom Nairn's notion of nationalism as Janus-like, Protestant unionism looks to the sectarian past, whereas Catholic nationalism looks to an ennobling future. While much evidence can be brought to bear to argue this case, what is elided is the secular individualism and the belief in civil society, incorporating a pluralist and federalist British Isles, to which Protestant unionism and culture give voice.

One stereotype is that Catholics are drawn to the arts as a working through of their perceived oppression, whereas Protestants, sitting in the majoritarian driver's seat, have not the same compulsions, and prefer to express themselves in non-fictional forms. In the film and television media, there may be some truth to this, as Protestant cultural workers have been able to practise their craft within the news and current affairs branches of the two television stations based in Northern Ireland (BBC-NI and UTV). For example, Bill Miskelly worked for most of his career in the BBC before freelancing as a director on projects such as *The Schooner* (1983) and *The End of the World Man*. Historically, Protestant directors found themselves seeking work in Britain. The aforementioned Brian Desmond Hurst is a noticeable example.[28] For the Protestant community, therefore, the media emphasis in Northern Ireland has been on television production and hard news-journalism. There may well have been reluctance on the part of Catholics to belong to the BBC, the major producing station, because of its British ethos. The contracting out and commissioning of programmes in the 1970s and 1980s created a more healthy and diverse environment for drama.

Ulster Protestants, broadly defined, have made a large cultural contribution. In fiction, St John Ervine, Jack Wilson, Maurice Leitch, Forrest Reid, Janet McNeill, Sam Hanna Bell, George Buchanan and Anthony West come quickly to mind;[29] in poetry, Michael Longley, Louis MacNeice, Derek Mahon and John Hewitt;[30] in drama, John Boyd, Sam Thompson, Graham Reid, David Rudkin, Christina Reid, Ron Hutchinson, Bill Morrison and Stewart Parker;[31] in the visual arts, Basil Blackshaw and Colin Middleton.

Protestant cultural production, therefore, does exist in qualitative and quantitative terms, yet cultural Protestantism is remarkably absent or underplayed in the films and videos I discuss in this book. Why is this the case? One simple reason is that a population of 900 000 Protestants will only produce a small number of filmmakers. Secondly, the majority of the Irish films produced are those made by southern (not northern) Catholics. Thirdly, the nationalist and republican communities in Belfast and Derry have been radicalised far more than the Protestant communities to produce visual alternatives to mainstream British film and television. Fourthly, the cultural workers on the Left in Britain, such as Ken Loach, have decided to identify with the Catholic, not the Protestant, working class.

What may be clear by now is that, in considering this field of study, I have chosen to enact as my methodological practice *cultural materialism* which, as Jonathan Dollimore and Alan Sinfield have aptly summarised, involves a "combination of historical and cultural context, theoretical method, political commitment and textual analysis".[32] In the heyday of deconstructionism in the 1980s, it became popular to talk about historical relativism, or even the politics of style, wherein cultural artefacts and products which mediated historical experience could be discussed within a framework that always threatened to deny the validity of what we normally refer to as historical facts or events. On the contrary, my study here assumes a reasonable degree of knowledge and acceptance of the reality of the Northern Ireland conflict. I opt to approach my topic conscious that no narrow methodology can account for the cultural products that such a situation has sparked into existence. Perhaps if one methodology worked, the bibliography on Northern Ireland's affairs would not be so vast.

I believe close analyses of these texts do help to address their overall conception. While such readings can run the risk of confusing film with literature and art with sociology, viewers apprehend films in a way to render them as stories for easier consumption. I have also thought to utilise and assume the persona of a "political spectatorship" in my attempt to situate the often neglected film spectatorship of the Ulster Protestant and unionist.[33] Furthermore, I implicitly draw upon political, historical and cultural studies (by Arthur Aughey, Paul Bew, Roy Foster, Tom Nairn and Edward Said, for example) to contextualise criticism which, if left alone, can be too subjective. At first glance, the influence of Said may appear to be a strange choice in a work that seeks to argue that anti-imperialism is a myth that has been overworked in Northern Ireland. Yet, Said has made fascinating intellectual journeys since his provocative *Orientalism* (1978). *Culture and Imperialism* (1993) is superbly balanced, undeterred from revealing the abuses of both nativist and imperialist actions and theories.

But, as this book is devoted to visual images and their power, I should outline what has informed my work within that discipline. In film studies of the last 25 years, interest in the relationships among feminism, psychoanalysis and semiotics has focused attention on the term "spectatorship". Spectatorship encompasses how audiences read films, and how filmmakers/screenwriters structure them, consciously and unconsciously, for desired responses. The process develops in two related ways. Firstly, screenwriters and directors actively consort to present images that privilege a certain reading and identification. Secondly, the "fluidity" of the viewer must be mapped or situated. Traditionally, spectatorship has evoked gender politics, where the viewer normally is said to adopt the male gaze with its nuances of sadism and voyeurism. This orientation, in turn, leads to the "masquerade". To Laura Mulvey and Mary Ann Doane, this masquerade can result in a female audience-member, for example, adopting the usually unnatural "male" roles of sadistic voyeur and consumer fetishist of the woman as screen object.[34] If acceptable (and there are those, such as Gaylyn Studlar, who argue for a masochistic aesthetic, and those, such as D N Rodowick, who argue for the recognition of the impossibility of rigid identification),[35] surely we can expand politically this concept of the masquerade – "fooling oneself but consciously" – to northern Irish-related cinema and its specific audiences. In particular, we can then more fruitfully discuss class and gender issues under the assumption that these masquerades can help us break out of the nationalist/unionist binary opposition. What I would like to add to this masquerade is the political and local dimension.

My main interest in spectatorship and the masquerade is to configure the Irish Protestant unionist from the North, or – as one government "information" film funded by the Republic of Ireland in the 1950s termed them – the "pro-British residents".[36] How do they view the same body of work as experienced by (a) mainstream Catholic Ireland; (b) the Dublin intelligentsia; (c) northern nationalists; and (d) the Left in Britain? What forced masquerades must they endure?

In recent academic media and film studies, as with debates in other disciplines, the question of audience reception is regarded almost as a central cultural studies methodological requirement. The argument here is twofold. Firstly, textual (and even contextual) analysis by one writer is of limited value, since he or she cannot speak for a community or a time, even one through which a writer has lived. I do not accept this assertion, since we are all imbricated in culture, and, while our perspectives may be restricted, they are still useful. Secondly, establishing popularity among productions tells us what the majority of the people favour at a given time. Popularity is, however, an ephemeral phenomenon, since it depends often on accessibility and calculated penetration of the market. With only so many screens available, getting a film shown can depend on such idiosyncratic factors as the good personal relationship between a producer and a major distributor. Nearly all the works mentioned in this book were not, I would assume, made with profit as their overriding concern, so marketing issues are not as pertinent as they would be in a consideration of mainstream commercial filmmaking.

Of course, it is valuable to have a general knowledge that, for example, Jim Sheridan's *In the Name of the Father* was widely popular in the Republic of Ireland, less so in Northern Ireland, and even less so in England. It confirms how the political winds are blowing. Since most of the productions I discuss have found their way to British television (watched in both Britain and Ireland), debates about distribution and exhibition/circulation, particularly since the arrival of Channel 4 in 1982, do not reveal much, except perhaps to point out that nationalists will often endeavour to receive (with special antennae) Radio Telefís Éireann (RTE) stations in Northern Ireland, whereas unionists would not dream of doing so. Both communities watch the British channels, and this is where the turf war is fought.[37]

Accurate audience reception is difficult to approach in any systematic, scientific way. One can trawl through reviews of films in newspapers and magazines; one can watch the odd feedback television programme; one can check how many critical comments were received after a broadcast; one can set out to manufacture artificial focus groups to test certain theories; or one can embark on a major research programme, which sets out to interview people of all ages on the most significant northern Irish-related films and television dramas they have seen. In this study, I draw on occasion from the first three of these procedures to balance my essentially theoretical pose as a Protestant unionist spectator.

In North American spectatorship studies, the initial pessimism mostly shared by feminists in considering the classical Hollywood films gave way to a rethinking of viewing. Instead of accepting the narrative line offered by the filmmaker, feminists began to write and discuss where the films break down, where their fissures and cracks are thinly veiled. An active and mobile spectatorship therefore exposes the lazy or virtual masquerade and forces viewers and critics by their responses to lead filmmakers and videographers to new strategies of representation that are more inclusive. This is the hope that I have of an active and mobile Protestant or unionist spectatorship of Irish film and video. Ideally, it may lead to the withering away of the need to adopt such a trajectory, as I propose, since film and video production will have been forced to address the innate intellectual weakness in the dominant nationalist cinematic heritage of Ireland – its exclusionary aesthetics.

I admit that one could legitimately say that there has simply not been a sufficiently wide variety of work, as yet, for such critical methodologies to be utilised and debated. We do have, however, representative films. I discuss a few briefly below to round out this chapter, and to give a taste of what is to come. One could devise an elaborate categorisation of the active or resistant spectatorship of the Protestant unionist, but different levels of engagement are required of different films, and I move from relatively simple texts – Tom Collins' *Dragon's Teeth* (1990), Desmond Bell's *We'll Fight and No Surrender: Ulster Loyalism and the Protestant Sense of History* (1987) – through ambivalent reworkings of the past (Kieran Hickey's *Attracta* [1983]) to the more fascinatingly complex (Stephen Burke's *81* [1996]). The following is, therefore, to borrow and twist a title from Linda Williams, "when the Ulster Protestant and unionist looks".[38]

Dragon's Teeth is a documentary about the irony of the preparations for political and economic union in Europe while roads between north and south in Ireland are continually blocked by the Army. Collins cleverly contrasts the media hype surrounding the European leaders' meeting in Dublin in 1990 with the "dragon's teeth", the barriers put across some unapproved roads on the border – here outside the town of Belturbet. Belturbet is only accessible from the south of Ireland since, it is claimed in the film, loyalists blew up the one bridge in the area which allowed movement between Fermanagh and Cavan.

Various interviews with the people of the town emphasise the geographic, economic and social nonsense of this isolation. No viewer would argue with the film's thesis that communities have suffered greatly from the security activities connected with the "Troubles", but what makes the unionist viewer despair at films such as this is the implicit assumption that this clearly Catholic community can be approached in isolation from other communities, and that, when it comes to selecting interviewees, the RUC, the Royal Irish Regiment (or the old Ulster Defence Regiment [UDR]), the British Army and, most importantly, the neighbouring Protestant community are all denied a voice or opinion on the terms of the filmmaker's thesis. Collins' technique invites the Protestant unionist spectator to masquerade (a false consciousness) as the aggrieved nationalist, or produces a resistant spectator who feels assured in exposing the intended masquerade, and interprets Collins' sins of omission as symptomatic of yet another IRA apologist. This criticism is not to take away from the seriousness of Collins' subject, which includes the disturbing killing of Aidan McAnespie at an Army checkpoint. Rather, this criticism is to point out that rhetorical strategies of exclusion underwhelm his argument.[39]

But even conducting interviews with the Protestant community, as Bell's *We'll Fight and No Surrender: Ulster Loyalism and the Protestant Sense of History* does, can equally create problems. Bell's work reveals many of the tell-tale signs of underfinancing and the proverbial shoestring budget, and my criticism here is not about its technical quality. This video documentary focuses on the history of the siege of Derry, and the commemorations in December and August relating to that event.

A sharper awareness of documentary theory would have forced Bell to reconsider the strategies he employs.[40] The videographer seems to appear as an "expert" on-camera, providing us with the information of how we are to view the subsequent images. He is assisted by an "authoritative" female voice-over. Together these "voices of God" make some remarkable and contestable statements which are not borne out by the images presented. Here are some statements from the video's controlling discourse which the active Protestant unionist spectator would find simplistic, tenuous or unreadable: the Museum of the Apprentice Boys "gather[s] dust" and is "a strange, jumbled collection"; the loyalists have a "culture of stultifying puritanism" and are a "people with no dream of the future". The interviews with working-class loyalists, many inarticulate, promote the videographer's thesis that these people are suffering from a false consciousness. Bell no doubt would say that these are the people he found; these are the Protestants speaking. Yet, filming the surface of reality and the surface of people's lives can often bring back a surface texture, subverting understanding. This is a criticism of "Direct Cinema", of course, and one levelled at all kinds of documentary filmmakers. I have sidestepped many good and educational aspects of Bell's video – the necessity to grasp historical consciousness, and the comment, "In the mind of the Ulster Protestant, the siege goes on" – but overall such brilliant insight is clouded by a desire, whether intentional or not, to delegitimatise the core beliefs of Protestant unionists. The invitation to the masquerade is subtler than in Collins' film, and therefore demands a more active spectatorship to resist it.

Most of the sophisticated films and videos dealing with Northern Ireland provoke, however, an ambivalent Protestant spectatorship. For example, Kieran Hickey's *Attracta*, based on the William Trevor short story, concerns an old southern Protestant teacher (Wendy Hiller) who works in a town 50 miles from Cork city, running a small Protestant school. She loses her bearings after hearing of the fate of Penelope Vade, the wife of an English soldier killed in Northern Ireland. Vade comes across to help in the peace movement, but is terrorised and raped, and finally commits suicide. The sacrifice of Penelope Vade unhinges Attracta's mind, forcing a re-evaluation of her own personal history. Attracta was orphaned at the age of three, because in a War of Independence ambush her parents were mistakenly killed by people from her own town. The leader of the attack, Mr Devereux (John Kavanagh), takes it upon himself to be kind to Attracta, and helps her education along. Attracta blames herself for forgetting that those who do not learn the lessons of history are doomed to repeat it. The problem is that she kept her personal history silent. Specifically, she blames herself for not – until her very last class – telling her charges that the people who killed her parents became her friends. It is a lesson she should have repeated at length throughout her teaching career.

The Protestant unionist viewer would feel ambivalent masquerading along with Attracta. Firstly, the film implies that the *silence* of the teacher, far from being part of her magnanimity, actually leads to the diminution of her Protestant community. Her school decreases in number; her spinsterdom suggests a dying community. Secondly, Mr Devereux, who has killed her parents, is a Protestant in the spirit of the United Irishmen. Protestant unionists are driven to distraction by Catholic clergy and others making statements that Protestants love Ireland as much as Catholics, and who then invariably go on to name only Protestant republicans. It is as ludicrous as saying that the Protestant directors of Field Day represented in their heyday the Protestants of Northern Ireland. Thirdly, the Orangeman in the film, Mr Purce (Joe McPartland), is represented as being not only absolutely crazed, but also possibly a sexual pervert. Is it any wonder that a Protestant unionist audience feels the resistant and active spectatorship emerging, refusing the masquerade invited by the film? For, even at the end, the ironic comment on Attracta's mental health – "disturbed not insane" – invites a double resistance, whereby Protestant unionist viewers have a choice of equally unsavoury spectatorships: either they are deranged, or they can never be accepted in Ireland.

However, there are films that encourage inclusivity, one of which is Stephen Burke's *81*.[41] In this half-hour film, funded in part by the Cultural Traditions Group, Burke constructs an interesting parallel structure between a Catholic and a Protestant family on either side of the Peace Line in Belfast (a wall dividing Protestant and Catholic housing areas). He sets the film at one of the key flashpoints of the Northern Ireland "Troubles" – the last few days of Bobby Sands' hunger strike in 1981. Burke is effective in casting light on the small and large differences between the two families by distancing techniques. One of these is the employment of a French television news team charged with seeking out the "story" of the "Troubles" and, in particular, the attitude towards Bobby Sands' hunger strike. It allows for both sides to articulate their respective positions.

As with Burke's earlier *After '68*, black humour is pervasive throughout, and yet dovetails nicely with the serious issues addressed. Furthermore, the clipped style, whereby scenes either end abruptly or are overly extended for contemplation, captures well the uneasiness and self-consciousness of conflicted individuals asked to defend their opinions. Burke also plays with generic forms, for the film is both a documentary and a fiction. It is not a "mockumentary", since the humour never dominates the sombre subject, nor is it a full-blown fiction, since real-life events are referred to. We hear, for example, the voices of Margaret Thatcher and unionist MP David Trimble on the television and radio as background.

Burke shows great care in his writing to achieve a balancing act without being saccharine. Whereas the working-class unemployed Protestant Ken Campbell (B J Hogg) buries his mother, the working-class unemployed Catholic Bernard Friel (Lalor Roddy) walks behind the funeral cortège for Bobby Sands. The wives Sara Campbell (Aine McCartney) and Clodagh Friel (Paula McFeteridge) are neatly contrasted in their respective domestic spaces, with little, if any, economic difference between them. Perhaps the funniest moment in the film is when Sara leads the French team out of the back door to the Peace Line, but makes them needlessly bend down because of the supposed gunfire. It is a rare moment in the history of Irish cinema: a Protestant with a sense of humour.

One false note is the decision to use actual footage of Bobby Sands' funeral. This footage is emotionally rendered with soulful background music; it threatens to overtake the gradual and equal accumulation of republican/loyalist "evidence". There can be no Protestant equivalent in 1981. If one made a film utilising footage from the Enniskillen Remembrance Day ceremony of 1987, when eleven Protestants were killed by an IRA bomb, one would also be faced with highly emotional material. Nevertheless, Burke's film gives voice to both Protestants and Catholics, loyalists and republicans, and thereby opens a space for each group or constituency to crossover to the other's political terrain. He gives each side a form of non-judgmental recognition.

This notion of recognition is a cornerstone to Francis Fukuyama's bestseller treatise, *The End of History and the Last Man* (1992).[42] In this work, Fukuyama argues that liberal democracies with a capitalist underpinning will prove to be the end of the evolutionary line of political history throughout the world. While he may sound unusually optimistic, perhaps naïve, a tremendous apologist for the "New World Order" of one superpower, Fukuyama continually points to the main reason for political action – not formal needs and desires, but the "struggle for recognition". This "thymotic impulse" drives change and resistance towards prevailing and static ideologies. This struggle for recognition is what the Ulster Protestant unionist community constantly seeks. This community is less interested in Benedict Anderson's definition of nationalism, with his strictures of limitation, sovereignty and community, than with the attendant recognition that Irish triumphalist nationalism creates a false consciousness in the political and cultural arena.[43] A pluralist Ireland, however agreed, cannot be achieved before this issue of recognition is fully addressed both culturally and politically. In this respect, Anderson's revision of his work in 1991 and his focusing on the census, map and museum as more appropriate metaphors for grasping late and postcolonial societies are, to a large extent, an admission that notions of nationalism are too often misunderstood by those sleepwalking their way to the politically correct pulpit of the day.[44]

I believe that turning away from Anderson and towards work in spectatorship studies may begin to free Irish images from the tyranny of stereotypes. Anne Friedberg has argued that the cinema is so prized because it combines the virtual gaze of photography with the mobile gaze of shopping and tourism.[45] It involves, in other words, transformation; it gives us the possibilities of crossing over (however temporarily) not only barriers of gender and race, but also those of politics. In short, understanding and appreciating the Protestant unionist spectatorship and that community's previously forced masquerades will help present and future Irish film and video practitioners to play a more constructive role in helping to solve the northern crisis. Failure to do so will condemn all communities in Ireland to perpetual and disabling mythmaking. Out of history such myths are made, and it is to the former that I turn in the next chapter.

Notes

[1]   Quoted by Jay Carr of the *Boston Globe* in "Fighting Irish", *Vancouver Sun* 24 October 1996: D5.

[2]   The Cadogan Group, *Northern Limits: Boundaries of the Attainable in Northern Ireland Politics* (Belfast: The Cadogan Group, 1992): 29.

[3]   Edward W Said, *Culture & Imperialism* (New York: Vintage, 1994): xiii.

[4]   *Irish Cinema: An Illustrated History* (Dublin: Anna Livia Press, 1988); as *World Cinema 4: Ireland* (Trowbridge: Flicks Books, 1989).

[5]   See also Kevin Rockett, Luke Gibbons and John Hill, *Cinema and Ireland* (London; Sydney: Croom Helm, 1987); Matthew Stevens, *Directory of Irish and Irish-Related Films* (Trowbridge: Flicks Books, 1989).

[6]   *Ireland on Screen: Film and Television Production in Ireland 1995+6* (Dublin: Film Ireland, 1995): 13.

[7]   I discuss *Some Mother's Son* in chapter 4. Jordan's film upset historians for its conflation of incidents and historical inaccuracies. It upset northern Protestants for the scene in which an Ulster police detective is blown up in his own car. This was not only anachronistic (car bombs were not part of the War of Independence), but also perilously close to bad taste. In the present "Troubles", numerous Protestant policeman have been killed by the IRA in this manner. In *Michael Collins*, this is the only scene in which an Ulster Protestant appears, and it lasts about five seconds. Historically, one needs to understand the unionist resistance to Irish nationalism to contextualise the Irish Civil War, but this is totally absent from the film. For a discussion of these issues, see Ronan Bennett,

21

Tom Paulin and Philip Dodd, "Ghosts From a Civil War", *Sight and Sound* 6: 12 (December 1996): 30-32, and Glen Newey, "Both gangster and Gandhi. Agency without blame: the significant omissions of *Michael Collins*", *The Times Literary Supplement* 15 November 1996: 20. See also my "History Without Borders: Neil Jordan's *Michael Collins*", in James MacKillop (ed), *Envisioning Ireland: Essays in Irish Cinema* (Syracuse: Syracuse University Press, forthcoming, 1999).

[8]   For an interesting critique of Seamus Heaney's currency, see David Lloyd, "'Pap for the Dispossessed': Seamus Heaney and the Poetics of Identity", in his *Anomalous States: Irish Writing and the Post-Colonial Moment* (Dublin: The Lilliput Press, 1993): 13-37. Lloyd's insistence on the political function of aesthetic production ties Heaney's work to 19th-century Irish cultural nationalism.

[9]   David Butler, "Broadcasting in a Divided Community", in Martin McLoone (ed), *Culture, Identity and Broadcasting in Ireland: Local Issues, Global Perspectives. Proceedings of the Cultural Traditions Group/Media Studies UUC Symposium, 21 February, 1991* (Belfast: Institute of Irish Studies, The Queen's University of Belfast, 1991): 102. Butler's views are elaborated upon in his *The Trouble With Reporting Northern Ireland: The British State, the Broadcast Media and Nonfictional Representation of the Conflict* (Aldershot; Brookfield, USA; Hong Kong; Singapore; Sydney: Avebury, 1995). See also my "The Repression of Communities: Visual Representations of Northern Ireland during the Thatcher Years", in Lester Friedman (ed), *Fires Were Started: British Cinema and Thatcherism* (Minneapolis: University of Minnesota Press, 1993): 92-108.

[10]   There is an argument to be made that in television drama this was not always the case since 1968/69; however, I argue that in the 1980s and 1990s television drama parallels developments in film and video.

[11]   The Cadogan Group, *Northern Limits: Boundaries of the Attainable in Northern Ireland Politics* (Belfast: The Cadogan Group, 1992). In 1992, the Cadogan Group comprised Arthur Aughey, lecturer in political science; Paul Bew, Professor of Political Science; Arthur Green, former Under-Secretary, Department of Education, Northern Ireland; Graham Gudgin, economist; Dennis Kennedy, journalist and former Head of the European Commission Office in Northern Ireland; and Paddy Roche, lecturer in economics.

[12]   See, for example, Maurna Crozier (ed), *Cultural Traditions in Northern Ireland: 'Varieties of Irishness'* (Belfast: Institute of Irish Studies The Queen's University of Belfast, 1989), and Maurna Crozier (ed), *Cultural Traditions in Northern Ireland: 'Varieties of Britishness'* (Belfast: Institute of Irish Studies The Queen's University of Belfast, 1990).

[13]   For the view of the Chairman of the Cultural Traditions Group funded by the British government, see Maurice Hayes, *Whither Cultural Diversity?*, second edition (Belfast: Community Relations Council, 1993).

[14]   While figures vary, it is generally agreed that the Protestant population in Northern Ireland between 1969 and 1997 hovered between 900 000 and 1 000 000; the Catholic population has fluctuated between

500 000 and 600 000. The 60%-40% split seems to be congruent with recent assumptions.

[15] These figures are approximate and are based on results in "Northern Ireland Election Results", *The Times* 1 June 1996: 10.

[16] R F Foster, *Modern Ireland 1600-1972* (Harmondsworth: Penguin Books, 1989): 563.

[17] A number of political scientists, in particular John McGarry and Brendan O'Leary in *Explaining Northern Ireland: Broken Images* (Oxford, UK; Cambridge, MA: Blackwell, 1995), insist that the Ulster Protestants are British nationalists fighting a political war against Irish nationalists. Despite their comprehensive consideration of the Northern Ireland predicament, many unionists would find their argument that unionists are British nationalists extremely imprecise and Procrustean. It is not surprising, therefore, that both authors heavily criticise The Cadogan Group and Arthur Aughey's writings, since both suggest a civic unionism as a way to gain widespread support for new governance in Northern Ireland. This view is in direct opposition to the revitalised power-sharing that O'Leary and McGarry have explicitly or implicitly favoured in their books on the conflict. The previous volumes which they have co-written or co-edited include *The Future of Northern Ireland* (Oxford: Clarendon Press, 1990) and *The Politics of Antagonism: Understanding Northern Ireland* (London; Atlantic Highlands, NJ: The Athlone Press, 1993).

[18] The contractual thesis is explored and explained cogently in David W Miller, *Queen's Rebels: Ulster Loyalism in Historical Perspective* (Dublin: Gill and Macmillan; New York: Barnes & Noble Books; 1978). A stimulating analysis of the importance of Scottish Presbyterian covenantal culture in understanding the Ulster Protestant political culture is Donald Harman Akenson, *God's Peoples: Covenant and Land in South Africa, Israel, and Ulster* (Ithaca; London: Cornell University Press, 1992). The way in which covenants move from the religious to the political in Northern Ireland can be gauged by the sacredness with which signed copies of the 1912 Ulster's Solemn League and Covenant is regarded in Ulster Protestant culture, often found framed and hanging on the walls of the family home. The republican parallel document would probably be the 1916 proclamation of the Republic.

[19] Liam O'Dowd believes that the unionist parties have been retarded by the way in which they have marginalised intellectuals from espousing their political philosophy. See his "Intellectuals and political culture: a unionist-nationalist comparison", in Eamonn Hughes (ed), *Culture and politics in Northern Ireland 1960-1990* (Milton Keynes; Philadelphia: Open University Press, 1991): 151-173. There is some merit to this analysis, since intellectuals are to be found in abundance in the Alliance Party and in the UK Unionist Party led by Robert McCartney, author of one of the Field Day pamphlets, *Liberty and Authority in Ireland* (Derry: Field Day, 1985). The Cadogan Group are also by no means traditional unionists. For an interesting critique of cultural unionism, liberal unionism and civic unionism, see Norman Porter, *Rethinking Unionism: An Alternative Vision for Northern Ireland* (Belfast: The Blackstaff Press, 1996).

[20] See the cultural essays in John Wilson Foster, *Colonial Consequences:*

Essays in Irish Literature and Culture (Dublin: The Lilliput Press, 1991), and John Wilson Foster (ed), *The Idea of the Union: Statements and Critiques in Support of the Union of Great Britain and Northern Ireland* (Belfast; Vancouver: Belcouver Press, 1995).

21   The literature on Irish cultural nationalism is large, but useful works include Seamus Deane, *Celtic Revivals: Essays in Modern Irish Literature 1880-1980* (London: Faber and Faber, 1985) and David Lloyd, *Nationalism and Minor Literature: James Clarence Mangan and the Emergence of Irish Cultural Nationalism* (Berkeley, CA: University of California Press, 1987). Debates of like nature occurred periodically within the Republic of Ireland concerning national film policies, particularly in the 1940s when the Roman Catholic Church founded the National Film Institute.

22   Conor Cruise O'Brien, *States of Ireland* (London: Hutchinson, 1972): 72-74. The reviews and contemporary commentary on the whole affair are marvellously captured in James Kilroy, *The 'Playboy' Riots* (Dublin: The Dolmen Press, 1971).

23   Edward W Said, *Orientalism* (New York: Vintage Books, 1994): 351.

24   Field Day had been influenced by *The Crane Bag*, probably the leading cultural journal in Ireland between 1977 and 1985, edited by, among others, Mark Hederman and Richard Kearney. They proposed the notion of a fifth province which would transcend the political arguments over the fourth province of Ulster. This vague concept merely smacked of old nationalism in new clothes to most unionist observers. For a sample of Field Day members' writing, see Seamus Deane (ed), *Ireland's Field Day* (London: Hutchinson, 1985). This book contains the contributions, originally in pamphlet form, of Seamus Deane, Seamus Heaney, Richard Kearney, Declan Kiberd and Tom Paulin. Brian Friel's *Translations* is perhaps the best-known dramatic nativist response to English imperialism and colonialism to come out of the group. The anthology emerged in three volumes – Seamus Deane, Andrew Carpenter and Jonathan Williams (eds), *The Field Day Anthology of Irish Writing* (Derry: Field Day Publications, 1991). A detailed balanced account of the first five years of the Field Day collective can be found in Marilynn J Richtarik, *Acting Between the Lines: The Field Day Theatre Company and Irish Cultural Politics 1980-1984* (Oxford: Clarendon Press, 1994).

25   To be fair, David Hammond made an award-winning documentary on the Protestant-dominated Belfast Shipyard, *Steelchest, Nail in the Boot and the Barking Dog* (1986), and Tom Paulin's *The Riot Act* (1984) and particularly Stewart Parker's *Pentecost* (1987) explored aspects of Protestantism and unionism.

26   For a good survey of the debates, see Shaun Richards, "Field Day's fifth province: avenue or impasse?", in Hughes (ed): 139-150. This article is considerably more nuanced than Richards' co-written book with David Cairns, *Writing Ireland: colonialism, nationalism and culture* (Manchester: Manchester University Press, 1988). This book is a very fast recounting of the postcolonialist view of Ireland's relationship with England. Although I share its cultural materialist assumptions, it very graphically fails in its last chapter to understand the complexity of the Northern Ireland situation. Few northern Protestant unionist writers are

mentioned; in stark contrast, Seamus Deane, Declan Kiberd, Brian Friel, Seamus Heaney and Tom Paulin are discussed as if these figures, with their nationalist and republican views, lead the way to a "natural" understanding of Northern Ireland. Cairns and Richards have nothing to say about the Ulster Unionists in the 1970s or 1980s. They do not seem to consider the possibility that the coloniser/colonised dichotomy comes unstuck once an examination of the Protestant community is embarked upon.

[27]   See Edna Longley, "Writing, Revisionism & Grass Seed: Literary Mythologies in Ireland", in Jean Lundy and Aodán Mac Póilin (eds), *Styles of Belonging: The Cultural Identities of Ulster* (Belfast: Lagan Press, 1992): 11-21.

[28]   For further information, see my articles on Brian Desmond Hurst's life and films: "Appreciation: Brian Desmond Hurst 1895-1986: Irish Filmmaker", *Eire-Ireland* 24: 4 (winter 1989): 106-113; and "British Filmmaking in the 1930s and 1940s: The Example of Brian Desmond Hurst", *Film Criticism* 16: 1-2 (autumn-winter 1991-92): 67-83.

[29]   See John Wilson Foster, *Forces and Themes in Ulster Fiction* (Dublin: Gill and Macmillan, 1974).

[30]   See Gerald Dawe and John Wilson Foster (eds), *The Poet's Place: Ulster literature and society. Essays in honour of John Hewitt, 1907-87* (Belfast: Institute of Irish Studies, 1991); and Gerald Dawe and Edna Longley (eds), *Across a Roaring Hill: The Protestant imagination in modern Ireland. Essays in Honour of John Hewitt* (Belfast; Dover, NH: The Blackstaff Press, 1985).

[31]   See Anthony Roche, *Contemporary Irish Drama: From Beckett to McGuinness* (New York: St Martin's Press, 1995): 216-278.

[32]   Jonathan Dollimore and Alan Sinfield quoted in David Cairns and Shaun Richards, *Writing Ireland: colonialism, nationalism and culture* (Manchester: Manchester University Press, 1988): vii.

[33]   There is historical and social scientific evidence to adopt what appears on the surface to be an uncompromising classification as the Ulster Protestant and unionist spectatorship. In a much-cited 1960s survey, Richard Rose found that differences between Northern Ireland Catholics and Protestants were very small; however, whenever political or constitutional issues were introduced, major differences opened up. See Richard Rose, *Governing Without Consensus: An Irish Perspective* (London: Faber and Faber, 1971): 324.

[34]   Laura Mulvey, "Visual Pleasure and Narrative Cinema", *Screen* 16: 3 (autumn 1975): 6-18. See also Mary Ann Doane, "Film and the Masquerade: Theorising the Female Spectator", *Screen* 23: 3-4 (September-October 1982): 74-87; and Mary Ann Doane, "Masquerade Reconsidered: Further Thoughts on the Female Spectator", *Discourse* 11: 1 (1989): 42-54.

[35]   Gaylyn Studlar, "Masochism and the Perverse Pleasures of the Cinema", in Bill Nichols (ed), *Movies and Methods volume II: An Anthology* (Berkeley; Los Angeles; London: University of California Press,

1985): 602-621; D N Rodowick, "The Difficulty of Difference", *Wide Angle* 5: 1 (1982): 4-15.

[36] This term is taken directly from the voice-over of *Fintona: A Study of Housing Discrimination* (1954). It is sobering to note the similarity in mainstream republican rhetoric between the 1950s and 1990s. It would not be hard to find such "contextualisation" today, as the following, taken from the same film commentary, shows: "The immediate reason for this discrimination usually is that the pro-British ruling class wish to create or to preserve a slender voting majority in a parliamentary constituency. Therefore, regardless of moral right, they give houses only to those who support them. This is the position in Fintona. Only by such a policy of discrimination can the six-county Belfast government and its henchmen maintain their, we hope, temporary ascendancy over those of the population who wish to see Ireland united and free...The situation at Fintona...emphasise[s] the moral weakness of the regime, in its constant striving to make the partition of Ireland permanent". The discrimination described did occur, but it is the language used to describe it that is so fascinating.

[37] The history of television reporting and Northern Ireland is littered with the out-takes of censored material. See Liz Curtis, *Ireland: The propaganda war: The media and the 'battle for hearts and minds'* (London; Sydney: Pluto Press, 1984). As far as Sinn Féin is concerned, the media are a battleground worthy of record. The Sinn Féin Video Collection, comprising over 100 tapes depicting how Sinn Féin was reported in the media, was copied in 1995 and lodged in the Northern Ireland Political Collection in the Linen Hall Library, Belfast. See also Danny Morrison, *Ireland: The Censored Subject* (Belfast: Sinn Féin Publicity Department, 1989).

[38] Linda Williams, "When the Woman Looks", in Mary Ann Doane, Patricia Mellencamp and Linda Williams (eds), *Re-vision: Essays in Feminist Film Criticism* (Frederick, MD: University Publications of America, 1984): 83-99.

[39] There are occasions where exclusionism is not necessarily disabling. One could cite many documentaries that concentrate on the Catholic nationalist community which appear to lament the reality of the "ghetto", but which equally applaud and celebrate the sense of community it has engendered. A recent example is Brendan Byrne's *The Kickhams* (1994), which profiles the Gaelic Athletic Association (GAA) and its members in the Ardoyne district of Belfast.

[40] Since the late-1970s, interest and advances in documentary practice and theory have been substantial. See, for example, Bill Nichols, *Ideology and the Image: Social Representation in the Cinema and Other Media* (Bloomington: Indiana University Press, 1981); Thomas Waugh (ed), *"Show Us Life": Toward a History and Aesthetics of the Committed Documentary* (Metuchen, NJ; London: The Scarecrow Press, 1984); Alan Rosenthal (ed), *New Challenges for Documentary* (Berkeley; Los Angeles; London: University of California Press, 1988); Bill Nichols, *Representing Reality: Issues and Concepts in Documentary* (Bloomington and Indianapolis: Indiana University Press, 1991); a special documentary issue

of *Wide Angle* 13: 2 (April 1991); Michael Renov (ed), *Theorizing Documentary* (New York: Routledge, 1993); and Brian Winston, *Claiming the Real: The Griersonian Documentary and Its Legitimations* (London: British Film Institute, 1995).

[41]   Others include Pat Murphy's *Maeve* and Orla Walsh's *The Visit*, both of which I discuss in chapter 5.

[42]   Francis Fukuyama, *The End of History and the Last Man* (New York: Avon Books, 1992).

[43]   Benedict Anderson, *Imagined Communities: Reflections on the Origin and Spread of Nationalism* (London; New York: Verso, 1991).

[44]   One could make this rather critical comment about Joe Comerford's *High Boot Benny*, discussed further in chapter 4. Arguably, it reinscribes myths of Protestants in the Catholic nationalist consciousness – an RUC man, brutal and sadistic, on the one hand, and, on the other, a decontextualised Protestant woman with insufficient herstory/history to convince the audience of the validity of the film's thesis that the border separating the north and south of Ireland perpetuates violence.

[45]   Anne Friedberg, *Window Shopping: Cinema and the Postmodern* (Berkeley; Los Angeles; Oxford: University of California Press, 1993).

2
Historical and political contexts

But the hard historical fact is that it has mattered, and still matters, enormously in Ireland to which religion a man belongs. (T W Moody)[1]

In essence, the 'problem' is very simple. There are a million Protestants in eastern Ulster who do not want to be ruled by Dublin and in no foreseeable circumstances will want to be. Maybe they should. Maybe the Israelis should want to belong to a united Arabia, or the Bosnian Muslims to a united Serbia, but they don't either. It is absurd and insulting to tell a people who they are and what they ought to want, as opposed to who they think they are and what they believe they want. (Geoffrey Wheatcroft)[2]

A chronicle

It is a bold person who can argue persuasively for a critical juncture in Irish history that can explain the current conflict in Northern Ireland. Most commentators focus on the early 17th-century plantation or settlement of Ulster by English and Scottish Protestants, many of whom were Presbyterian. This plantation was fundamentally political in nature. To quell the most contrary of provinces, James I, who had inherited the bloody aftermath of the Elizabethan Wars in Ireland, came to believe that the only way to secure the "back door" to England from possible French and Spanish influence and from periodic Irish uprisings was to colonise the land. Settlement in Ireland was not new. Both the Vikings and the Normans had invaded and settled in parts of the country in previous eras, but, whereas these groups gradually assimilated into the mainstream Catholic population, the English and Scottish Protestants were more resilient. The 17th century also contained the momentous events of the 1641 Irish Rebellion; the English Civil War and the beheading of the King, Charles I; the rule of Cromwell; the restoration of Charles II in 1660; and the ascent of James II in 1685 as a Catholic King. English Protestant resistance to James II led to their inviting Prince William of Orange from The Netherlands in 1688 to invade England and to ascend the throne as William III. James fled to Ireland where his mostly Catholic-supported army lay siege against the city of Derry. The Protestant inhabitants of the city resisted, risking starvation, until the embargo was lifted by William III's forces after nearly eight months. Protestant fortitude and loyalty to the new Protestant King and the British Crown reverberate to this day. William's defeat of James' army at the Battle of the Boyne in July 1690 is likewise celebrated in northern Protestant culture as a great victory, even though William's success in Ireland against the Jacobite forces was less conclusive overall, demanding treaty negotiations. Nevertheless, the defeat of James II put paid to the prospects of Catholics in Ireland assuming a role in the governance of the country. Penal laws against Catholics were passed in the Irish Parliament, ranging from the loss of the franchise to severe restrictions on owning property and land. The rule that Catholics could not own a horse worth over £5 was only one of a number of mean-spirited and clearly sectarian measures passed by the Anglican Establishment. By the late-18th century, many of these penal laws had been repealed, with Catholics given the franchise in 1793, but unfettered freedom to vote and hold parliamentary office did not come until 1829.

Strangely, the radical ideas stemming from the American and French Revolutions of the late-18th century did not succeed in fomenting mass support for the expulsion of British rule. The reasons for this failure are many, but they include the fact that the American Revolution was sparked and led mainly by Protestants, poor role models for the majority Catholic population of Ireland. The French Revolution, however, seemed to influence the Presbyterians in Ulster, who, somewhat like the Catholics, were treated as second-class citizens by the established Anglican Church, the Church of Ireland and the British state. In 1791, the Society of United Irishmen was formed first in Belfast, and then in Dublin. This organisation, which launched a series of abortive military actions in 1798, with the tardy assistance of the French, sought to secure liberty, equality and fraternity among all Irishmen, Protestant, Catholic or Dissenter (non-Anglican Protestants). One of the reasons they failed was that they were too secular for their time, since the Catholic population was not prepared to give up their religion to be merely Irish. For many Catholics, Catholicism denoted Irishness. Furthermore, the forces of unionism were not inconsiderable among the Protestant population. This revolt is often referred to in republican mythology and in some of the films and videos discussed in this book, because it is one of the few occasions in modern Irish history where it appeared that Protestants and Catholics combined, however weakly, against the British state.[3] The revolt did help to force the passage of the Act of Union (effective 1801) which integrated Irish Members of Parliament with those from England,

Scotland and Wales at Westminster.

The north-east of Ireland prospered in the 19th century as Belfast became part of the British industrial revolution. The big industries of shipbuilding, engineering, textiles, rope-making and tobacco ensured that links between Northern Ireland and Great Britain were strong, unlike in other areas of Ireland. This probably explains why the Irish famine (1845-49) did not affect the north-east as severely as it did the rest of the country. The close rivalry between the Tories and Liberals in Westminster gave the Irish contingent considerable influence. Eventually, a home rule bill for Ireland emerged out of this exercise of political leverage. From 1886 to 1914, three home rule bills were defeated or held up either by the House of Commons or by the House of Lords. Finally, at the point when unionists seemed to be making headway in allowing the north-east counties to opt out of any home rule, deliberations were postponed because of the First World War. One could argue that the introduction of the first home rule bill in 1886 set in motion the divisions we see so markedly today. It galvanised both sides to articulate their positions more strongly and militarily. In 1913, the Ulster Volunteer Force (UVF) was formed to preserve the union; later in the year, their opponents established the Irish Volunteers and the Irish Citizen Army. Thus, the "physical force" tradition is linked to both unionists and nationalists.

The onset of war encouraged members of the Irish Republican Brotherhood, set up in 1915, to consider ways and means to promote Irish independence, under the adage that "England's difficulty is Ireland's opportunity". The Easter Rising of 1916 – when the Irish Volunteers led by Patrick Pearse, and the Irish Citizen Army led by James Connolly, took over several prominent Dublin buildings, including the General Post Office, while declaring an Irish Republic – was crushed within a few days with some 3000 casualties, including 450 dead. The leaders of the Rising were executed. The series of executions changed the mood of the majority of Irish people away from their initial rejection of the aims of the Irish Volunteers. This atmosphere of sympathy set the scene for the beginning of a guerrilla war of attrition against the British.

In December 1920, while the Irish War of Independence (1919-21) raged, the Government of Ireland Act was passed by the British, a statute which provided for the setting up of a six-county parliament and administration in the North. This new political and geographical jurisdiction included the counties of Antrim, Armagh, Derry, Down, Fermanagh and Tyrone. These were only six of the nine counties of traditional Ulster, since Cavan, Donegal and Monaghan were excluded. Two thirds of the population of this new state were Protestant, and one third Catholic. The northern Parliament was officially opened by George V in June 1921. The British government imposed partition as a way to solve a political and military problem.[4] The unionists were strongest in the North, and threatened to make a possible united and Sinn Féin-dominated Ireland completely ungovernable. Instead of a civil war erupting between unionists and nationalists to establish a new polity, this struggle was displaced to the new Irish Free State's 26 counties in 1922-23, when former comrades-in-arms were divided over the acceptance of the Anglo-Irish Treaty. This treaty was signed in December 1921, and debated and approved by a fairly small margin in the southern Parliament (Dáil Éireann) during 1922. While the Free State moved into a short and bitter civil war over the acceptance of the treaty's partition provisions, one of the most controversial pieces of legislation was passed in the North: the Civil Authorities (Special Powers) Act. As Sabine Wichert summarises, the act included "search and arrest without warrant, appropriation of documents and other property, destruction of buildings, questioning of witnesses, banning of meetings and publications, and the prohibition of approach to specific places. Later these were extended, originally as temporary measures, to internment and exclusion orders."[5] In 1933, this act became permanent. Naturally, the existence of this legislation and the formation of Special constabularies from 1920 onwards (the most notorious being the 'B' Specials) went a long way to ensure that unionists dominated all aspects of northern society, including local councils.[6] Allied to the latter's gerrymandering was the use of the English model for plural voting for property- and business-owners. Since most of these owners were Protestant, the Catholic and nationalist minority was further disenfranchised.

What is surprising to the historian of Northern Ireland is not that these inequities existed between 1922 and on into the Second World War, but that they continued after April 1949 when Éire (the name which the Irish Free State had become via the new Irish Constitution of 1937) formally changed to the Republic of Ireland and left the Commonwealth. The Ireland Act of June 1949, passed at Westminster, guaranteed Northern Ireland's position within the UK as long as the latter's parliament (Stormont) so wished. Given the solid unionist majority at Stormont, there could not have been a greater assurance from London. Yet, only two years later, in 1951, the Northern Ireland Parliament passed the Public Order Act which, if invoked, allowed the internment of any individual suspected of subversion. By all accounts, the 1950s were, relative to previous decades, economically beneficial for all of Northern Ireland's citizens. Nevertheless, the IRA did begin acquiring weapons after the 1949 constitutional activity in England and Ireland. The IRA was afraid that it had become irrelevant, and a border campaign was waged between 1956 and 1962. It did not catch the imagination of the Catholic minority in the North, perhaps because of prosperous times and the dominant quiescent attitude among a growing Catholic middle class, not to mention the concerted efforts of both governments to undermine the IRA insurgency.

The arrival of Captain Terence O'Neill as Prime Minister of Northern Ireland in 1963 appeared to offer a possibility that a more equitable arrangement between the two communities could be achieved within the Northern Ireland state. Unfortunately, his rather paternalistic liberalism gave mixed signals to the Catholic nationalist minority, and infuriated sections of the Protestant unionist community. Historian J J Lee argues that much of the sorry turn of events since 1968 is due in large part to the wrong man with the right ideas being in charge (Terence O'Neill), or the right man in charge too late (Brian Faulkner).[7] O'Neill was a member of the landed aristocracy, and his Eton education and upper-class accent were regarded by many as ill-suited to the realities of necessary change in Northern Ireland. In the 1960s, O'Neill knew that modernisation of the economy was necessary, and prosperity for the province required the minority population to feel they had an equal stake in its future. Hence his willingness to meet with Irish prime ministers south of the border, and to visit Catholic schools. He seemed to begin a path towards reconciliation that allowed the Nationalist Party in Northern Ireland to take its seats in Stormont in 1965. But there were always ominous signs: as the working-class Protestants began to lose their jobs in the general decline of mass labour, they were attracted to the exclusionist rhetoric of Ian Paisley, the firebrand Free Presbyterian Moderator, who talked openly of his distaste for Catholicism and the Republic of Ireland. Paisley was the man, after all, who introduced to the Oxford Union the motion "that the Roman Catholic Church has no place in the twentieth century".[8]

1966 was the 50th anniversary of both the Easter Rising and the Battle of the Somme (where mostly Protestants in the 36th [Ulster] Division were heavily involved, with great loss of life). These memorials undoubtedly contributed to the raising of tension, as each community identified with different military sacrifices. A Catholic barman was murdered by the Ulster Volunteer Force (UVF) in 1966 just before Paisley was arrested and imprisoned for unlawful assembly and breach of the peace. The Northern Ireland Civil Rights Association was formed in 1967, and led protest marches in 1968 to campaign for better housing, mainly for Catholic families, and for a reformed local electoral system. These marches were obstructed by the police. The Marxist People's Democracy Movement, which emanated from Queen's University in Belfast, became involved in protests in late-1968 and early 1969, including a march from Belfast to Derry which was attacked by Protestants along the route. By the end of 1969, O'Neill had resigned, replaced by James Chichester-Clark; riots in Belfast and Derry were commonplace; British troops had arrived; the disbandment of the 'B' Specials was in process, and "one person − one vote" was instituted in the local government franchise. 1970 and 1971 saw the split between the Official and Provisional IRA; Paisley's election to both Stormont and

Westminster; the foundation of the nationalist SDLP; the succession of Brian Faulkner to Prime Minister of Northern Ireland; the introduction of internment; and the rise of Paisley's DUP. 1972 brought not only the infamous "Bloody Sunday" (30 January), when fourteen Catholic civilians were killed by the British Army in Derry following a banned civil rights march, but also "Bloody Friday" (21 July), when the Provisional IRA exploded over twenty bombs in Belfast, killing five Protestants, two Catholics and two British Army soldiers, while injuring over 130 civilians. Politically, the year brought the suspension of Stormont and the imposition of direct rule from Westminster.

The new Secretary of State for Northern Ireland, William Whitelaw, began secret negotiations with the IRA, but without tangible results. Next, Whitelaw promoted a power-sharing executive which did have the support of Faulkner's official unionists, the nationalist SDLP, and the moderate Alliance Party. This executive was installed in January 1974, but collapsed under hard-line Protestant unionist and mostly working-class resistance in a strike in May, which practically closed down the province. The failure of the executive was precipitated by the loss of legitimacy for Faulkner's supporters within the Official Unionist Party, as the General Election in the UK of February 1974 gave all the unionist seats to those opposed to the executive power-sharing arrangement. In this sense, the strike (while noted for massive intimidation at ground level) did have intellectual and democratic support. Direct rule was reimposed, provoking a stalemate between nationalists and unionists, the IRA and the Protestant paramilitaries. British government policy appeared to move into simple reaction mode. When the "Peace People" emerged in 1976 (a movement begun by Mairéad Corrigan – the aunt of three children killed by a car driven by an IRA man who was shot by pursuing British soldiers – Betty Williams and Ciaran McKeown), government and media attempted to frame the events as an opportunity for real peace, but, as the general revulsion towards violence strove to get down to specifics, the old divisions arose.

When Margaret Thatcher came to power in 1979, she inherited the problem of "special category" status for republican prisoners. From 1976 onwards, the British government had withdrawn the right of prisoners to be regarded as "political" and thereby having special privileges. Those incarcerated began to refuse to wear prison uniform, preferring to go "on the blanket".[9] This situation escalated into the "dirty protest", with inmates daubing the walls of their cells with their own faeces. Finally, a hunger strike was embarked upon. In total, ten men were to die. Bobby Sands, the first and most famous to die, was elected an MP while dying. Although the hunger strikes did not break Thatcher's will, they amounted to a major diplomatic disaster for the British government, bringing Sinn Féin and IRA aspirations to a national and international audience.[10] In the long term, it also helped Sinn Féin to gain confidence at the ballot-box; their support rose from 10% of the northern Irish electorate in local assembly elections in 1982 to over 15% in the local assembly elections in 1996.

The assembly elections of 1982 did not produce any viable solution, and the SDLP under John Hume's leadership turned to the Republic of Ireland's government-sponsored "New Ireland Forum" to contemplate external ways of creating an "agreed Ireland". The impetus behind the new debate pushed Dublin and London to sign the Anglo-Irish Agreement (AIA) in 1985, which allowed Dublin for the first time to have a consultative role in the governance of Northern Ireland. Although strongly resisted by the unionist parties, the vagueness of the AIA, which managed not to define the present status of Northern Ireland, did not provide an easy target, ensuring the Agreement's survival.

In the early 1990s, after "three-strand talks" foundered (so named to describe political possibilities within Northern Ireland, between Northern Ireland and the Republic of Ireland, and between the Republic of Ireland and Great Britain), John Hume began meeting Gerry Adams of Sinn Féin to establish a nationalist coalition, in which he argued that the unionists, not the British, needed to be persuaded of the advantages of a united Ireland. Hume's link to the Irish government laid a path to the Downing Street Declaration in December 1993, which was notable for its statement that the British government had "no selfish, strategic or economic interest in Northern Ireland". In turn, the IRA declared a cease fire in August 1994 (as did the Protestant paramilitaries in October), which was followed by a framework document written and agreed to by the British and Irish governments, and released in early 1995. It was at this point that the process for implementing talks slowed down over issues over the decommissioning of weapons. Former US Senate Majority leader George Mitchell delivered a report to the British government suggesting the gradual and parallel handing over of weapons as peace talks progressed. Unionists demanded decommissioning before Sinn Féin could be allowed into the talks. In the midst of these disagreements, the IRA ended its cease fire in February 1996. British Prime Minister John Major pressed ahead with elections in the province in May, and in late-1996 the talks began with all parties except Sinn Féin. By early 1997, the IRA campaign appeared to be back in action while all participants awaited the call for a general election in the UK (and, to a lesser extent, in the Republic of Ireland), in the hope that new majority governments would be able to make radical decisions to jump-start the peace talks into dealing with substantive issues. To some degree, this hope was realised after Tony Blair's Labour Party's landslide election victory in May 1997. There soon followed in July an "unequivocal" cease fire from the IRA. Substantive talks, including Sinn Féin, began in September 1997 with a closure date of May 1998, when referenda were held in both parts of Ireland on the same day. Citizens of the Republic of Ireland voted 95% in favour of amending the Irish constitutional articles 2 and 3, effectively removing the territorial claim over Northern Ireland. The electorate in Northern Ireland voted 71% in favour of what became known as the Good Friday Agreement. Eight of the ten parties elected to the Peace Forum signed on to the accord (Ian Paisley's DUP refused to participate in the talks, while Robert McCartney's UK Unionists withdrew during the discussions). In reality, the 71% vote indicated that perhaps only 55% of the Protestant population supported the agreement, with many upset that most prisoners would be freed within two years. Nevertheless, the majority vote paved the way for elections in June 1998 to set up a Northern Ireland Assembly to be followed by cross-border bodies and stronger links between Great Britain and Ireland. In the elections, 80 of the 108 seats went to those supporting the agreement. David Trimble, leader of the UUP, was elected First Minister in July, with Seamus Mallon of the SDLP as his deputy. Splinter paramilitary groups on both sides threaten to disrupt this political process, and it will be difficult for the UUP to be on committees with Sinn Féin, but a way to take violence out of Irish politics has now begun. It remains to be seen whether the 1968-98 period will be regarded as the final violent phase of the Irish conflict.

Revisionism and its discontents

The foregoing chronicle lays out many of the important events in Irish history pertinent to present-day Northern Ireland, but it requires a gloss to put some flesh on several bones of contention. Even if we can establish what actually happened with broad brush strokes, it does not automatically confer meaning or illumination. With partition in 1921, and the emergence of two separate states, a number of intellectual disciplines and social activities were also split. In an effort not to succumb to the vulgar nationalist and unionist ideologies pouring out of Dublin and Belfast, historians sought common speaking ground. In February 1936, the Ulster Society for Irish Historical Studies was founded at Queen's University, Belfast, to promote the scientific study of Irish history; as a counterpart, in November 1936, the first meeting of the Irish Historical Society was held in Dublin at the Royal Irish Academy. The influential secretaries of these organisations were the historians T W Moody and R Dudley Edwards, who were to become joint editors of the important journal *Irish Historical Studies.*

Ireland has always been home to feisty periodicals and newspapers which have claimed to examine the past in a more enlightened way than their predecessors or competitors. There is nothing new to this debate, as each generation of historians has striven to make sense of the past, although not always through the standards of that past. Inevitably, a writer must bring his or her own experience, political and personal, to the appreciation of historical circumstances. This is particularly true at a time when an issue so fundamental as the unification of Ireland remains unresolved. This tension must affect the current crop of historians and political scientists.

Revisionism in Irish history has been understood as an attempt to bring some objectivity when reassessing nationalist/republican and unionist/loyalist assumptions about the past. For example, the myth of one-nation Irish nationalism has been the target of many of these studies. This myth's reliance on the supposed linear progression of (Catholic) Irish experience – conquest, oppression, rebellion, partial freedom and inevitable full unification – has been heavily scrutinised. For Roy Foster, author of the impressive and now-standard *Modern Ireland 1600-1972*, it is important to observe the contradictions and rejections of this myth.[11] Note the opening line of Foster's foreword to *The Oxford Illustrated History of Ireland* (1989): "One of the marks of maturity in Irish historical studies has been a growing interest in pinpointing discontinuities rather than ironing out elisions".[12] Probably the word "maturity" is the most problematic, as it implies that the revisionist orthodoxy is disinterested, which other commentators have contested.

Conor Cruise O'Brien is fairly regarded as one political revisionist historian, whose *States of Ireland* in effect called for a more realistic link between nationalist rhetoric in the Republic of Ireland and reality in Northern Ireland.[13] The reality I speak of here is the presence of 900 000 unionists on the island of Ireland, and the movement of the Republic of Ireland's citizens onto the modern stage, where Anglo-American and European culture and values have become increasingly powerful over Irish imaginations and aspirations. This modernisation of the Republic of Ireland, which is normally attributed to the election of Seán Lemass as Prime Minister in 1959, has arguably created the sense that the country *is* a separate state from British and militant republican-influenced Northern Ireland.[14] The desire for modernisation was voiced as early as the 1940s by Seán Ó'Faoláin. Editor of the journal *The Bell*, Ó'Faoláin had pointed out the dangers of the Gaelic cult, even making a few mischievous parallels with Nationalist Socialist mythology.[15]

The revisionist project and its detractors have provoked a fascinating debate, questioning not only how history should be written, but also how historians should confront the northern crisis. One of the tasks Roy Foster and other political scientists and historians such as Tom Nairn and Paul Bew have achieved is to complicate the nationalist line of thinking that partition was an innate evil, and that British influence was invariably bad for Ireland. Counter-revisionists such as Brendan Bradshaw, Desmond Fennell, Brian Murphy and Seamus Deane attack the project for attempting to paint militant republicanism as irrational, for trying to create an intellectual space for the current Republic of Ireland to reject its violent genesis and to relinquish its nationalist constitutional aspirations, and for failing to empathise with the very real Catholic Irish grievances against British and unionist hegemony.[16]

These are strong charges, whether they are brought against reassessments of the famine (truly a national trauma often evoked) or against the Northern Ireland "Troubles". As Roy Foster and others imply, there exists a fair degree of evidence that little continuity in the "one-nation" struggle can be deduced. Retroactive mythologies are perhaps the most difficult to dispel. One revealing trajectory is the evolution of the Provisional IRA and Sinn Féin in Northern Ireland, and its intellectual basis. It is true, for example, that the condition of the republicans in 1968-69 (and immediately before) was of a precarious nature. There was no armed IRA to speak of, no consistent ideology, and little resistance towards the hegemony of unionist-run Stormont. In Frank Martin's video *Behind the Mask* (1989), Gerry Adams refers to the joyous disbelief of one old man, who had been around for partition in 1920/21, at the fall of Stormont in 1972. The yoke had certainly (and remarkably) been broken. As the years went by, as the mostly peaceful "ethnic desegregation" after 1972 went on (as distinct from the many violent moves in 1970/71), the republicans built themselves up militarily and politically as "protectors" of Catholic ghettos in Belfast and elsewhere. When Gerry Adams lost his Westminster seat in 1992 to the SDLP member Joe Hendron, he claimed that the seat had been "stolen" from the people of West Belfast. The "people", of course, to him were Catholic republicans.[17]

Given that, when it finally got involved in elections, Sinn Féin polled an average of 40% of the nationalist vote and 12% of the overall northern Irish electorate, one should not overestimate its democratic importance. Although the assembly elections of 30 May 1996 gave Sinn Féin its best result, it was only a marginally higher percentage of its usual nationalist vote (42%, as opposed to the 58% of the SDLP).[18] Yet, it is a fact that the agitation created by Sinn Féin forced John Hume into two series of talks with Gerry Adams. Much-touted as the statesman of the era, Hume has surprisingly reactionary views towards the Protestant population. He has consistently seen the unionists as analogous to the Afrikaner in South Africa: "The unionist mind-set based largely in the Protestant population of Northern Ireland, is akin to that of the Afrikaner who believes that, surrounded by hostility that is real or apparent, the only way to protect his people is to concentrate power in their own hands to the exclusion of others".[19]

This is a clever ploy of Hume's: it suggests that the Protestants continue to rule badly (yet, since 1972, they have not been allowed to do so by Britain); that the Catholics were denied like blacks in

South Africa from voting (untrue at the national and provincial level, and only partly true at the local level where a property qualification was required of both Protestant and Catholic: this statement is usually countered by arguing that Catholics were disproportionately represented in rented accommodation, and the key decisions on housing and employment were made at the gerrymandered local level, but research has shown that, where Catholics controlled councils, similar discrimination occurred);[20] and that the Protestants will eventually see the sense of a united country (but the Ulster Protestants wish to belong to a larger unit – the United Kingdom; in contrast, the Afrikaner did not want to remain connected to The Netherlands or Great Britain). There is also a historical irony in Hume's analogy between the Ulster Protestants and the Afrikaners. In the Boer War (1899-1902), John McBride, a member of the Irish Republican Brotherhood and one of the men executed in 1916 by the British, fought for the Boers, although certainly not for the native black population. Politically ingenious as it is, Hume's analysis is flawed and, from a unionist perspective, unhelpful because it legitimises claims for a united Ireland when, in fact, no basis of cross-community consent actually exists on the national question.

In what still remains one of the best and most even-handed assessments of the Northern Ireland crisis, Tom Nairn has provided the intellectual context for Hume's views and for those of Gerry Adams: the myth of anti-imperialism. As Nairn has succinctly explained, the anti-imperialist myth has the virtue of simplicity. It argues that unification was prevented by an imperial conspiracy, requiring the help of "deluded lackeys" (the northern Protestants). Furthermore, the Protestants can be "dismissed from history" because they foolishly identify with the imperialist power of Great Britain. In this framework, Protestants are suffering from a false consciousness. To allow this myth to work, the Protestant proletariat must be ignored, as must the fact of two diverse ethnic communities inhabiting the same land.[21]

I share with Nairn the concern of unchecked nationalism and also his belief that, if there is to be change and a solution of sorts in Northern Ireland, the answer will lie not with Great Britain or the strength of the republican/nationalist movement, but with a strategy to address the hopes and fears of the Protestant community, which we have still fully to witness.[22] The Protestant community is fragmented by politics and by religion. Anglicans, Baptists, Evangelicals, Free Presbyterians, Methodists and Presbyterians cross class lines and may vote with equal conviction for the Alliance Party, the UUP, the DUP or even fringe unionist parties with connections to paramilitaries, such as the UDP and the PUP.[23] This diversity is in keeping with a Dissenter culture, although it is one often foreign to many Irish Catholics, and to many in England and the United States. Nairn's observations, however, prove to be uncannily accurate in understanding the cultural area of film, television drama and video to date. This myth of anti-imperialism to varying degrees informs all of the work which I discuss.

As with all myths, fiction becomes confused and intermixed with verifiable reality. Myths do not tell outright lies, but they harness and embellish selective truths. In this vein, one might profitably bear in mind Edward Said's distinction between imperialism and colonialism: "'imperialism' means the practice, the theory, and the attitudes of a dominating metropolitan centre ruling a distant territory; 'colonialism', which is almost always a consequence of imperialism, is the implanting of settlements on distant territory".[24]

Looking at these definitions with Ireland in mind leads us into complex areas of debate. London is a powerful influence over Ireland both north and south, although it might now be argued that the imperial centre has shifted to the United States, certainly in cultural attitudes. The 17th-century plantations of Ireland by English and Scottish settlers are generally agreed to mark the major colonisation of the country. The descendants of these settlers form the majority of the 900 000 Protestants present today in Northern Ireland. Arguably, it is the failure fully to grasp the fact that Northern Ireland's problems are due to a colonial experience and reality, rather than an imperialist conspiracy, that retards any peace or political agreement. Ireland may have been regarded as a distant territory in the 17th century, but, with its next-door location to Britain, and the constant travel and commerce between the two islands so commonplace, it is less easy to view the smaller country in the same light as Canada and Australia.

Revisionism in history and in the reading of literature connected to the Northern Ireland "Troubles" has thus been embarked upon. In a much more modest way, this book seeks in part to deliver a revisionist reading of Irish film and video to help this debate about the past and near past to come more clearly into cultural focus, and I think it is fitting to begin with one of the most popular representations of Northern Ireland on film: Carol Reed's *Odd Man Out*.

Notes

[1]   T W Moody, "Irish History and Irish Mythology", in Ciaran Brady (ed), *Interpreting Irish History: The Debate on Historical Revisionism 1938-1994* (Blackrock: Irish Academic Press, 1994): 81.

[2]   Geoffrey Wheatcroft, "Northern Ireland: the game neither team wants to win", *The Globe and Mail* 10 June 1994: A25.

[3]   The republican strain in mainly Presbyterian culture has been championed on many occasions by Catholic nationalists and republicans. It has also been championed by born unionists, such as Tom Paulin, who "converted" to the constitutional nationalist cause. See Paulin's selections

of this Presbyterian strain in "Northern Protestant Oratory and Writing 1791-1985", in Seamus Deane, Andrew Carpenter and Jonathan Williams (eds), *The Field Day Anthology of Irish Writing*, volume III (Derry: Field Day Publications, 1991): 314-379. A clear and succinct exposition of the travails of Presbyterians in the crucial period of the late-18th century and the early 19th century is John McCann, "The Northern Irish Liberal Presbyterians 1770-1830", *Canadian Journal of Irish Studies* 21: 1 (July 1995): 96-114.

[4]   The border between the two new states was always a fictive construct, since it was clearly a compromise between all of Ireland staying within the union and none of it staying. Critics have argued over the naturalness or otherwise of this border. Some see it as a natural extension of economic and cultural difference; others see it as a mainly artificial political construct. See Tom Garvin, "The North and the Rest: The Politics of the Republic of Ireland", in Charles Townshend (ed), *Consensus in Ireland: Approaches and Recessions* (Oxford: Clarendon Press, 1988): 95-109; and Joe Clery's admittedly problematic "'Fork-Tongued on the Border Bit': Partition and the Politics of Form in Contemporary Narratives of the Northern Irish Conflict", *South Atlantic Quarterly* 95: 1 (winter 1996): 227-276, particularly 273. Clery's hostility to the revisionist project of Roy Foster and Conor Cruise O'Brien is so pervasive, and his sympathy for the republican thesis so obvious, that it undermines his otherwise useful readings of Bernard Mac Laverty's novel *Cal* (Belfast: The Blackstaff Press, 1983) and of *The Crying Game*. For example, Clery seems fixated by a contrast between northern Irish (Catholic) nationalism and British/ northern Irish (Protestant) statism; he strangely rejects the notion that southern Irish statism exists which is antinationalist, and the notion that both Cal and Fergus, the leading characters of the above narratives, are in search of a suitable state to call their own; rather he sees them weakly "returning" to British statism.

[5]   Sabine Wichert, *Northern Ireland since 1945* (London; New York: Longman, 1991): 16-17.

[6]   Cornelius O'Leary remarks that "[i]n Derry city there was still a Unionist majority on the council, although there were more Nationalist voters in one ward than Unionists in the entire city". Quoted in Paul Bew, Peter Gibbon and Henry Patterson, *Northern Ireland 1921-1996: Political Forces and Social Classes*, revised and updated edition (London: Serif, 1996): 9.

[7]   See J J Lee, *Ireland 1912-1985: Politics and Society* (Cambridge: Cambridge University Press, 1989). In his chapter on Northern Ireland 1945-85, Lee is clearly no friend of the Ulster Protestants, but the value of his work is in concisely pinpointing the major elements of the "Catholic complaint" in the northern state. These included the inequality of industrial development west and east of the Bann River (the Catholic-dominated west was undeveloped compared to the Protestant-dominated east); the decision to locate the new University of Ulster in Protestant Coleraine, rather than in Catholic Derry; and the creation of a new town, Craigavon, between Lurgan and Portadown, named after the first prime minister of Northern Ireland, James Craig (noted for his comment that Northern Ireland had a "Protestant parliament for a Protestant people").

This name did little to appeal to the sensitivities of the minority Catholic population.

8   On 23 November 1967, Ian Paisley took part in a televised debate at the Oxford Union with Norman St John Stevas. Paisley supported the motion "That the Roman Catholic Church has no place in the Twentieth century"; he lost the debate. See Clifford Smyth, *Ian Paisley: Voice of Protestant Ulster* (Edinburgh: Scottish Academic Press, 1987): 19-20.

9   The blanket protest was an attempt to fight for the status of political prisoner, whereby prisoners could wear their own clothes and not standard issue. Since they refused to wear prison clothing, they wore only blankets.

10   One of the best accounts of the hunger strike and its political resonance is Padraig O'Malley, *Biting at the Grave: The Irish Hunger Strikes and the Politics of Despair* (Boston: Beacon Press, 1990).

11   R F Foster, *Modern Ireland 1600-1972* (Harmondsworth: Penguin Books, 1989).

12   R F Foster (ed), *The Oxford Illustrated History of Ireland* (Oxford; New York: Oxford University Press, 1989): v.

13   Conor Cruise O'Brien, *States of Ireland* (London: Hutchinson, 1972). O'Brien's role in Irish affairs and his writings can be comprehensively perused in Donald Harman Akenson, *Conor: A Biography of Conor Cruise O'Brien. Volume I: Narrative & Volume II: Anthology* (Montreal; Kingston: McGill-Queen's University Press, 1994).

14   Note, for example, Dermot Bolger's comment: "Although some commentators still speak simply about two cultures existing in Ireland – a Catholic/Nationalist and Protestant/Unionist one, the response of the largely untouched South to the frequent barbarism of both sides in the North has been such that recent statistical analysis has shown the citizens of the Irish Republic to feel now that they have more in common with the Scottish, Welsh and English than with any section of the population in the North." See Dermot Bolger (ed), *The Picador Book of Contemporary Irish Fiction* (London: Picador, 1993): ix.

15   See Luke Gibbons' prose selections in his "Challenging the Canon: Revisionism and Cultural Criticism", in Seamus Deane, Andrew Carpenter and Jonathan Williams (eds), *The Field Day Anthology of Irish Writing*, volume III (Derry: Field Day Publications, 1991): 561-680. Gibbons includes selections from Seán Ó'Faoláin, T W Moody, Roy Foster, Conor Cruise O'Brien and Edna Longley, among others. Gibbons' introduction is interesting as it shows him to be a counter-revisionist. He argues, although not very convincingly, for the liberal strand in nationalist thinking, and accuses the revisionists of conservatism.

16   A guide to the debates may be found in Ciaran Brady (ed), *Interpreting Irish History: The Debate on Historical Revisionism 1938-1994* (Blackrock: Irish Academic Press, 1994). Essays by T W Moody, R D Edwards, F S L Lyons, Oliver MacDonagh and Roy Foster set the stage to quite virulent criticisms by Desmond Fennell, Brendan Bradshaw, Brian Murphy and Seamus Deane. Further reflections on the debate may be found in D

George Boyce and Alan O'Day (eds), *The Making of Modern Irish History: Revisionism and the revisionist controversy* (London; New York: Routledge, 1996).

[17] See Fionnuala O Connor, *In Search of a State: Catholics in Northern Ireland* (Belfast: The Blackstaff Press, 1993): 85.

[18] In the May 1997 election, Sinn Féin polled 16% of the vote, and 17% in the local elections later that month. For the first time, Belfast unionists lost control of the city of Belfast (26-25 seats). In 1997, Belfast had a SDLP mayor.

[19] John Hume, "A New Era Beckons for Ireland", *Guardian Weekly* 2 October 1994: 19.

[20] See Donald Harman Akenson, *God's Peoples: Covenant and Land in South Africa, Israel, and Ulster* (Ithaca; London: Cornell University Press, 1992): 200.

[21] Tom Nairn, *The Break-Up of Britain: Crisis and Neo-Nationalism*, second expanded edition (London: Verso, 1981): 231.

[22] Nairn's point that nationalism is Janus-like, having both a liberatory and a reactionary potential is nowhere truer than in Northern Ireland. Recently, Nairn has reformulated his ideas. He no longer sees an independent Northern Ireland winning out, but nor does he see the "assimilative nationalism" of Sinn Féin doing so. Stormont will never return, nor will full integration with the United Kingdom be possible, but a Swiss-style cantonal or civic nationalism may work. See Tom Nairn, "On the Threshold", *London Review of Books* 17: 6 (23 March 1995): 9-11. The concept of civic nationalism is also the preferred path of Michael Ignatieff in *Blood and Belonging: Journeys into the New Nationalism* (London: Vintage, 1994). Cosmopolitan civic nationalism imagines a practical geographical entity functioning under the rights of citizenship and the rule of law as against the self-determination push by ethnic nationalists with their rhetoric of exclusion and imposition. The work of historian R F Foster also seems to present an interest and precedent for civic nationalism; as a generally acceptable concept, it appears implicit in Foster's *Modern Ireland 1600-1972*.

[23] Although the religious identity of the Protestant community in Northern Ireland is hard to quantify accurately, Presbyterians account for approximately 50%, Anglicans (Church of Ireland) 40%, and the rest, including Methodists and Baptists, 10%.

[24] Edward W Said, *Culture & Imperialism* (New York: Vintage, 1994): 8.

3

The Rorschach test: anti-imperialism in Carol Reed's Odd Man Out

The political angle you may completely ignore, as the director has wisely ignored it. In essence it is just another cops-and-robbers film. Why the 'hero' robbed a bank is his own business, not ours. It may have been to get his 'doll' a mink coat, or funds for his political party. All that concerns us are his reactions when, having killed a man, he, wounded and desperate, seeks to escape in a city which has been roused against him. (*Belfast Telegraph*)[1]

There is no doubt that it is a really good film. There equally is no doubt that, in its essence, it amounts to a glorification of the I.R.A.! If I had been a youth, emerging from the Theatre Royal on Sunday night, and saw on the walls of Trinity College the slogan 'Join the I.R.A.,' I have not the least doubt that I should have been sorely tempted to do so! All the romance is on the side of 'the Organisation.' (*The Irish Times*)[2]

The tyranny of stereotypes, disabling myths, and subtle or forced masquerades for the spectator are to be found in abundance in Carol Reed's *Odd Man Out* (1946). This fascinating film does not need to be "reread" in the 1990s in order to demonstrate to a new generation of viewers that it is worth seeing and discussing.[3] An important work in British film history and in the assessment of Carol Reed's œuvre, *Odd Man Out* showed that film noir was not a totally American phenomenon, and underscored the humanist credentials of its director.[4] And yet, *Odd Man Out* is more than its great photography, its film noir stylistic conventions, and its narrative imperatives of seeking closure. It is simply the first major fiction film to depict the state of Northern Ireland.[5] It is a film that questions the status quo, and implies that the Protestant community in Northern Ireland is akin with militarism. More to the point, I believe it is productive to read the film as an earnest exploration of the anti-imperialist arguments that Tom Nairn views as a believable fiction or myth dominant within the nationalist community.

What is interesting is the intersection between British and Irish culture articulated by the film. This criss-crossing, this interrogation of a state under duress, is surely symptomatic of nearly all films and videos produced since 1968 on the subject of Northern Ireland. *Odd Man Out* sets the standard from which further dramatisations can be compared and contrasted, and from which filmmakers and screenwriters have modulated their own visual constructions.[6] The film frames Northern Ireland (specifically Belfast), unfortunately perhaps, as a place where a police state exists, where the common people are oppressed, and where revolutionaries struggle to achieve self-determination.

Critics have pointed to the British ideology that runs through the film. This bias, it is argued, includes the affirmation and validation of state violence, the undermining of the cause of the IRA through its atavistic urges, and the apparent general decontextualisation of Northern Ireland's status. While there are elements of truth in this analysis, the more detailed the reading of the film, the more a sympathetic republican/nationalist position emerges. Far from ignoring the republican issues, the film invites viewers to see Belfast (inaccurately) as a Catholic-dominated working-class city, with a populace not only unhappy with their poverty, but also resentful of the militaristic Protestant policing. This implicit sympathy is superficially masked by the "main" story of the state seeking to find a killer at large. And, in the love interest, so often cited as the weakness of any political reading of a film, we can actively see the clinching argument, for Kathleen's (Kathleen Ryan) decision to take up the gun and run into martyrdom is quintessential mythmaking of the kind that generates political passions.

Politically-oriented or -implicated films invariably reach some form of compromise with the demands of commercial filmmaking. Audiences do not like to listen to a lecture. In this film, it would appear that the ingredients of romantic melodrama win out to the detriment of the political "message", although this natural tension is not as clear as it appears at first glance. Characterisation and action often push the political context into the background, but do not erase it. What I suggest is that in *Odd Man Out* the political topography can nevertheless be mapped, even from the very opening titles:

> This story is told against a background of political unrest in a city of Northern Ireland. It is not concerned with the struggle between the law and an illegal organisation, but only with the conflict in the hearts of the people when they become unexpectedly involved.[7]

Critics have complained that Reed, or whoever was responsible for these titles, is imprecise in the first sentence, since Belfast is not specifically named.[8] I find this an odd criticism. Whenever we watch

44

British social realist films such as *Room At the Top* (1959) and *Saturday Night and Sunday Morning* (1960), we do not know the nuances that differentiate one northern English town from another. Similarly, *Odd Man Out* could have taken place in (London)Derry city without any loss to the narrative dynamics.

The truly curious aspect of these titles is the second sentence. Here we have an interpretation of the narrative which attempts to garner sympathy for those caught up in illegal activities. The paragraph of Reed's titles begs the question: who are "the people" who actually have a conflict in this film? Many, such as Gin Jimmy (Joseph Tomelty), Shell (F J McCormick), Tober (Elwyn Brook-Jones), Lukey (Robert Newton) and the barman Fencie (William Hartnell) become unexpectedly involved, but they could hardly be said to have a conflict about their meeting Johnny McQueen (James Mason). They either use him or jettison him as quickly as possible. Kathleen wants to have him to herself; Lukey wants to paint him; Tober wants him to practise his long-forsaken medical profession; Shell wants to exchange him for money, while Gin Jimmy and the barman simply wish to offload Johnny onto someone else. In fact, the only scene of true conflict concerns the two Englishwomen Rosie (Fay Compton) and Maudie (Beryl Measor) and the Englishman Tom (Arthur Hambling) posted to Northern Ireland. These individuals have the choice to phone for the police, but act humanely towards Johnny, providing him with some treatment and a drink before sending him on his way. Luckily for Johnny (and the narrative), he is momentarily "rescued" by these English people and not discovered by the local Protestant community, who presumably would have handed him in immediately. It would not be surprising, therefore, that the English audience would find that the true conflict is an English one, not an Irish one. Even in 1946, Reed's film locates the English influence in Northern Ireland as "above" the "real" conflict. For the most part, the English are neutral observers.

One of the most interesting features of Reed's film is his contemporary look at Northern Ireland. His 1946 Belfast shows the "two up-two down" terraced houses familiar to most Northern Ireland residents (only recently cleared), the waste ground and fallout from the bombing during the Second World War (Belfast was targeted as a port city), and the poverty of the working-class kids, who beg for money, tease the police and re-enact Johnny McQueen's actions. Today, this re-enactment has an emotional power, which was probably lacking in 1946. These children take as their hero an IRA activist who has killed a civilian. Given Reed's choice to hire the local boys to act out these scenes, one wonders at the irony that, twenty years later, these kids most likely became part of the civil rights marches and the renewed IRA struggle. Despite the low-level IRA campaigns since partition, which were hardly on the scale of the 1970s campaign, ongoing nationalist politics allowed republican mythology to be reactivated, notwithstanding the sobriquet I Ran

Away at the beginning of the "Troubles". A 1990s viewer of the film might be mystified by the presence of the British troops (who significantly voice their desire to leave), and by the request of police for identity cards when checking civilians. The stationing of the troops in Northern Ireland was a result of the war, and ID cards were in force in the UK until the early 1950s. However, the impression conveyed is of a militarised, Big Brother state, which fed (and continues to feed) republican arguments over Northern Ireland.

Reed's arrival in Belfast in the 1946/47 period coincided with many difficulties for the Conservative unionist Stormont government in its dealings with the new Clement Attlee Labour government in Westminster.[9] As Paul Bew, Peter Gibbon and Henry Patterson have observed, Northern Ireland's political leaders were lukewarm at first to the establishment of a welfare state, in case it decreased the autonomy of the Stormont government and affected many unionist businesses, including the very dominant linen industry.[10] For a while in 1946 and 1947, Stormont Cabinet Ministers and UUP members considered the value of seeking Dominion status (which would have allowed an opting out of any national legislation). In fact, Attlee never wanted to upset the unionist hegemony, and the Northern Ireland government finally realised that not going along with reforms might allow the partition of the country to be reopened as a political question, particularly if benefits from the union with Great Britain could not be seen by working-class voters.

Novelist and screenwriter F L Green and director Reed clearly saw the symbolism of the robbery of the textile mill as an attack on one of the key Protestant-owned (and mostly conservative) industries in Northern Ireland. In the film, it is significant that our view of the mill is from Johnny's dazed perspective. The mill is shown twice: firstly with what appears to be a dutch tilt from inside the car, and secondly with a low-angle shot from outside the front door. Both shots focus on the tall brick chimney bellowing black smoke. The chimney conjures up allusions to German Expressionist films, especially Fritz Lang's *Metropolis* (1926). One may indeed see the connections that Green and Reed are making between the exploitation of the workers in Lang's film with those who must work for this Protestant-owned business.[11]

In establishing the nationalist rhetoric of the film, it is instructive to look closely at a few key scenes and sequences. The first of importance is the discussion in the upstairs bedroom between Dennis (Robert Beatty) and Johnny after the orders for the textile mill robbery have been given. This scene has the narrative purpose of revealing to the audience that Johnny is the leader of the organisation in the city; that he has been sentenced to seventeen years for gunrunning; that he escaped after serving only eight months; and that he has spent the last six months hiding in this house. Dennis is concerned that Johnny will not be well enough for the "mission", and intimates that Johnny has changed while in prison. Whereas Green's novel begins with the robbery, this addition to the screenplay firmly plants Reed's sympathies with constitutional nationalism. But, as the film progresses, focalised as it becomes through Kathleen, we are shifted to unconstitutional nationalism.

The scene is prefaced by Johnny telling Pat (Cyril Cusack), who is waving his handgun, not to encourage violence. After Pat and his two compatriots Nolan (Dan O'Herlihy) and Murphy (Roy Irving) have left, Kathleen, Dennis and Johnny remain. The following discussion can be understood as a gentle debate between a would-be constitutional nationalist (Johnny) and a "die-hard" nationalist (Dennis), who sees violence as absolutely necessary to further the "cause":

Dennis: Your... your heart's not in this job, Johnny, is it?
Johnny: I won't be sorry when we're back.
Dennis: You don't believe in anything?
Johnny: I believe in everything we're trying to do. But this violence isn't getting us anywhere.
Dennis: You were sentenced to seventeen years' imprisonment for bringing guns and ammunition to the dumps. You talk about violence?
Johnny: In prison, you have time to think. What if we could throw the guns away and make our cause in the parliaments instead of in the backstreets?

From this dialogue we can see that Johnny is a "soft" constitutional nationalist, a reluctant robber/terrorist. Highly significant is his reference to parliaments, presumably including Stormont, Westminster and Dublin. Johnny's change of thinking is underscored by the way in which the scene is shot and choreographed. The camera during the above exchange is positioned opposite Kathleen who sits on the bed between the two men. We are encouraged to associate with Kathleen as the "quiet" listener to this debate, weighing the pros and cons. For Dennis' lines, the camera has been panned left with a slight low-angle position. For Johnny's lines and, in particular, his last speech above, the low angle is much more pronounced, given that Johnny rises to stand on the end of the bed. His body fills the frame imposingly, thus naturally giving greater authority to his pursuit of an eventual constitutional struggle devoid of violence. Kathleen's "neutral" role here locates her as the source of "common sense", a person who seeks love and warmth. This initial reaction is important because of her changed actions later in the film. She fully understands the politics, since her father is absent due to activities associated with the "organisation". Her choices, given that she represents a new generation, are critical for audience-identification.

The second scene of importance is when Johnny is picked up by the two Englishwomen Rosie and Maudie. He has fallen on the road as a long vehicle passes by. The women think he has been hit by the vehicle, when in fact he has just fallen from the pain of his gunshot wound. Rosie and Maudie bring him inside and argue over how to look after him. This scene is partly comic, allowing the audience a moment of respite, and providing the "neutral" English audience with the conflict expressed in the film's titles: what would an English person do, if faced in Northern Ireland with a dying gunman in his or her front room?

Reed's choice to have it become an English dilemma, rather than an Irish Protestant one, is worthy of comment. In Green's novel, it is clear that Rosie, Maudie and their husbands are Irish Protestants. Both women are strong independent thinkers who, Green makes clear, consider their Protestant community as containing intolerant people. For example, in the novel, Rosie struggles in argument against her husband Alfie:

> 'I have never had such hard things to decide,' he remarked in a soft, troubled tone.
>
> Rosie snorted contemptuously. 'Hard things? It is only hard because o' the politics and all that in you! Sayin' hard things all your life and callin' them politics, and knowing all the time that they's bad and against Christian feelings. And then findin', like now, that your true heart was never in the hard words, but was only stirred by the bad blood was raised up in you. ...'
>
> 'That's treason, and you know it!' Alfie said.
>
> She met his horrified glance boldly.
>
> 'Is it?' she exclaimed. 'I am loyal to king and country and I fear God. My sons and my daughter is in the Services. I'm actin' on what my conscience tells me is human and kind when I see a dyin' man, and I don't want no politics or religion to tell me I must put him out. I hold nothin' against anyone on this earth, except the king's enemies. Maybe, this fellah Johnny is one o' the king's enemies; but he is dyin' and that's what matters now. Let the ones who like living at daggers drawn with their neighbours come in and put him out!'[12]

Green attempts to draw attention to the many contradictions of a divided Christian community of Protestants and Catholics. The novelist's work labours to encourage support of a loyal, non-sectarian community. Green's status as an Englishman who came to reside in Belfast perhaps explains his tendency not to see beyond this Christian surface. Rosie seems to speak for Green, for she is the enlightened one who strives to persuade her more hard-line Protestant husband to see in his Christianity the equality of all men and women before God. These sentiments comprise Green's view of how Northern Ireland's majority Protestant community needed to reassess their attitudes towards the working-class Catholics in the city. In this sense, Green's novel is a plea directed to the Protestant community to embark on a modernised approach to old prejudices.[13]

By erasing the Irish Protestant character of these individuals, Reed and his screenwriters Green and R C Sherriff promote a specific reading of the situation in Northern Ireland. This change implies that the non-Catholics in the film are "passing through", and are people with no real commitment to the land in which they live. As Nairn ironically remarks, they can be "dismissed from history".[14] Naturally, this attitude serves to increase the audience's sympathy for Johnny, coupled with the striking fact that the only potential Protestant representations are the prison officer Donald (a mute role) and the Head Constable (Dennis O'Dea), both twinned to military-like repression.[15]

The debate in the film between Rosie and her husband Tom functions to place the Christian themes foremost, but also, as I have suggested, to underscore the point that the English are effectively non-combatants at heart in this "conflict". If this viewpoint is accepted, the "cause" of Irish "liberation" is more easily justified. For, the logic runs, if Northern Ireland is populated mainly by people such as Rosie and Maudie, all that is required for an early British exit is a "raising of consciousness". The latter assumption has always been part of Sinn Féin's political ratiocination, somehow reckoning that removing British control and troops will bring the Irish Protestants into the republican fold. Additionally, this scene in the film tends to perpetuate the anti-imperialist myth so dear to republican readings of the film. Here we see the colonial masters' representatives – three English people – *agree* not to interfere with Johnny's journey; in fact, they actually give him rudimentary medical help, as if they are simply good Samaritans. Rosie even offers to send Maudie out to find Johnny's friends.

The third scene of critical importance takes us back again to Kathleen. She has been warned by the Head Constable to give up Johnny to the law, since he has killed a man. In this scene, Kathleen helps Granny (Kitty Kirwan) to hide an incriminating gun; she wears her father's jacket; she listens to Granny's story of how the latter avoided conflict in her life by not chasing after a revolutionary. In a classic Lacanian-like mirror stage scene, Kathleen stares into the mirror on the fireplace.[16] We view her regarding herself. It is an intensely self-conscious moment, a point from which there is no true return to the old world that Kathleen has known. She takes the gun, then attempts to find and rescue Johnny. When finally Kathleen does come across her lover, and the police are closing in, she has only a few choices, none of them particularly appealing. She could hand Johnny in; she could kill him herself; she could fire a volley at the police. In the end, she chooses to play with all three possibilities by firing without enthusiasm at the police who gun them both down. Her rebellion against the

Northern Ireland state is therefore framed in the most attractive terms possible. She and Johnny become the doomed lovers of many a romantic melodrama, but they also become part of the republican mythology of blood sacrifice. The Law of the (Protestant and English) Father is rejected by outright rebellion and refusal to serve. Furthermore, the film's ending is highly significant in its placing of the deciding direction of events in the hands of a young woman brandishing a gun – what better call to arms in a traditional society? The ending of the film is of particular historical interest, since, in the novel, Kathleen kills Johnny and herself. Reed's change was apparently motivated by the American censor Joseph Breen, who suggested that such an ending would give the impression that Johnny was escaping justice; Breen wanted Johnny killed by the police as he attempted to escape. Reed claims that he only partially relented: "I agreed, but I got out of it. While the police are following them, she understands that Mason will never make it to the boat, so I had her turn around, fire at the police, and thus cause them to return fire and kill both. Everybody was satisfied. But I made her clearly fire toward the ground."[17]

In fact, Reed uses this "device" twice. Earlier in the film, Pat and Nolan are shot dead by the police after the two men fire first on leaving Teresa's (Maureen Delany) drinking and gambling den. With regard to the end of the film, Reed's comment above is less than true. Close analysis of the final sequence shows that Kathleen's firing is *not* towards the ground. The effect of this action is remarkable. Undoubtedly, the narrative pace convinces the viewer at first that this tragic sacrifice is committed on the spur of the moment and is motivated by her love for Johnny. On subsequent viewings, taking into account her awareness of the political arguments (her father also appears to be on the run), and the scene with Granny, Kathleen's decision to fire becomes far more political in nature. In this sense, Reed moves his film uneasily between constitutional and non-constitutional nationalism. Neither the published screenplay nor Reed's own unpublished and annotated shooting script contains any mention of this separate shot.[18]

Tom Nairn's "myth of atavism" may indeed work quite powerfully for some spectators of *Odd Man Out*. These critics argue that the film displaces social and political issues, preferring instead to privilege fate, melodrama, and irrational and unjustified violence.[19] Yet, one could equally say that Nairn's "myth of anti-imperialism" is endorsed by the film's subtext, as my scene analysis implies. Given the extremely high regard filmmakers and critics have for Reed's film, it is logical that this myth has been reworked and reformulated in later years. As the two newspaper quotations at the start of this chapter suggest, reading *Odd Man Out* may be likened to a Rorschach test, one which allows the individual to reveal more about himself than the object at hand. The northern reviewer seeks to dismiss the political content almost completely, leaning towards the "myth of atavism", while the southern reviewer favours the "anti-imperialist myth". I favour the latter reading, but I concede that it is unresolved. This ambiguity is arguably less present in more recent fiction films, as the next chapter reveals.

Notes

1   Harris Deans, "Here is a Really Great Picture", *Belfast Telegraph* 1 March 1947: 2.

2   Nichevo, "An Irishman's Diary", *The Irish Times* 15 March 1947: 7. This reviewer admits to a Presbyterian upbringing, which no doubt explains his unwillingness to deny the republican rhetoric in the film. The reviewer also points out that Johnny McQueen in his delirium speech appears to remember lines not from the Roman Catholic bible, but from the King James authorised Protestant bible! A wonderful irony, but one that was hardly intentional.

3   In recent years, Reed has been the subject of a biography by Nicholas Wapshott, *The Man Between: A Biography of Carol Reed* (London: Chatto & Windus, 1990), and a biocritical study by Robert F Moss, *The Films of Carol Reed* (London: Macmillan, 1987). *Odd Man Out*'s editing and music are analysed as models for teaching technique in Karel Reisz and Gavin Millar, *The Technique of Film Editing*, enlarged edition (London: Focal Press, 1970): 261-270; and Roger Manvell and John Huntley, *The Technique of Film Music*, revised and enlarged edition (London; New York: Focal Press, 1975): 123-133.

4   The British film noir theory has been advanced by Laurence Miller, who sees *Odd Man Out* as pivotal. See his "Evidence for a British Film Noir Cycle", in Wheeler Winston Dixon (ed), *Re-Viewing British Cinema, 1900-1992: Essays and Interviews* (New York: State University of New York Press, 1994): 155-164.

5   There were other narrative films that used Northern Ireland as subject-matter or setting between 1921 and 1947. They include *The Luck of the Irish* (Donovan Pedelty, 1935), *Irish and Proud of It* (Donovan Pedelty, 1936), *The Early Bird* (Donovan Pedelty, 1936), *Blarney* (Harry O'Donovan, 1938) and *Devil's Rock* (Germain Burger and Richard Hayward, 1938), Maurice Wilson's *Crime on the Irish Border* (1946). These are relatively minor works, mostly "quota quickies". See my *World Cinema 4: Ireland* (Trowbridge: Flicks Books, 1989): 24-27, and my "Appreciation: Brian Desmond Hurst, 1895-1986: Irish Filmmaker", *Eire-Ireland* 24: 4 (winter 1989): 106-113. See also Geraldine Wilkins, "Film Production in Northern Ireland", in John Hill, Martin McLoone and Paul Hainsworth (eds), *Border Crossing: Film in Ireland, Britain and Europe* (Belfast and London: Institute of Irish Studies in association with the University of Ulster and the British Film Institute, 1994): 140-145. The most notable fiction film set firmly in Northern Ireland between *Odd Man Out* and the current "Troubles" was Roy Ward Baker's *Jacqueline* (1956), which focuses on the alcoholic problems of a Belfast shipyard worker. Of most interest in this film is the fact that it is set at the time of the Coronation street parties in honour of Queen Elizabeth II. It is a rare northern Irish-related

film: not only does it not question the Britishness of Northern Ireland, it actually celebrates it. In one school scene, a boy produces a map of Ireland with Northern Ireland and the Republic of Ireland clearly marked as separate entities. One should also mention two other British attempts to address republican violence: Basil Dearden's *The Gentle Gunman* (1952) and Tay Garnett's *A Terrible Beauty* (1960), neither of which overshadows the achievement of Reed's work.

[6] Connections between *Odd Man Out* and Neil Jordan's *The Crying Game* could be usefully pursued, down to the actual words spoken by Fergus (Stephen Rea) and the general passivity of the main character.

[7] As James DeFelice observes, these titles are not present in the advance screenplay. See his *Filmguide to Odd Man Out* (Bloomington; London: Indiana University Press, 1975): 19. The screenplay is published in Roger Manvell (ed), *Three British Screen Plays* (London: Methuen & Co., 1950). Only small changes between the published screenplay and the shooting script are evident. For example, Kathleen in the film was originally given the name of Agnes. Catherine de La Roche is the first to argue that the story is detached from its setting, the titles imprecise, and that Reed was uninterested in politics. She argues that "a story based on evasion cannot achieve universality" ("Carol Reed", BBC 3rd Programme Talk [n.d., but probably 1947], Carol Reed Collection, item 17, British Film Institute, page 3 of 6. La Roche also argues that Reed's interest in children reveals the director's intent, as children generally do what they are told to do. If true, the idolisation of Johnny McQueen by these children puts Reed in the nationalist, and even republican, camp.

[8] For example, Kevin Rockett, Luke Gibbons and John Hill, *Cinema and Ireland* (London; Sydney: Croom Helm, 1987): 158.

[9] Reed was reported to have been obsessed with local accuracy and authenticity, employing Joseph Tomelty of the Group Theatre, Belfast, as an adviser. See Wapshott: 183-184. It is hard, therefore, to believe that Reed would have been unaware of the political elements of his film. *The Catholic Herald* (7 February 1947) claimed that Reed had the help of two priests on the set.

[10] Quoted in Paul Bew, Peter Gibbon and Henry Patterson, *Northern Ireland 1921-1994: Political Forces and Social Classes* (London: Serif, 1995): 81-110.

[11] Nor should one miss the overdetermined phallic nature of the imposing chimney. Johnny McQueen symbolically rejects the Law of the Father (read Protestant unionist business interests) and significantly kills the cashier on the steps below this chimney. It is as if his attack on the abusive father is understandable but carries a fatal retribution.

[12] F L Green, *Odd Man Out* (London: The Book Club, 1946): 133.

[13] To some degree, Captain Terence O'Neill, Prime Minister of Northern Ireland in the 1960s, regarded such modernisation as quintessential to Northern Ireland's economic survival. The changes advanced, however, unleashed what Tom Nairn calls "the myth of atavism", or a periodic outbreak of violence and intolerance within the Irish context. As Nairn and many others have argued – often in relation to the French Revolution

– at the very moment that conditions appear to be improving for a minority or disadvantaged community, the majority or élite community often loses control of the pace of change. See Tom Nairn, *The Break-Up of Britain: Crisis and Neo-Nationalism*, second expanded edition (London: Verso, 1981): 222.

[14] Nairn: 231.

[15] In an otherwise straightforward and entertaining commentary on the film, Dai Vaughan argues that the Head Constable must be a Catholic, since the priest refers to him by his first name. If true, although it is not supported by the published screenplay nor by the annotated shooting script, Reed has set up a tantalising tale of a community fighting amongst itself. See Dai Vaughan, *Odd Man Out* (London: British Film Institute, 1995): 54. Both Wapshott and Vaughan inaccurately state that the film was put on general release in the UK on St Patrick's Day, 17 March. The film had a three-week run in Belfast starting on 3 March 1947.

[16] The mirror stage in Lacanian psychoanalysis is the moment when the child sees the difference between the image of herself and her real self. The mirror image often supplies an idealised self, one may even say a romanticised self, which has no basis in reality. The point here is that, at this moment, Kathleen weighs up her possibilities to remain, like Granny, as a domesticated woman (the symbolic order), or to take charge of her own destiny by taking up the gun and seeking to join/rescue Johnny against the forces of the state (the imaginary order). She chooses the latter option.

[17] Quoted by Wapshott: 186. According to the Production Code Administration files for *Odd Man Out* in the Margaret Herrick Library in Beverly Hills, California, Joseph Breen was concerned that Kathleen not kill Johnny nor commit suicide herself, to let them escape from the police. The Managing Director of Rank, Filippo del Giudice, replied to Breen that it was not Reed's intention that Kathleen kill Johnny.

[18] The annotated shooting script is available in the Carol Reed Collection, deposited in the Special Collections Division of the British Film Institute.

[19] This is John Hill's argument in his chapter "Images of Violence", in Rockett, Gibbons and Hill: 147-193. It is repeated in his description and evaluation of *Odd Man Out* in Nicolet V Elert and Aruna Vasudevan (eds), *International Dictionary of Films and Filmmakers, 1: Films*, third edition (Detroit; New York; Toronto; London: St. James' Press, 1997): 725-727.

4

Troubled fictions: contemporary Irish film

I hope that we can negotiate our way out of the unnecessary British influence in this country. There are certain elements of it that might have been helpful – that part of our history which is British may turn out to contain some benefits – but their continuing involvement in governing part of this country is not helpful. And I don't feel ashamed at saying that...That doesn't mean that you are an IRA supporter if you say those things although I know people in the IRA and a lot of them joined out of a sense that there were principles at stake. (Stephen Rea)[1]

There is no understanding of the Protestant mind in Catholic Ireland and the common belief that Northern Protestants can be accommodated in a thirty-two-county all-Ireland state is delusionary – their obdurate resistance to being incorporated into one is a primary component of their identity. Catholic Ireland does not understand them and makes little attempt to do so. It does not take them seriously; it treats them, at best, with benign condescension, at worst with benign bigotry. (Padraig O'Malley)[2]

You're a Prod. They don't have souls. (Beth in Neil Jordan's *Angel*)[3]

If Carol Reed had been alive when Neil Jordan's *The Crying Game* was released in 1992, he might well have wondered to what extent Jordan had considered *Odd Man Out* as a model from which to break away. The same may be said, in conceptual terms, of other narrative films produced in the 1980s and 1990s. Each forces a particular masquerade on the viewer not unlike that found in Reed's film. This chapter discusses seven feature films that take Northern Ireland's "Troubles" as their subject. It is a sign of the polarisation of Irish society that these films can be made with little, negative or no reference to the Ulster Protestant community, and count on a warm critical, if not popular and commercial, response to their work

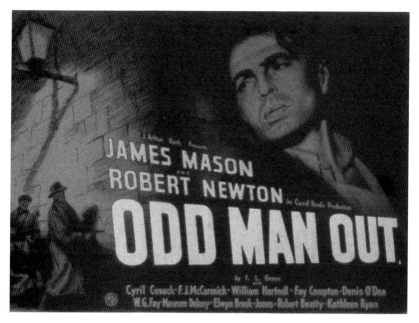

Odd Man Out

A Sense of Loss

The Patriot Game

The Patriot Game

Maeve

Angel

Attracta

Harry's Game

Acceptable Levels

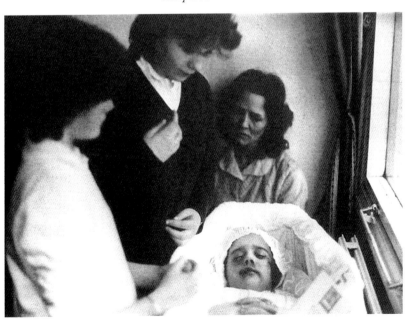

Cal

Four Days in July

Irish News, British Stories

Contact

Picturing Derry

Mother Ireland

in North America and the Republic of Ireland. The "progressive" debate in these films is arguably locked in a rethinking of the nationalist cause, but may be explained as illustrating a conversation between different tactics, rather than different strategies in addressing the northern crisis.

Neil Jordan's *Angel* (aka *Danny Boy*) and *The Crying Game* are important works in the corpus of films depicting Northern Ireland. That they come from the writer-director hands of Ireland's most successful contemporary filmmaker adds to their general interest for an Irish and international audience. Both stories on which the films were based were written around the same time in 1982, according to the director.[4] The 1970s and early 1980s were a particularly violent time in Ulster, and they spawned many literary works.[5] Only a few Irish critics have discussed the earlier film in any detail, and therefore it will serve my purpose well to be generous in my description and analysis.[6] What I argue in respect to Jordan is that, while a sensitive and gifted filmmaker, he has not been able to push dramatically beyond Nairn's atavism and anti-imperialism myths. *The Crying Game* is certainly a much more complicated film than *Angel*, and it does show a development of thought on the "national" question, yet it is still framed within a Catholic nationalist consciousness which displaces the "problem" of the Protestant community onto "representatives" of the British government.

I am not attacking Jordan's films on any arbitrary historical-realist criteria, since they are certainly effective and demanding thrillers. Rather, I want to make clear that, while they are works which emerge out of the filmmaker's interest in interrogating mythmaking, the films happily subscribe to myths of their own. That Jordan would be fascinated by myths is unsurprising on at least two counts. Firstly, his mentor and executive producer on his first film, John Boorman, is renowned for his explorations in mythical and archetypal figures in such films as *Zardoz* (1974) and *Excalibur* (1981);[7] secondly, Jordan's own writing, particularly *The Dream of the Beast* (1983), shows a keen interest in the fantastic or Gothic.[8]

From the UK title, *Angel*, one can see that Jordan likes to play with words. It connotes both good and evil, as in the term "re/avenging angel". The film opens at "Dreamland", a ballroom out in the countryside of south Armagh, otherwise known as "bandit country" in Northern Ireland because of its violent incidents.[9] Danny (Stephen Rea) is a saxophone player who seems carefree with both women and music. He flirts with the deaf mute Annie (Veronica Quilligan), the lead singer Deirdre, or Dee (Honor Heffernan), and a new bride (Lise-Ann McLaughlin) within one evening at the dance. Meanwhile, during the banter between the manager Ray (Peter Caffrey) and the drum player Bill (Alan Devlin), we learn that the band is in an area that might require protection to be safe. As it turns out, Ray has already paid such a group, presumably the IRA, or so he tells a rival twosome whom he throws out of the ballroom.

At the end of the evening, Danny meets Annie outside and makes love to her. The underage sex is glossed over visually and aurally by the mystical-looking wishing tree with fairy lights nearby, a Verdi-like chant, and the advances of Annie, rather than those of Danny. While they are recovering from their amours, two cars with four occupants draw up outside the ballroom. A bomb is planted and Ray is shot, apparently for paying protection money to the wrong group. Annie steps out from hiding to see better, and is shot by one of the assassins just before the ballroom explodes. Danny cradles the dead body of Annie in a *pietà* composition. It is this total loss of innocence, as represented by Annie, that appears to drive Danny to seek revenge. Sex and death are linked here for the first time as Danny comes under a kind of spell. Jordan has remarked in interview that Danny's revenge is really a matter of not taking a moral stand – he drifts into violence and cannot seem to stop:

> [H]e's a victim of his own lack of logic, he supplies no logic himself, but the relentless logic is supplied to him by forces that are outside of him. And these are the forces of politics, sectarianism, the forces of social hate really, and I think they are forces which assume a momentum that is larger than human beings. And that's the terrifying thing I find about the world at the moment, that ideas and ideologies and common constructs that are created by human beings assume a power that is actually larger than the sum of those human beings. And that is really what I wanted to show in the film.[10]

While it is true that Jordan strives for the metaphysical, this quotation also presents someone intent on questioning the ideological role of Irish and British nationalism and its relationship to violence. It is puzzling that Jordan prefers not to articulate what this alternative ideological stand could be, for if he were just interested in violence or ideology, he would not need potent Irish settings.

Questioned by the RUC detectives Bloom (Ray McAnally) and Bonner (Donal McCann), Danny declines to reveal his only clue – that one of the assassins was wearing an orthopaedic shoe. Gradually, Danny seeks out and kills three of the murderers (one in his home, one on a beach, and one in a car). Finally, the fourth, who turns out to be Bonner, is shot by Bloom before he can kill Danny.

Jordan and other critics have asserted that the characters' identities as Catholics and Protestants are very well-hidden, but this is not the case. The four assassins are clearly part of a Protestant grouping, since two of them are identifiable: John (Ian McElhinney) is named a "Prod" by his Catholic girlfriend Beth (Anita Reeves), and Bonner's position in the RUC, a predominantly Protestant force, helps to make their paramilitary UDA/UVF identity more apparent. Perhaps of most interest is the identity of Danny who, in conversation with Dee, implies that he is a Protestant, whereas both Dee and Annie are "convent girls" and therefore Catholic.[11] When Danny visits his Aunty Mae (Marie Kean), there are no Catholic religious icons in the house, and when he is left off home on one occasion, he meets a Salvation Army band, who are tied strongly to the Protestant tradition.[12] A deranged Protestant gunman killing violent Protestant paramilitaries is a curious mischaracterisation of the Northern Ireland "Troubles". It is as if Jordan wants a secularised Protestant to be touched by mysticism, sometimes Catholic, sometimes not. As Jordan makes clear, the "metaphysical language in which the film speaks is a very Catholic one, [it's] to do with sin and guilt".[13]

The "magical" in the film includes Annie's sexual advances in front of the wishing tree; Aunty Mae's ominous card-reading; Dee's feelings of being spellbound by Danny after they have made love; Danny's wearing of a dead man's clothes; and the faith-healer's laying on of hands right at the end of the film. These magical elements are the supertext over the traditional narrative of the thriller. In a sense, they are moments of contemplation, showing how a murderer can so easily justify heinous acts by projecting himself into a world of make-believe. Furthermore, two sequences in particular direct our attention to the possibilities of mental illness as the key problem created by the real world which Danny wishes to escape. The most overt is the gig in the mental asylum where, in an eerie atmosphere, the residents stand silently as Danny plays. Then, as Dee begins singing, one woman starts clapping alone in the crowd and removes to a corner of the building. Equally distressing is Mary (Sorcha Cusack) whose dead husband's clothes Danny puts on. She speaks of her former hatred for her husband, the priest's advice that she stick to him, and the loneliness now that her husband is dead. Mary takes Danny's gun while he sleeps and kills herself. Conventional religion cannot keep people on the rails, and, significantly, it is after this gory incident that Danny returns to the burnt-out ballroom. Here he encounters the faith-healer Francie (Macrea Clarke), a seventh son of a seventh son, and the ultimate in mystical power, working at the edges of Catholic institutional belief.

It is fitting for Jordan's Gothic universe that the Jewish police detective Bloom should kill Bonner, the former thus becoming a third religious presence to act as some kind of godly arbiter. It lets Jordan off the hook in not having to delineate more clearly Danny's motivations in any final "confession scene". Protected by the mystical presence of the faith-healer, as well as the gun of Bloom, Danny is released back into the wasteland that is Northern Ireland, as if newly baptised and cleansed.

No such political ambivalence is found in *The Crying Game*, in which Stephen Rea plays Fergus, an IRA volunteer. Neil Jordan's drama has an interesting history. He had the usual trouble of financing the project, mostly due to the Irish dimension in the first part of the film. Indeed, when it was sold to North America, Miramax, the distributor, cunningly succeeded by marketing it as a gender bender or sex shocker with a twist. Siskel and Ebert fell out briefly for giving the "secret" away on television. This marketing was all hype, of course, and told us more about North American society than Neil Jordan's intentions, his film or its relationship to Ireland. Subsequently, much of the writing on *The Crying Game* has focused upon issues of race and gender. Feminists have been particularly critical of the film, arguing that the only heterosexual woman, Jude (Miranda Richardson), is demonised. Moreover, Jordan appears to approve of the way male homosexual relationships can appropriate the feminine. In short, heterosexual women have no place in this film (nor lesbians for that matter). Of course, the introduction of bisexual and homosexual black characters, Jody (Forest Whitaker) and Dil (Jaye Davidson), runs the risk of equating otherness with "exotic" sexuality, in a kind of racial and sexual tourism. Jordan's desire to explore how a man (Fergus) can choose the feminine to his benefit, and how a woman (Jude) can choose the masculine to her detriment can lead to a male-oriented agenda, however unconventional his intent.[14] This emphasis on race and gender is not without merit, but what is ignored or elided by commentators, and primed viewers, are the issues of nationality that surface in the film.

Certainly race, gender and nationality are interwoven in Jordan's film, but, as the filmmaker's introduction to his published screenplay makes clear, the national context is, at the very least, an equal partner. He mentions the lineage of his film, stretching back to Frank O'Connor's story, "Guests of the Nation", in the 1920s, and Brendan Behan's *The Hostage* (1958) in the 1950s. The added ingredient for Jordan's reworking is the possibility of a sexual attraction.[15]

Clearly, when Jody is captured, we are struck by the fact that, as a black soldier, he is undeniably a member of a group more oppressed than that of his captors. That he plays cricket and lives in Tottenham in London throws into sharp relief the complexity of national identities. To be British and black is, one suspects, to the likes of Fergus – working-class like his prisoner – as mystifying as to be Irish Protestant and unionist. Jody's role in the narrative is to unsettle the archetypal Irish Catholic IRA volunteer. The black soldier is convinced that the IRA will kill him because it is in their "nature", although Jody makes a distinction between Fergus and his "people". Fergus will not kill him, Jody reasons, because he has seen his true "face" and tested his humanity, whereas kowtowing to the concept of the "people" or "nation" – as the IRA commander Maguire (Adrian Dunbar) does – can allow "righteous" killing to occur.

Many intentional national ironies abound in the film. As Fergus leads Jody out to be shot, they argue over cricket and hurling, one a sport that has been co-opted, enjoyed and paraded by the former colonies, the other a sport only played seriously in Ireland and symbolic of a monochrome nationalism. It is no accident that Fergus dreams of Jody in his white flannels moving in slow-motion bowling a cricket ball. Nor is it accidental that Fergus finds construction work in London overlooking a cricket ground, the apparent essence of Englishness. Nor is it out of pure derangement that Fergus clips Dil's hair into a masculine cut and makes her wear Jody's white cricket clothes.[16] Fergus is trying to turn Dil into Jody to assuage his conscience, but he is also in some small way attempting to accept alternative identities, as if acknowledging that former colonies can have a life of their own even within the general parameters of the original coloniser.

Jody's riddle of the scorpion and the frog, where the latter is persuaded to carry the former across the river despite its tendency to sting, is at the cusp of the mythmaking concerning nationality. The scorpion stings the frog even though it means certain death for both of them. Jody explains that it is in the nature of the scorpion and the IRA to kill, even when against their best interests. Fergus is indirectly affected by this anecdote, since his political beliefs seem to extend only to the conviction that the British Army should not be in Ireland. When asked for a personal story to define who he is, he is lost for words. Indeed, all he can really come up with is a half-remembered biblical line (I Corinthians 13: 11): "When I was a child, I thought as a child. But when I became a man I put away childish things." The line is the same one that James Mason's Johnny utters in Carol Reed's *Odd Man Out*. Interestingly, Mason's character speaks his line when in a state of delirium in which he clearly questions the IRA role that he has played up to that point in the narrative. Fergus' nationalism is skin-deep, as thin as his provincial notions of race and gender boundaries. This delimiting provincialism is the subtext of Jordan's film on nationality and nationalism: Fergus advances through his experiences with Jody and Dil to see that all kinds of identities are fluid and equally legitimate. And, if legitimate, his IRA activities, with their theoretical underpinnings of Irish pureness (read Irish and Catholic), cannot be justified. The deaths of the two committed IRA members Maguire and Jude act as a collective purgation of monochrome nationalism, as well as monochrome racialism and sexuality. Despite the sometimes prurient hype around the film, *The Crying Game* attempts to accept the barriers between and among people, and asks us to make the effort to imagine our relationships differently.

One of the curiosities about Jordan's work is that in both these films Danny and Fergus are bereft of immediate family. In direct contrast, Jim Sheridan's *In the Name of the Father* charts a more conservative but realistic route by highlighting a family relationship, illustrating the link between personal and political decisions. This Academy Award®-nominated film based on the Guildford Four and the Maguire Seven cases relies upon standard conventions and icons within the "wrongly imprisoned" genre film: a suffering family; a working-class milieu; a petty thief with bad timing; a father with a heart of gold; a maniacal IRA man having to rub shoulders with a maniacal prison godfather; and an outrageously flawed criminal justice system. However, Sheridan has two major targets: the British justice system and the IRA. Fundamentally, the film explores and develops the relationship between father and son. Put more precisely, the film asks: who *is* the proper father or role model for the likes of Gerry Conlon (Daniel Day-Lewis)? On the one hand, we have the abusive father of the IRA hardman, Joe McAndrew (Don Baker), who committed the real bombings and who continues his assault on the British system within the prison by torching the warden (John Benfield). This ideological father is contrasted with the insidious police interrogator Dixon (Corin Redgrave) and the simply corrupting godfather figure of the prison bully (Frank Harper). Countering all these false fathers is the biological father – Giuseppe Conlon (Pete Postlethwaite), a religious man who is physically sick from having been exploited at work when he was a young man. On numerous occasions, Sheridan explores the difference in perspective between the two generations of northern Irish Catholics. For Giuseppe, his life has been one of restraint, of feeling lucky (as a Catholic) to have a job in the shipyard in Belfast. But to Gerry, such self-effacement denied him a healthy father. To the son, the father had always been a victim, whether at work in Belfast or incarcerated in an English jail. Sheridan's zeroing in on the different forms of protest (Gerry's occasional involvement in violent action vs. Giuseppe's legal, letter-writing campaign) mirrors in an uncanny way the Sinn Féin doctrine of fighting with both the Armalite and the ballot-box. Gerry's withdrawal from his aggressive posture pushes him to follow the legal path of appeal initiated by his father by working with the English lawyer Gareth Pierce (Emma Thompson); this tactic eventually produces results.

It is significant that Gerry Conlon decides to sign his "confession" to the police after his biological father is threatened. The central interest of the film is, of course, the educative power of Giuseppe Conlon to steer his son away not particularly from the drug culture in prison, which provides much-needed humour (and an alliance between blacks and Catholic Irish), but from the IRA man's influence. Although Gerry dismisses the religious flavour of his father's spirituality, he is drawn to the basic moral goodness that it inspires. This influence allows him not only to be able to put out the flames engulfing the English warden, but also to be confident in rejecting to his face the IRA man's ideology – an ideology, it has to be remembered, for which he is doing time.

Clearly, Sheridan's film is a conservative document in many ways. It places trust in Catholicism (despite Gerry's curt dismissal of the priest after his father's death) and in the belief that a grievous wrong will eventually be righted. The major scandal that the film highlights at the end is that no police officers have been jailed for their extractions of confessions from the Guildford Four, Birmingham Six and Maguire Seven. What the film does strike at is the need for individuals to find their nationality and their sense of self-worth outside republicanism and outside the colonial grasp of the British government. Sheridan's film looks for that middle path, but cannot articulate what that new nationalism should comprise, except non-violent principles. Controversially, Sheridan's film may be seen as a perfect visual vehicle for SDLP-like constitutional nationalism, for that appears to be the middle position that Sheridan implies through Gerry Conlon's story.

Much of the debate over the film in Britain centred on the lack of accuracy of the events depicted. Given that it was based on real-life occurrences over fifteen years, and that Gerry Conlon was involved with the film's production process, this criticism is to be expected.[17] Additionally, the fact that the Guildford Four, Maguire Seven and Birmingham Six were all proved to be innocent has cast an unmistakable cloud over the British judicial system, a system (by force of these cases alone) shown to be unequal to the task of ensuring fair treatment to the disadvantaged and poor. If Sheridan's film may be conventional in morals and filmic style, it earns its laurels rightly for exposing the gross injustice meted out to Irish people, such as Gerry Conlon, who happened to be Irish in England at the wrong time.[18]

Rather neatly, *In the Name of the Father* has found its female counterpart in public consciousness with Terry George's *Some Mother's Son*. George and Sheridan worked as co-writers on both films. Whereas Sheridan hails from the Dublin theatre world, George, according to Toby Harnden of the British *Daily Telegraph*, "is a former terrorist linked to the Irish National Liberation Army [INLA] who served three years in the Maze prison after being convicted in 1975 of possessing a loaded gun with intent to endanger life".[19] Whatever George's background, his personal knowledge of the debates surrounding the period of the late-1970s and early 1980s is very assured.

The film contrasts middle-class Catholic Kathleen Quigley (Helen Mirren) and working-class Catholic Annie Higgins (Fionnula Flanagan) in their reactions as mothers to their sons' participation in the 1981 hunger strikes. These sons, Frank Higgins (David O'Hara) and Gerard Quigley (Aidan Gillen), are responsible for an attack on a British Army patrol, and are later captured in a shootout when the security forces raid Annie's home. Once incarcerated, both refuse to wear prison clothing and join the blanket protest, which escalates from daubing the cell walls with their own faeces to fully-fledged hunger strikes. Although we see little of the chemistry between Gerard and his cellmate, the historical figure Bobby Sands (John Lynch), we become aware that Gerard has become a true disciple to the bedraggled Sands, who indeed looks, as Gerard initially remarks, like Jesus Christ. The main focus of the narrative, however, is charting the emotional and practical steps that the two mothers must address in trying to support, yet also save, their sons.

The combination of Helen Mirren as associate producer and actress, and Terry George as director/co-writer allows the film to achieve an enviable aesthetic distance from these very emotional events. Instead of a disabling overt republican premise, George is able to be reflective on the range of Catholic nationalist and republican thought, even if a Protestant spectatorship is largely disallowed. This maturity of representation is varied. Firstly, there is the conflict among the Catholic community itself over the right approach to the hunger strikes; secondly, the division among British political opinion is explored; thirdly, although the Protestant community is militarised, it is not completely demonised in the way in which other films have chosen to depict them.[20]

Mirren has remarked that an earlier draft of the script basically set out to show how a middle-class woman was politicised to realise that "the IRA is *great*".[21] Not surprisingly, she was not content with this stereotypical characterisation, and helped to bring some realism and complexity to the project. She was instrumental in securing Castle Rock's funding for the film at a time when the IRA cease fire was in place. One realistic aspect is the juxtaposition of the two women's class positions. Kathleen is a pacifist schoolteacher who is the widowed mother of three children (we do not know the circumstances of the father's death). Her main interest is in keeping her children happy and away from the external conflict. Annie, however, is a small farmer (also without her husband) who has already suffered the loss of one of her sons to the guns of the British Army. She is an avowed republican, with strong sympathies for Sinn Féin and the IRA. Whereas Annie is fully knowledgeable about Frank's involvement, Kathleen is shocked at Gerard's; whereas Annie is willing to trust the political thrust of the Sinn Féin spokesperson Danny Boyle (Ciarán Hinds), Kathleen is far more sceptical and willing to consider almost any means to save her son's life; and, most tellingly, whereas Annie cannot sign the form to allow her son to receive life-saving medical treatment, Kathleen eventually does.

These differences are also worked through on a more comic level: whereas Kathleen drives a car, Annie only knows how to ride a bicycle. Kathleen takes Annie to the beach and allows her new friend to learn to drive. She is not very successful, and the car gets stuck in the sand with the tide racing in. Only with the arrival of a few British troops is the car saved, much to the chagrin of republican Annie. The two women converge and diverge in specific areas. Each criticises the Mother Superior at the Catholic girls' school, and each believes that the election of Bobby Sands will force the British government to reach a compromise on the hunger strike issue. In the latter hope they are both wrong.

Annie chooses to accept her son's wishes and the prisoners' bargaining position. In contrast, Kathleen looks for a compromise, just as the local priest does in the face of an equally belligerent Sinn Féin and Thatcherite military intelligence officials. As the local priest and Danny Boyle of Sinn Féin argue over a compromise wording to end the strike, Kathleen tunes out their voices and looks at them as if for the first time: angry men fighting over an issue of pure ego. This perception drives her to sign the medical release form. Of course, this decision is easier for Kathleen, since she lives in a middle-class area, less prone to the peer pressure evident in working-class and lower-middle-class areas, where support for such a radical departure from the prisoners' wishes would be more difficult to find. In fact, her middle-classness allows her to accept the soldiers' help on the beach, to drink in a Protestant-owned pub, and to tolerate, to a degree, the "Diplock" courts.[22] Her struggles are more conflicted, if less dangerous. Kathleen sparks the disapproval of her employer for her electioneering for Bobby Sands (apparently, to the Mother Superior, a distinctly working-class republican occupation), and she must endure the pain of her daughter Alice's (Geraldine O'Rawe) decision to resign her position from a mainly Protestant-staffed bank because her co-workers feel they cannot trust her. Alice's barely concealed frustration at Gerard's hunger strike position and her leaving Ireland for a job in England speak volumes about the exclusion of women from this messianic-like struggle.[23]

If there are differences in attitude among Catholics of different classes, the same may be said about the relationships among Sinn Féin, the prisoners and the Roman Catholic Church. For the Catholic Church, in both film and real life, the dilemma centred around how to defend members of its flock, even those who murder and maim for the republican cause. The local priest Father Daly (Gerard McSorley) feels that it is his duty to condemn the IRA murders of prison officers, despite the Sinn Féin accusations made vocally *inside* the church that he is being soft on the British. Yet equally, Sinn Féin knows it needs the moral authority of the Catholic Church to exert pressure on the British government on behalf of the prisoners. Perhaps the most striking image in the film is the Cardinal of Ireland giving communion to the kneeling, blanketed, bearded cadre of prisoners, while in the background the prison authorities defumigate the faeces-daubed cells. It is a complex image, suggesting how state, Church and revolutionary groups uneasily interrelate. Within the Irish context, it reaffirms the standard view that the IRA is bonded and supported, however unfortunately and unintentionally, by the Roman Catholic Church.

Terry George sets the scene well: the arrival of Mrs Thatcher at 10 Downing Street in 1979, about to start her eleven years in power, quoting the platitudes of St Francis of Assisi to nearby reporters; cut to the mincing Thatcherite strategist who redesigns the British approach to the IRA by emphasising "isolation, criminalisation, demoralisation". (Other policies in the real world included normalisation and Ulsterisation, an attempt to put as many security jobs as possible into the hands of the local RUC.) George is shrewd to concentrate on this new policy of criminalisation, as it did lead directly to the hunger strikes. The stakes were raised to provoke a trade mark Thatcherite battle of wills, a stubbornness later noted in her fight over the Falklands in 1982 and the miners' strike in 1984-85. As far as the IRA was concerned, however, she may have won the battle, but lost the war of public opinion.

Although George shows restraint in his depictions of the Protestant community, he still fully believes in the anti-imperialist myth, which explains his dwelling on the divisions between Sinn Féin and the British government, and his representation of the Protestant community as militarised (the arresting policemen, the head prison officer, and so on). We do see two short sequences where two of the prison officers are murdered, one in front of his children, and anonymous (presumably Protestant loyalist) people throw urine into the face of Kathleen Quigley. George uses a number of close-ups on the head prison officer (who says very little), as if to communicate his grudging respect for the prisoners' fortitude. On the other hand, these close-ups may be interpreted as George's take on the Protestant "deluded lackeys" that Tom Nairn speaks of in his explanation of the anti-imperialist myth.[24] It is unfortunate that George's nuanced analysis of the conflict, of which he has written at length, is underdeveloped in the film.[25]

Sheridan and George continued their writing partnership with *The Boxer*. Directed by Sheridan, this film had the good fortune to arrive at a time of actual attempts at full negotiations among the various parties in Northern Ireland. It is a "cease fire film", in which ex-IRA man and ex-boxer Danny Flynn (Daniel Day-Lewis) emerges from prison after fourteen years, and, with the help of his old boxing coach Ike (Ken Stott), starts up a cross-community boxing gym in a republican working-class district of Belfast. Gradually, he begins to succeed in his efforts, aided by an IRA cease fire, and in returning to boxing, but he cannot stop himself from wanting to reignite a relationship with his former girlfriend Maggie (Emily Watson), who is now married to an imprisoned IRA man, the mother of a young boy, and also the daughter of the IRA leader Joe Hamill (Brian Cox). The relationship is fraught with danger, since such an extramarital affair, if consummated, would likely mean Danny's murder.

If this were not enough to deal with, Danny must negotiate the barbs of Harry (Gerard McSorley), the hard-liner who has no time for peace processes or cross-community initiatives, and with whom he shares a dark although mostly unexplained history. In a similar plot to Ronan Bennett's *Love Lies Bleeding* (BBC-2, 1993), Sheridan and George appear to suggest that for peace and reconciliation to be achieved, men such as Harry must be eliminated. From an aesthetic viewpoint, the rewards of Sheridan's film are many: an intense rapport between the two leads, a clear awareness of the boxing film genre, and some marvellous moody cinematography by Chris Menges. Despite the few occasions when Protestants appear – one of the most moving moments of the film is when Ike reads out the name of a deceased Protestant boxer in the presence of his elderly parents – Sheridan and George continue where *Some Mother's Son* left off in concluding that the main action in Northern Ireland is the struggle among the Catholic population itself, and not that between the two communities. This conclusion avoids discussion of the nature of the compromises that the Protestant side has endured and will have to endure in the future.

The remove to England and the "meat market" boxing circuit for the benefit of rich English patrons fits uneasily within the framework of the film as a whole. Its metaphoric suggestion, that Irish (and black) pugilism is manipulated by English political and business interests, is too simplistic, however visually powerful Danny's refusal to complete a bout with a Nigerian boxer may be. Danny knows that the violence by the IRA has to stop, and he begins that process himself – in the ring. Powerful as the love interest and the boxing scenes are, the political dynamics are at times too formulaic.

Formulaic is not a word one associates with the work of Joe Comerford. In an interview, the director has explained how the genesis of *High Boot Benny*, which took five years to complete, was rooted in a family story. In the 1930s, Comerford's father attended an alternative/independent school, which attempted to accept the different traditions on the island of Ireland, including republicans and southern unionists. The demise of the school was occasioned by the narrow Roman Catholic character of the new Irish Free State, which did not brook competition in the area of education. Comerford's interest in this subject arose from the fact that the closure of the school was symptomatic of an intellectual closure of many issues in Ireland, and not just the unresolved situation of partition.[26]

Tellingly, the film relies upon setting for much of its effect. The border between Northern Ireland and the Republic of Ireland is used as a potent metaphor for the many divisions present in modern-day Ireland. Teenager Benny (Marc O'Shea) lives with the owners of an independent school run by the Matron (Frances Tomelty) and Manley (Alan Devlin), with the sometime help of Father Bergin (Seamus Ball). Benny is first spied poaching a rabbit, skinning it, and daubing its blood over the border sign, "Hoping You Make a Return Visit to Northern Ireland". His rebellion towards authority is thus quickly established. We see the British Army and an RUC man enter the Republic of Ireland and lie in wait. Benny discovers a naked dead body covered only in rubbish bags. The patrol pounce upon Benny, and it becomes apparent that the school's caretaker is the dead man and was an informant for the British forces. The RUC man (David McBlain) berates Benny, and, in his attempt to find out who killed the caretaker, the policeman reveals that Benny is known to him and has a lurid past, which is left unexplained (perhaps child abuse?).

Meanwhile, Father Bergin wants Matron and Manley to close the school, called "The Mount", a school for boys, which sports a plaque with the inscription, "Independence in Education is a dangerous aspiration". But Matron, who is a Protestant, sees her role as providing a much-needed corrective to the schooling on both sides of the border. She is a history teacher who seems to have lost faith in the traditional teaching of her subject, remarking, "How can I teach you people history? You have to live with it." Matron seems more interested in having a child, as if trying to eradicate the memory of an earlier abortion. She sleeps with Manley, a silenced priest, but harbours sexual desires for Benny.

Benny discovers that the IRA is hiding a wounded colleague. He deliberately bumps into a mute orphan (Fiona Nichols) who is carrying blood containers. Angered, it seems, at the IRA for killing the caretaker, Benny bursts a number of these receptacles. For this act, he is taken to a hill, tied up, and tarred and feathered. His revulsion at the IRA is put on hold, and reversed, when the Army and RUC hit squad stake out the Mount school and kill Manley (who was responsible for informing on the caretaker's actions) and Matron. Benny's final act is to join the IRA.

This summary is arguably disabling, as what comes across strongly in Comerford's film is the rough texture of these individuals' existences. Shot in a desolate and windswept landscape (possibly Donegal), there is a strong sense that we are dealing with the periphery of civilisation. The problem with the film is that its metaphors do not cohere. At one level, we have the straightforward nationalist rhetoric, as depicted in the propaganda "history" film shown to the boys by Father Bergin, which the pupils short-circuit (past or southern Irish history is no use to them). At another level, we have the odd comparison between Benny's tarring and feathering and Manley and the boys "playing native Indians". It seems that Comerford is trying to link the barbarism and primitivism of Benny's punishment with some form of idolisation of the indigene. This *is* a "primitive"-oriented film, from its naked aggression to its isolated mountain school, defrocked or silenced priest, and random murderous activities. Equally odd is Benny's love of his red cowboy boots; the boots are symbolically transferred to Matron, who puts them on. It is not clear to what end Comerford is using this prop, except to imply that the rules of the Wild West apply to contemporary Ireland. Presumably, Benny's Mohican haircut links him to the "savage", while the tall red boots link him also to the "settler".

The film simply works as a sympathetic piece about marginalised individuals in a very intolerant society. Yet, it is cold, indifferent to characterisation, and far too reliant on explosive violence for its narrative drive to make any significant statement about Northern Ireland or Ireland's "Troubles". We are left, therefore, with a few wonderfully unique scenes to savour, particularly the funerals of Matron and Manley, at which the boys throw all the school's musical instruments into the graves as a final act of rebellion against Father Bergin's formality.

One critic has referred to the film as a "no punches pulled pro-republican testament", which in turn led other critics to rebuff this remark with amazing speed, thereby revealing how tense the culture and politics battlefield in Ireland remains.[27] I do not find the film sufficiently cogent in itself to make such vitriolic attacks and desperate defences. That Benny chooses to side with the IRA is presented just as much as a lack of choice as a deliberate action. After all, the school is shut down, his adoptive parents have been murdered, and he appears unwilling to return (if that is what it would be) to Northern Ireland where he may be terrorised by the RUC. Taking a charitable view, the film documents the dilemma for young Catholics in both Northern Ireland and the Republic of Ireland. The élites or political/military classes – whether the RUC, IRA or the Roman Catholic Church – do not necessarily provide young people with a safe emotional and physical space in which to prosper. This claustrophobia is what Comerford exposes.

Searching for a safe emotional and physical space is at the heart of Pat O'Connor's *Cal*. The eponymous "hero" is, by all appearances, a nineteen- or twenty-year-old unemployed Catholic (John Lynch) who lives with his father Shamie (Donal McCann) on an estate dominated by Protestants. Shamie works in the apparently Protestant-run local abattoir, together with Crilly (Stevan Rimkus), who is a gunman and thief for the IRA. Cal is the sometime driver for Crilly on these "missions", including one in which a policeman is killed. Gradually, Cal gets to know Marcella (Helen Mirren), the wife of the murdered policeman. By the strong hand of fate, Cal finds work at the farmhouse where Marcella and her Protestant in-laws live. A sexual relationship develops between Cal who feels guilty, and Marcella who feels lonely. It is short-lived, however, as Cal is picked up by Crilly for another "job", although this time the Army intervenes, killing the IRA leader, Skeffington (John Kavanagh), and arresting Crilly who, it seems, names Cal as a conspirator. The film ends with Cal, having suggested his past actions to Marcella, punched and beaten by the police as they take him away for trial.

Based on Bernard Mac Laverty's novella, the film proves to be a very faithful adaptation. Both works are interested in detailing how isolated and trapped young Irish Catholics feel in a predominantly British and Protestant culture. Both raise a critique of Irish nationalism and British nationalism by focalising the narrative through Cal, who is energised mainly by his attraction to the opposite sex. Of course, in Marcella he sees the possibility of redemption, and this is why, when they finally make love, the scene is interspersed with images of the shooting of Marcella's husband and accompanied by an ominous, jarring soundtrack. This scene is very unconventional in the "love story" genre, upon which *Cal* draws, but, because of the politics of Northern Ireland, one senses that no true happiness is possible.

What the film shows best is a typical Catholic's feeling of disenfranchisement in Northern Ireland. The foreman at the farm, Cyril Dunlop (Ray McAnally), remarks to the effect that if they (Catholics) were all like Shamie, things would be different. Dunlop means that Shamie is not a *provocateur*, but a good citizen who appears by his outward quiescence to accept the status quo in Northern Ireland. This is not exactly the case, as we hear Shamie remark that Dunlop is a "bastard"; Shamie also keeps a gun handy because of the intimidation he feels in his neighbourhood. Through Cal's symbolic narrative, we see Dunlop's hatred of the Roman Catholic religion and his cosy relationship with the security forces; the victimisation of Catholics on the streets; and the burning of Catholics out of Protestant areas. The Orange parade that stops outside Cal's house is as ominous as the evangelical Protestant preachers who hammer signs with biblical quotations onto the local landscape. Compounding this view of the Protestant as prejudiced Other is the fact that Marcella is a Catholic who married a Protestant, but whose relationship was an unhappy one. Marcella explains to Cal that Robert, her husband, told lies; now, for the sake of their child, she stays with her severe Protestant in-laws. A strange Oedipal twist is suggested when Shamie has a nervous breakdown after losing his home, and Cal ends up wearing the clothes of the murdered Robert. Cal is without a biological mother, and Marcella, a mother-figure in her own right, provides a form of the forgiveness and reassurance that he seeks, despite Cal having "killed the father and slept with the mother" in the traditional Oedipal triangle.[28]

Clearly, the doomed love story, ably supported with an Irish folk-style score by Dire Straits' Mark Knopfler, allowed the film to be successfully marketed. Yet, the film does attempt to make linkages, as in Jim Sheridan's *In the Name of the Father*, between political and social action and various father-figures. Shamie tries to keep Cal on the right side of the law, but fails to persuade him to stick at a job at the abattoir; Skeffington, the IRA leader, tussles for Cal's soul with republican rhetoric and invocations of 1916 and "Bloody Sunday", because he knows Cal is not a crude psychopath like Crilly, and requires a different approach to be kept in the IRA. It is true that Cal has very little space in which to take any rational decisions, and so atoning for his sins by "giving" to Marcella and by refusing to hide from the police at the end does suggest a new life for him, even though that may be in prison.[29] Skeffington and Crilly as representatives of the IRA are not welcoming figures, and, like Sheridan, O'Connor appears to be earnestly searching for a middle path that is not snared with political traps. Their characters look for a state they can call their own.

These films by Jordan, Sheridan, George, Comerford and O'Connor confront a topic of which the world has grown tired, and it is to their credit that each persevered to bring to fruition their vision of the "Troubles". Nevertheless, these visions are problematic in that they concentrate primarily on the Catholic community, as if that were where the answer to the conflagration lies. The representation of the majority Protestant community is so perfunctory in these films that the viewer could not be blamed for thinking that the British government is entirely at fault for the violence and instability. By eliding the Protestant unionist claims, these filmmakers tell us, in the end, only half of the tragic story.

Through another optic, it can be equally argued that these films, including *Some Mother's Son*, are male fictions, which tell us little about how women regard the "Troubles". To what extent the "Troubles" have been a male construct is a pertinent question. The next chapter surveys films – far less commercial than those discussed above – that have endeavoured to confront this inequity of perspective within narrative fiction and the nationalist and republican traditions.

Notes

1   Stephen Rea, "The Acting Game" [interview with Paul Power], *Film Ireland* 49 (October/November 1995): 19.

2   Padraig O'Malley, *Biting at the Grave: The Irish Hunger Strikes and the Politics of Despair* (Boston: Beacon Press, 1990): 284-285.

3   Neil Jordan, *Angel* (London; Boston: Faber and Faber, 1989): 41.

4   "Celtic dreamer" [Marina Burke interviews Neil Jordan], *Film Ireland* 34 (April/May 1993): 16-21. In this sometimes confrontational interview, Jordan reveals that he added new dimensions to the first outline of *The Crying Game* story written in 1982.

5   The 1970s were a particularly gruesome time for tit-for-tat killings between the IRA and the various Protestant unionist paramilitaries. The worst period was actually 1974-76, not the late-1970s and early 1980s to which Jordan refers. See Malcolm Sutton (compiler), *Bear in mind these dead...: An Index of Deaths from the Conflict in Ireland 1969-1993* (Belfast: Beyond the Pale Publications, 1994). The "Troubles" have been the background of innumerable novels and "potboilers". Established Irish writers have ventured into this troubled landscape, such as Benedict Kiely (*Proxopera* [London: Victor Gollancz, 1977]), Brian Moore (*Lies of Silence* [London: Bloomsbury, 1990]) and David Martin (*The Ceremony of Innocence* [London: Secker and Warburg, 1977]).

[6]   Two useful critical readings of *Angel* are Richard Kearney's "Avenging Angel: An Analysis of Neil Jordan's First Irish Feature Film", *Studies* 71: 283 (autumn 1982): 296-303, reprinted in a slightly altered version in Richard Kearney's *Transitions: Narratives in Modern Irish Culture* (Manchester: Manchester University Press, 1988): 173-183; and a section of John Hill's "Images of Violence", in Kevin Rockett, Luke Gibbons and John Hill, *Cinema and Ireland* (London; Sydney: Croom Helm, 1987): 178-181. Just as enlightening is Michael Open's interview with Neil Jordan after *Angel*'s success at Cannes in 1982, "Face to Face with Evil", *Film Directions* 5: 17 (1982): 3-5, 16.

[7]   John Boorman's role in helping Jordan to get his first film made cannot be underestimated. Channel 4 put up at least £800 000 and the Irish Film Board around £100 000. The latter figure was half of the Film Board's budget, a board on which Boorman served. This seeming conflict of interest resulted in Boorman's resignation, and various attempts to ostracise Neil Jordan within the Irish film scene. In numerous interviews, Jordan has commented on his often being made unwelcome by other Irish filmmakers. See, for example, the interview in my *World Cinema 4: Ireland* (Trowbridge: Flicks Books, 1989): 114-118.

[8]   Some of Neil Jordan's creative writing can be perused in *A Neil Jordan Reader* (New York: Viking, 1993).

[9]   I am speculating here from the manager's offhand reference to Danny as the "Stan Getz of south Armagh". Although the film moves from urban to rural landscapes, it is extremely hard to establish where in Northern Ireland they are supposed to be. This is certainly one area where the lack of specifics in locations lends to Jordan's metaphysical musings.

[10]   Quoted in "Face to Face with Evil": 4.

[11]   After the second killing, Danny sleeps with Dee. Just before they sleep together, they exchange the following dialogue which suggests that Dee is Catholic and Danny is Protestant:

Danny: Are you a convent girl?
Dee: I'm a woman, Danny.
Danny: Tell me what a sinning is.
Dee: It's a habit Catholics indulge in.
Danny: What about Protestants?
Dee: They don't know what sin is. You do, though.

[12]   One can speculate about Rea's influence on the script. He had by this time set up Field Day Theatre Company with Brian Friel. He is the son of a Protestant bus driver, but clearly holds views more in keeping with mainstream Catholic nationalist and perhaps even republican sentiments. In interview, he remarked on his days at university in Belfast: "The only good thing for me at Queen's was these Border Catholics coming in and seeing the whole thing as a sham. The austerity of Michael Farrell and the appropriate disrespect of Eamon McCann, took the place and showed it to be a pile of shit." Quoted in Marilynn J Richtarik, *Acting Between the Lines: The Field Day Theatre Company and Irish Cultural Politics 1980-1984* (Oxford: Clarendon Press, 1994): 84.

[13]   "Face to Face with Evil": 16.

[14] For a discussion of these issues, see Robert M Payne, "*The Crying Game*: Crossed lines", *Jump Cut* 39 (1994): 7-14; Aspasia Kotsopoulos and Josephine Mills, "*The Crying Game*: Gender, genre and 'postfeminism'", *Jump Cut* 39 (1994): 15-24; Kristin Handler, "Sexing *The Crying Game*: Difference, Identity, Ethics", *Film Quarterly* 47: 3 (spring 1994): 31-42.

[15] See Neil Jordan, *The Crying Game* (London: Vintage, 1993): viii.

[16] Haircutting and changing clothes are powerful metaphors also tapped in *Angel*, when Danny asks Mary to cut his hair and to give him new clothes, which also turn out to be those of a dead man. In addition, Cal in Pat O'Connor's *Cal* puts on the dead Robert's clothes.

[17] Michael Mansfield QC gives a legal opinion on some of the "creative" licences Sheridan takes with the fifteen-year ordeal of Gerry Conlon in "Jurassic Justice", *Sight and Sound* 4: 3 (March 1994): 7. Other useful reviews of the film are Martin Bright's in the same issue of *Sight and Sound*: 41-42, and Martin McLoone, "In the Name of the Father", *Cineaste* 20: 4 (1994): 44-47. Gerry Conlon's "actual" story can be perused in his *Proved Innocent* (London: Hamish Hamilton, 1990).

[18] Of course, the evil and duplicitous representation of the Chief of Police Dixon is overwrought and rather stereotypical. For some viewers, it takes away from the attack on the *institutionalised* problems of British justice in relation to Irish people. Such details did not ruffle the feathers of Gerry Adams, who visited the United States (on a special visa) for 48 hours in February 1994. Appearing on *Larry King Live*, a caller asked him what he thought of Jim Sheridan's film. The Sinn Féin President replied that he thought it was a "good dramatic representation". Beautifully diplomatic, Adams deliberately declined to interpret the film, thereby marginalising the inherent critique of the IRA and, by extension, the long-standing wishes of the majority in both Northern Ireland and the Republic of Ireland for peaceful negotiation.

[19] Toby Harnden's article from *The Daily Telegraph* was excerpted and reprinted as "Promoting the IRA", in *The Province (Vancouver)* 12 January 1997: A39.

[20] The anti-imperialist myth is nevertheless apparent to some commentators as ultimately central. As Harnden (ibid) states: "Like other Hollywood films, *Some Mother's Son* depicts the conflict in Ulster as being between the oppressed Irish and the British. The only Protestants in the film are neanderthal Unionists who bray and boo during an election count."

[21] See Ken Eisner, "Daring Bosnian Women Inspired Mirren's *Son*", *The Georgia Straight (Vancouver)* 19-26 December 1996: 52.

[22] Since the 1970s, terrorist-related offences in Northern Ireland have been tried in special courts, named after the judge who recommended them, Lord Diplock. These courts provided for only one judge and no jury. While appearing to contravene normal due process, these courts were a reaction to the fact that juries for such serious offences were difficult to find, and that it was virtually impossible to prevent jury members from being intimidated by terrorist organisations. They also avoided the political trauma of having to decide on the ratio of Catholics to

Protestants on each jury selected.

[23] There were women "on the blanket" at the women's prison in Armagh, but they were few by comparison to what went on at Long Kesh/the Maze. It should be noted that the name of the prison is even contested in Northern Ireland. Protestants tend to call it the Maze, while Catholics call it Long Kesh.

[24] Tom Nairn, *The Break-Up of Britain: Crisis and Neo-Nationalism*, second expanded edition (London: Verso, 1981): 231. George has openly called his film "partisan", and this is clear from the promotional website that accompanied the film (http:\somemotherson.com). The website included pages on the history and politics of Northern Ireland. Errors and overly neat glosses occur in the information provided. For example, whereas George's information on the hunger strikes is fascinatingly detailed (although he never states why these men were originally incarcerated), his approach to events in 1972 is selective. While he is correct to refer to "Bloody Sunday" when fourteen civilians were shot dead by British troops, he does not check his facts on "Bloody Friday", when there were 22 explosions (not 20), killing at least nine people (not five) and injuring 130 (unmentioned), an act admitted by the Belfast Provisional IRA. George's comment that the "timing was coordinated to demonstrate to the British that there was really no defence against such attacks" is small comfort to the Protestant community that bore the brunt of this bombing campaign. In George's suggested further reading, of the 34 authors and their works cited, there are many references to republican-influenced history and political analysis by Gerry Adams, Tim Pat Coogan and Michael Farrell, but no mention of revisionist historians Paul Bew, Roy Foster and Conor Cruise O'Brien. George provides an abbreviated version of this republican history in his preface to the screenplay. See Terry George and Jim Sheridan, *Some Mother's Son: The Screenplay* (New York: Grove Press, 1996). Politics, history and film are intertwined further in this book by actual photographs of the real hunger strikers beside stills from the film.

[25] See, in particular, Terry George's comments in Gary Crowdus and O'Mara Leary, "The 'Troubles' He's Seen in Northern Ireland: An Interview with Terry George", *Cineaste* 23: 1 (1997): 24-29.

[26] See Laoise Mac Reamoinn's interview with Joe Comerford, "Crossing the Border", *Film Ireland* 43 (October/November 1994): 10-11.

[27] David Butler's initial review of *High Boot Benny* is to be found in "Reviews", *Film Ireland* 38 (December 1993/January 1994): 30-32; the ripostes by Desmond Bell, Gerry McCarthy and Gaye Lynch are in *Film Ireland* 39 (February/March 1994): 36-38.

[28] A useful interview conducted by Michael Open with producers David Puttnam and Stuart Craig, director Pat O'Connor and writer Bernard Mac Laverty on *Cal*'s production can be found in "The 'Cal' Team interviewed", *Film Directions* 7: 25 (1984): 3-5.

[29] Of course, the desire to be incarcerated by the Northern Ireland state could also be read as a sign of his inability to extricate himself from political forces.

5

Irish herstories; or what feminism thinks of republicanism

> Being a woman is a nationality I carry around with me.
> (Maeve in *Maeve*)

> But Rockey, like all his sort, puts women down the list. He'd
> rather by far be running his hand along the barrel of a gun
> than along his own conjugal equipment. (Nelson in Ron
> Hutchinson's *Rat in the Skull* [1984])[1]

A quick survey of the female characters in six of the seven films
discussed in the previous chapter would force one to come up with
abrupt summaries: apolitical Dee in *Angel*; terrorist fanatic Jude in
The Crying Game; mercurial Matron in *High Boot Benny*; victimised
Marcella in *Cal*; anguished Kathleen and Annie in *Some Mother's
Son*; and politically passive Maggie in *The Boxer*. Irish women do not
figure largely in *In the Name of the Father*.[2] To discover more
thorough and challenging representations, one has to move away
from the mainstream. The four films discussed below develop and
explore the sometimes troubled relationship between feminism and
republicanism. All four films conclude that, although men and
women with a republican agenda may have similar political
aspirations, the equity goals set by women have less support among
men, at least beyond mere tokenism. When the civil rights marches
began in 1968, one of the slogans was "one *man* – one vote". It has
since taken many years for social and political struggles to be seen
as gender-inclusive. Yet, equality of choice, treatment and
opportunity between men and women does not come easily in any
culture. Indeed, the problem facing most feminists is how to argue
for equity (as distinct from literal equality) while also demanding
respect for difference. This statement implies that true equality is
a mirage, and some kind of flexible asymmetrical exchange between
men and women must be attempted. Each of these films at some
level raises the question of "women's bodies", not simply to consider
issues, for example, of pregnancy and abortion, but more to consider
the totality of women's social experience in the constructed past and
present.

By far the most complex of these films is Pat Murphy and John Davies' *Maeve*, which has garnered a fair amount of critical commentary, certainly more than most Irish films.[3] Apart from the occasional television broadcast, it is currently only available for rental on 16mm from the British Film Institute, who backed it financially, and therefore my description and discussion are fairly detailed to give a good sense of the film's importance.

In terms of plot, little happens in this two-hour film.[4] Maeve Sweeney (Mary Jackson), in her early twenties, returns from London on a visit to her family home in Belfast which is located in a Catholic nationalist area. From there, she clashes ideologically and emotionally with her mother Eileen (Trudy Kelly), sister Roisin (Brid Brennan), father Martin (Mark Mulholland) and boyfriend Liam (John Keegan). Intercut during this familial and ideological journey are flashbacks to Maeve's past, which show how the ideological state (and non-state) "apparatuses" of family, community and school forced her to rebel and leave Ireland for England. Her return is a complicated one. She believes that she is a feminist, one who questions the status quo of northern Irish society, but, like all such returns to the hearth, there is a bitter-sweet taste in her mouth. No triumphalism in her character is evident or endeavoured, but rather a desire to seek a reconcilement in some areas and an empowerment in others. Strangely, no great struggle with the Roman Catholic Church is depicted.

One of the best ways to begin discussion of the film is to trace the childhood of Maeve, sequences of which are interspersed throughout. For a film so concerned with understanding the past, it is fitting that time shifts occur frequently. Film, after all, is a time-machine, and Pat Murphy's rather overwritten script takes the viewer on a personal and political journey backwards. Flashbacks are not signalled in any obvious way, such as with the use of dissolves or sentimental music (in fact, the film is devoid of non-diegetic music), but by simple cuts. Murphy seeks to simulate the way in which the mind wanders from the present to the far past and near past, and the way in which "locations" can spark a memory picture, or even an elongated memory sequence. There are also some sequences in the film that appear to emerge in a timeless zone, such as Maeve's father's solitary speech that ends the work, where he expresses aloud his innermost fears.

The film does have a "present" consciousness. *Maeve* opens with the father Martin, forced into the scullery because of a bomb scare, sitting in the semi-darkness writing a letter to his daughter, who is in England. We cut to the London scene in which Maeve is seen partying. From then onwards, Maeve's journey is backwards to Ireland, its troubles and its past. As she arrives in Ireland, the flashbacks interweave with the present, and clarify the issues raised.

I have counted eleven flashbacks in the film, which can be divided into three types: (A) those of Martin and Maeve, when she is about eight years old (five sequences); (B) those of Maeve aged around fifteen (two sequences); and (C) those of Maeve with Liam when she is around eighteen (four sequences, including one when Liam visits Maeve in London). No clear chronology is established among the sequences within each division, although those sequences between Liam and Maeve can be reasonably disentangled.

I think it significant that, in terms of memory pictures, it is those of Maeve at a young age with her father that dominate. The first such sequence in (A) depicts Martin and Maeve travelling in a van in the country. He stops at a mound covered with trees, and relates the story that the incline was not levelled because people were spooked by narratives of the "wee people" inhabiting the area. Martin here educates his daughter about myth and superstition, and how such magical tales can have effects on people's actions.

In the second flashback, we are still in the van with Martin telling his daughter how her grandfather was killed in the 1920s, and how, as a child, her father was sent off to the country to an "activist" family. There, under the tutelage of a woman, he was indoctrinated with republican ideology. When this woman visited him years later in Belfast, she criticised him for working for an *English* supermarket company. In the next flashback, the van has arrived in a small Ulster town, where Martin is delivering cakes and bread to the local bakery. As Maeve waits for her father, she is sharply spoken to by a man in the square who sees that her van has southern Irish number-plates. The clear implication is that they have arrived in a mainly Protestant town among people who do not take kindly to "Free State cakes", even if these Catholics live in Belfast. The fourth flashback in this section involves a short sequence when Martin is unloading his van of televisions (has he lost his supermarket job and been reduced to selling old televisions out of the back of his van?) on the apparent orders of an Army patrol. The image of the televisions lumped on top of one another while a helicopter noise is heard above and while young Maeve looks on conveys to her at a young age her father's impotence in the face of British authority. It also raises the ongoing criticism of media images of Northern Ireland, what might be termed the "newsreel culture" which this film attempts to redress. The final sequence in this section finds the young Maeve walking beside a stone wall and ending up in a tree behind her father, while his voice is heard first offscreen. We end up watching Martin, looking straight into the camera as he tells his magical tale of meeting a bard of Irish poetry in a dream. These scenes imprint upon Maeve not only the legends of Irish mythology and just a sense of her father's personal republican-influenced past, but also a context to understand why men, the spinners of tales or fictions, appear to structure the *terms* of the present, however flawed these may be.

The two sequences of section (B), when Maeve is about fifteen, show her burgeoning physical activism. In the first sequence, we see her coming home from school, walking underneath a loyalist "bridge" only to discover that her sister Roisin has been hit by a Protestant neighbour. Maeve then goes out and slaps the boy who did it, who, in turn, threatens her with a stone. Later, when the whole family is soberly watching the Protestant 12 July celebrations on television, a stone crashes through their window. Due to such intimidation, the family is forced to move back into a Belfast Catholic "ghetto" away from their more suburban mixed area. The second sequence begins with the fifteen-year-old Maeve at convent school, clearly disliking the nationalist ballads (ones valorising female sacrifice) that she has been forced to learn and recite. Particularly oppressive are the framing of the nun teacher with a map of Ireland behind her, and the highlighting in red of Northern Ireland. There then follows a cut to a hospital bed where Maeve has been recuperating from having been beaten up by the police on a demonstration, much to the anger of the three nun teachers who visit her. Oppressed by the nuns on one side, she seems more gently oppressed on the other side by a crazed old woman, presumably Protestant, singing "Abide With Me".

The arguments and debates between Liam and Maeve in section (C) also chart a political trajectory in Maeve's development. Both in flashback and in the "present", Maeve and Liam struggle to find a liveable and consistent perspective for young republicans in and around 1980. Chronologically speaking, the second flashback is actually the first. Here we see an eighteen-year-old Maeve, with Liam, being frisked as they enter a republican social club. Our view of them at first is through surveillance cameras. Although just in time for a quick and quiet drink, they are dragged over to the table of Maeve's uncle who was an IRA activist in the 1950s. Here the male bravado is much in evidence, as Martin's brother reveals that Maeve's father was imprisoned for a year in the 1950s for refusing to name the people who had hoarded guns on his property. Maeve gets annoyed and smashes the beer glasses on the table and storms out, angry that this brother does not appreciate that Maeve's mother had an extremely hard time coping while her husband was in jail. Maeve wants to escape this narrow-minded situation, although Liam's only misguided response here is to say that he will move out from his parents' home and get a flat. Then we assume that the first flashback occurred, when Maeve visits Liam living above the spiritualist Mrs McIlroy (Sheila Graham). This scene occasions for a wry joke as the spiritualists seated around their table hear the groans of lovemaking of Maeve and Liam above. Afterwards both lovers discuss the utility of "political work". Maeve wonders if there is not a way for different but equally valuable work to be done. She thinks "we have barricaded ourselves in". The point Maeve is making (while Liam is only concerned if his lovemaking is satisfactory) is that we create our own fantasies and structures to work within. She implies that Liam's "political work/ideology" is only one such fantasy/structure.

The third flashback sequence begins with Maeve's voice-over offscreen, "A centre, a landmark, laying a foundation...", and both Maeve and Liam are discovered overlooking the city of Belfast, possibly halfway up Cavehill Mountain, which has United Irishmen associations. In their discussion, although often it seems more like two monologues, Liam reveals his desire to break away from his father's thinking and his 1950s nationalism. Maeve argues that this movement away from the 1950s myths is not enough, for it fails to include the role of women. Liam believes that one can take hold of the myth and control it, arguing that, without myths, there is no story to adhere to. Maeve counters that the past is a way of reading the present, and unfortunately some myths, such as the nationalist ones, are false memories. Her major critique is that these nationalist myths provide no space for her as a woman. The feeling of neglect explains why she "blew up" at the older men's nationalist stories, which were either oblivious to women's suffering or dismissive of them.

This overwritten section of the film is very strained and uncinematic, and the actors seem unable to believe in some of the lines. This criticism would be more serious in a conventional narrative film, which *Maeve* is not, and so a different perspective must be taken. Normally the film critic objects to such stylised and articulate lines without seeing greater character motivation for their utterance or greater situational motivation. Neither is particularly evident here. But I do not want to "load" the film with expectations that it did not initially seek to fulfil. Maeve is an angry, young, articulate and politically educated woman. It is believable that she is prone to extreme conflicting emotions, between the selfish but necessary desire to escape the narrowness of the Belfast ghetto, and a grander theory that would explain the feminist plight within the republican/nationalist behemoth. The personal is definitely the political, yet she cannot argue at a high level of political discourse with her mother and father, nor for that matter with her younger sister Roisin. A different kind of emotional language must be found here, some of it unspoken.

The fourth and final flashback concerning Liam and Maeve is set in London when Liam visits. Here we see Maeve much more at peace, albeit dislocated. House-sitting in a professional's flat would appear to be a middle-class goal for Maeve. Her spoken desire is to study photography at a college in London, and she regards the English metropolis as a "centre of energy" that allows people of different cultures to interact fruitfully. Interestingly, she believes England has disconnected itself more successfully than Ireland from its false memories. Liam is resentful, since he believes that Ireland is still suffering from England's "colonial aftermath", as if all the sins of the past have been transported to Northern Ireland and evacuated from England. Again, part of Liam's anger towards Maeve revolves around a common experience. Back in Belfast at one point they were both stopped and searched by the British Army. When Liam was temporarily arrested, Maeve chose to contact Liam's mother instead of his father, and this decision upsets Liam's sense of maleness. Liam thinks Maeve has opted out, run away from her country's responsibilities, but she declares the right not to know what she is doing or where she is going. Behind Liam's accusation is obviously a fear that Maeve has taken a bold individualist stride forward: she has stepped out of the nationalist rhetoric, and, by travelling to England, has been offered a better view than Liam will allow himself.

By the time Liam and Maeve meet for the last time in the present, we have journeyed with both of them visually and aurally over a number of years, and do not expect a reconciliation between them, only a mutual respect for their political views. They meet by accident and go for a walk in Clifton Street cemetery, where the United Irishman Henry Joy McCracken is buried. The location is natural for Liam, for he seems to represent the republican desire for Protestant, Catholic and Dissenter to embrace an united independent Ireland, but for Maeve it is an ambivalent location, given that the name of the organisation, "United Irishmen", tends to erase the contribution of women.

To Maeve, there are some parallel lines between her feminism and Liam's republicanism: "Look at the South", she remarks, "we are fictions of their nationalisms". What she means here is that the Republic of Ireland pays lip-service to the nationalist struggle in the North because it appeals to its sense of history, pride and constitution, although not to any "reality", political or otherwise. But more pressing to Liam is that Maeve's feminist views threaten to splinter the republican movement, and he accuses feminists of being "anarchists". Maeve retorts that their struggle is control over their bodies, and that women's bodies are being subordinated: "You're in possession of us; you occupy us like an Army". Their general incompatibility of views is encapsulated by Maeve's outburst, "Being a woman is a nationality I carry around with me".

The above scene, which comes near the end of the film, appears to set down the parameters of Murphy's political discourse. Both feminism and republicanism can and do follow similar paths, but they can also diverge quite radically. (This is a point taken up historically in Anne Crilly's *Mother Ireland* [1988] in chapter 9.) The contest, however, between the two former lovers (an interesting metaphor in itself) does breed a respectful distance for a common cause: to decolonise Ireland without disenfranchising its different peoples.

In establishing her personal and ideological past, therefore, Maeve finds the narrowness of Liam unsatisfying, her religious schooling inadequate, and her father impotent in the face of the war around him. Significantly, we begin and end the film with Maeve's father. The patriarchal discourse, which he would seem to embody, is frequently undermined. The opening shots show him lit up by the light of the television screen, as he watches an "old war movie". He then gets up only to see the British troops run around his street. The soldiers call on his home, warning that a bomb has been reported in the next avenue. The final images of Martin feature his monologue about being hijacked by a gunman and caught between the IRA and the security forces. This monologue reinforces the notion that the "Law of the Father" has ceased to be operative in any real or moral sense. He still is living *his* old war movie.

Very little connection is made between Maeve and her father in the present. He is either a strong memory impression or a spinner of tales. Almost as soon as she arrives back in Belfast for her visit, her mother begins to tell her a story of some local incident, but is immediately interrupted by her father who insists on giving his version of events, much to her mother's frustration. In this scene, as in later ones, Martin looks directly at the camera, almost as if his discourse assures us that it is the object of the camera's gaze. The irony, of course, is that the film displaces this apparently sutured position in favour of Maeve's resistance.

Much more difficult to address is Maeve's relationship with her mother. In her memories/flashbacks, Maeve's mother keeps the family together when Martin is imprisoned for a year; tends to Roisin when, as a young girl, she is hit by a Protestant boy; and appears to keep faith to her Catholic religion, which is symbolised by regularly adding to her icon collection. Although initially thinking her mother too passive, Maeve is encouraged by Roisin's story that her mother risked being shot at an Army checkpoint for losing her temper at a young British soldier. The story is related to convey the pent-up rage inside her mother, which Maeve has inherited yet refuses to repress. Maeve has no qualms in telling an amorous drunk to "fuck off", or in rejecting her boyfriend's arguments. She is strong in her own right, representative of a new generation.

But while this strength may be palpable, one discussion between Maeve and her mother is extremely tense, and during it the daughter has few responses. Her mother alights upon the time Maeve left for the airport to travel to England, and how Maeve did not wave her goodbye. These small "slights" are personalised, and Maeve cannot construct any political discourse to argue back – as with Liam – for this is not how her mother sees the world. This pervading sense of emotional loss is why the penultimate scene of the film, featuring Maeve, Roisin and their mother walking on the Giant's Causeway, is important. The scene links the women together, taking control of a male mythological site,[5] replete with a crazed man shouting the loyalist slogan into the sea, "Ulster will fight and Ulster will be right". Despite these distractions, the women, even with their differences, have reconciled and bonded in a common struggle for recognition and solidarity.

The relationship between Roisin and Maeve is apparently a good one. They share stories, show concern for their mother, and have a "realistic" attitude towards the lot of women in northern Irish society, typified by the scene in which they are forced to jump up and down by British troops, and when they spot a soldier making love to an Irish woman. This woman's bored face, as the soldier goes about his business, only confirms to Maeve and Roisin the inadequacy of traditional male values. The level of intimacy between these two women is underscored by the fact that both feel comfortable naked in each other's presence. This desexualised nudity is important, for *Maeve* is certainly one of the first Irish films to think and show male and female nudity as natural.

Whereas *Maeve* looks at the choices available to an educated single woman, Orla Walsh's *The Visit*, winner of a prize at the Oberhausen Short Film Festival, explores the responsibilities of Sheila (Magael Maclaughlin), a married woman, without children, whose husband Sean (Ger Carey) is in jail for terrorist activities. Her husband seems to be incarcerated for murder, as his sentence is long, and references are made to "going on the blanket". Sheila's life revolves around her work, her visits to the jail, and "reporting" to her mother (Stella McCusker) and mother-in-law (Sally McCaffrey) on her situation. The atmosphere she must endure is one of great repression and claustrophobia, whether at the jail, on the minibus journey to and from the jail, or simply being the faithful "prisoner's wife" in the part of the city in which she lives.

One telling scene occurs in a bar where Sheila and her female friends are chatting. They look over at three men who are eyeing them up. Two of the men goad the third to go over and strike up a conversation, but just as he is about to do so, they pull him back, telling him that they are "prisoners' wives" and therefore "out of bounds". Sheila cannot have a sanctioned emotional relationship with Sean, except in the public view of the prison officers, who observe their every conversation and action. It is little wonder that she finally breaks this stony fortitude when a co-worker Tom (Brendan Laird) invites her out for a drink, and convinces her that it should not be her who is "in prison" as well. Nevertheless, they must have this drink clandestinely. The relationship is consummated, and Sheila becomes pregnant. Tom offers to live with her and move to Dublin, but Sheila argues that she will keep the baby and attempt to reconcile with her husband. To Sheila, the pregnancy is about her alone, not about her new relationship. In this way, Walsh's script tries to give Sheila some autonomy in this cloistered and repressive society. More ambitiously, Sheila intends to tell her husband of her pregnancy at her next visit. Her reasoning is from a feminist position: she had stuck to him all these years he was in trouble; now she expects him to stand by her. The boyfriend believes this expectation to be naïve, and the film ends at the point of revelation without us knowing what the results will be. In a sense, it does not really matter, for Sheila's decisions to develop an extramarital relationship *and* to tell her husband are what empowers her as an individual. These decisions are all the braver, since she is told about one woman who, unfaithful to her prisoner husband, was brutally treated.

Throughout this short film, Walsh makes us aware of the heavy surveillance and monitoring that Sheila feels. Images of Army patrols, helicopters and security cameras are plain enough to interpret. But equally suggestive is the Belfast City Hall and the statue of Queen Victoria, representative of tradition. The nod to Queen Victoria is of interest as she is mythologised as one who stayed in mourning after the death of her husband Albert (although rumours abound that she may have had at least one affair). In Sheila's predicament, Victoria conveys a traditional (ironically British) role model for a woman – literally to stand by her man to appease society's mores. Wherever Sheila turns she is reminded of those responsibilities – in conversations with her mother, mother-in-law, and Sean. Even the simple task of getting to the prison involves her having to take a black taxi (the bus service in West Belfast) and run the verbal gauntlet of other women in a similar situation. As she waits for the Long Kesh/Maze jail bus, she stands in front of a mural of Bobby Sands, the IRA prisoner who died on hunger strike, which declares: "Everyone Republican or otherwise has his/her own part to play". The rhetoric here implies that Sheila, who has withstood seven long years of this twenty-year sentence, must simply endure. This nationalist/republican dogma, however, as in *Maeve*, leaves little room for the personal needs and desires of women.

Both idealism and realism are explored in the film. If nationalism is the progressive force that it claims to be, Sheila wants her feminism to be recognised. As she tells Tom: "This whole thing [the affair] was never about you or him. It was about me. Everything has always been decided for me. Now I'm going to have my own life, my own life with this baby...If this is a problem for people, they're going to have to deal with it. Same as Sean. I stood by him through it all, the blanket, the dirt, and the deaths. Now I'll see if he's got the strength to stand by me...but if it was to go on between me and Sean it would have to change anyway."

We can see the connections between *Maeve* and *The Visit* in the way in which both women must fight for a space for themselves which is not preordained or circumscribed by male roles. We can also see the stylistic connections in that the use of flashbacks is favoured to accompany Sheila's final journey to tell Sean. In a sense, such technical choices resist the conventional linear narrative with its assumption of coherence. If one thing is clear in both films, it is that a smooth path for socially and politically aware women is not easy to find.

Much more straightforwardly than these two films, Margo Harkin's *Hush-A-Bye Baby* also addresses women's issues, particularly for teenage girls in the nationalist areas of Derry in

Northern Ireland. The main ethos of the film is that of Catholic nationalist Ireland with its ambivalent relationship with the Roman Catholic Church and its teachings. Another ethos is that of the 1980s when there were many incidents that brought the issues of abortion and women's rights into the limelight. Yet another is the awareness that the mid-1980s were the period of "supergrass" trials, symptomatic of the continuing war with the British and unionist population.

Hush-A-Bye Baby emerged out of a very specific combination of events. Firstly, in 1983, an abortion referendum was held in the Republic of Ireland and was massively defeated, thereby making abortion illegal within the confines of the state, as well as within the doctrines of the Roman Catholic Church. Northern Ireland also outlaws abortion, as the 1967 liberalisation of the law in England, Scotland and Wales did not automatically transfer across the Irish Sea. Secondly, in 1984, there was a series of appalling incidents in the Republic of Ireland mostly due to the atmosphere created by the referendum result. In one case, Anne Lovett, a fifteen-year-old schoolgirl, died giving birth to a stillborn baby in a field in County Westmeath. She was found dead in a grotto to the Blessed Virgin. In County Kerry that year, Joanne Hayes was *falsely* accused by the Irish police (Gardaí) of the murder of a baby who had been stabbed 28 times and found washed up on a beach. Thirdly, 1984 saw the formation of Derry Film and Video Workshop, which was set up to counteract the images of Northern Ireland propagated in the British and foreign media, and, in particular, to counteract those images of women and women's issues.

For over two years, the script of *Hush-A-Bye Baby* was developed with local people, drama workshops and interviews with Irish women who had experienced pregnancy outside marriage. Margo Harkin's film naturally involves the "Troubles", as it is set in 1984 in the "North of Ireland" and focuses on the Catholic nationalist community of the Creggan and Bogside in Derry. Just as there is a "war" on two fronts in *Maeve* and *The Visit* (feminism and republicanism, respectively), *Hush-A-Bye Baby* raises the point that, while there is an infrastructure for republicanism, even when it is under stress, a lamentable absence exists when it comes to catering for young women and their needs.

The plot of *Hush-A-Bye Baby* is fairly transparent. A fifteen-year-old schoolgirl Goretti (Emer McCourt) falls in love with a slightly older boy Ciaran (Michael Liebmann). Ciaran is picked up by the Army and held under the Prevention of Terrorism Act. Goretti realises that she has become pregnant, and attempts to hide it from her family. She seems to be rejected by Ciaran and believes her Catholic family and child-oriented community will also reject her. Abortion is not an option. The film ends with Goretti frightened and hysterical as the stress of the situation overwhelms her, and she is discovered pregnant by her mother and sister.

That this film hit a chord with a southern Irish audience can be gleaned by the high rating it achieved when it was screened on RTE-1. An estimated 650 000 people watched the film, making it the seventh highest viewed programme for that week. The RTE switchboard received thirteen calls of complaint, mostly criticising the "foul language", although it is hard to gauge the true reason for one-word criticisms such as "sick", "disgusting" and "disgrace".[6] Clearly, the reaction in Northern Ireland, with its majority Protestant population, would have been more complicated. At this time (the late-1980s), the film naturally found a slot on the UK's Channel 4, although this would be in the context of an international or art cinema programme for which the channel is noted. Although set in Derry, the Protestants in Northern Ireland and perhaps those in Derry would view the film as an extremely localised event within the nationalist community for a number of social reasons. Whereas contraception and family planning services, including the option of abortion, can be taboo subjects in some Catholic neighbourhoods, the same cannot be said with the same confidence about Protestant neighbourhoods. I hasten to say that the taboo of abortion is a real issue among Protestants in Northern Ireland, but whereas politically and socially Protestants tend to look to liberal England, Catholics tend to look to the more conservative Republic of Ireland.

Significantly, the Republic is utilised in the film as a location (Donegal), where both Goretti and Dinky (Cathy Casey) go for a holiday and to be in the Gaeltacht (the Irish-speaking community). It is while she is in Donegal that the issues of pregnancy, abortion and religion come to the fore. In an amusing reversal of attitudes to language, Goretti listens secretively to an English-speaking radio programme which is discussing the lack of abortion rights in Ireland. Particularly notable is the voice of a woman on the radio who is heard remarking, "Abortion cannot be described as anything other than murder". To a fifteen-year-old girl, this is a dramatic and damning accusation, since Goretti in her heart knows she is not ready to be a mother. At this moment, Harkin pictures Goretti, in slow-motion, breaking an egg into a bowl of flour. It is a very striking image, conveying the fragility of the fertilised egg now growing inside her body. Also significant during this sojourn in Donegal is an acknowledgment of the "moving statue phenomenon" (which became, rather like crop circles in the UK, a mystical *cause célèbre* in Ireland). Goretti and Dinky come across a statue of the Blessed Virgin Mary. Dinky instructs it, humorously, not to "fucking move". To Goretti, it is a more serious and sobering symbolic image for her predicament. In her dreams, she sees this statue of Mary moving and appearing to be impregnated. Goretti naturally interprets these images as a condemnation of her physical state. This apparition perhaps explains the voice-over of the prayer (the Memorare) at the end of the film. It seems that Goretti is trapped within the religion she fears, and within the fear of condemnation by her family.

Harkin sets up an interesting dynamic by using the Donegal holiday as the catalyst for Goretti's philosophical awareness of her entrapment. It is a journey into "old Ireland" in more ways than one. Both Dinky and Goretti are not truly committed to learning Irish, and one senses that the recreational aspects of their Irish-language classes are what drives them to the community centre (it is there that Goretti meets Ciaran, after all). Harkin's contemporary image of Derry through the eyes of four fifteen-year-old schoolgirls is both realistic and humorous. British soldiers patrol the streets (one of whom even tries to engage in conversation with Ciaran in Irish), Father Devine at school preaches high and mighty about the sanctity of marriage, and parents and older siblings demand a family-oriented culture. When we see Goretti framed in front of the famous graffiti, "YOU ARE NOW ENTERING FREE DERRY", we understand that, for women, it is a limited freedom at best.

The arrest of Ciaran, the worry of his mother in particular, and the political education he seems to be receiving from his fellow prisoners all seem to run counter to Goretti's problems as a young pregnant woman. Ciaran's late offer of marriage and repentance "for getting you into this mess" are somewhat beside the point, as Goretti wants more options which are denied her. Harkin's framing of Goretti alone on the rocky beach in Donegal, her frightening montage-like dreams of an ominous Virgin Mary statue, and the visual references to the washed-up dead baby of real-life Ireland of 1984 all create an oppressive world for the teenager to whom the narrow political/republican issues are simply irrelevant. This marginalisation of the generally accepted "political" is what ties *Hush-A-Bye Baby* to *Maeve* and *The Visit*.

The opening shot of Harkin's film – a mixture of hair, fabric and dissonant sounds under water (which turns out to be a child's dunking of a doll into a bath-tub) – captures supremely well the sense of young women in a state of confusion in 1980s Ireland. In this work, Harkin intended to counteract the generalised and often foreign visual depictions of the North in favour of a more realistic day-to-day accounting of people's actual lives. In that respect, she has certainly succeeded.

Stephen Burke's 30-minute *After '68* is a remarkably mature cinematic exploration of the turbulent period between 1968 and 1972. Set also in Derry, the film begins just before the "Troubles". In utilising a female voice-over throughout the work – as opposed to diegetic sound – Burke achieves an aesthetic and political distance from the events described. Frieda (Deirdre Molloy)'s monologue gives shape to these occurrences, a delivery which is surprisingly lukewarm to the tumult around her. The rather deadpan, matter-of-fact tone desensationalises the violence. As Frieda recounts, 1968 was a significant year internationally – student riots; the proliferation of the Vietnam War; the invasion of Czechoslovakia by the Soviet Union; and the assassination of Martin Luther King Jnr. On the periphery of Europe, (London)Derry city added its voice for change.

Frieda's view of the situation is nicely complicated, since she is the illegitimate child of a mixed liaison: her Protestant father Mr Craig, a city councillor and part-time UDR man (Brian McGrath), apparently separated from her Catholic mother (Ger Ryan) before or soon after Frieda was born, and then married a Protestant woman (Fidelma Murphy). The film charts a number of the key political movements of those early years: the civil rights marches; the Burntollet incident; the Battle of the Bogside; the arrival of the British Army; the IRA split; the first murders; "Bloody Sunday"; and the dissolution of Stormont in 1972. Each segment is punctuated by a formal caesura: a black screen. Throughout the film, actual footage of the period is interspersed, whether of Northern Ireland's lame-duck prime ministers Terence O'Neill or James Chichester-Clark, or of British Prime Minister Harold Wilson, or, in fact, of the Provisional IRA patrolling the streets. These period pieces add a general feeling of authenticity and of isolation, since they appear irrelevant to the basic concerns of Frieda and her mother.

Feminism and republicanism working together would appear to be suggested by the mother's actions in becoming involved in the civil rights movement, but, whereas the former is undeniably embraced, the latter is partly disavowed. Frieda's mother berates the nuns in the convent school for hitting her daughter, and removes her from the school, deciding to tutor her alone. When the two move to Donegal, however, Frieda is seemingly forced to return to the repressive Catholic ethos of convent schools. Moving to the Republic of Ireland does not therefore change that reality.

While her mother involves herself in marches and social and political struggle, Frieda, like most teenagers, starts dating, smoking and listening to pop music. Meanwhile, once the payments from Mr Craig stop coming, Frieda's mother visits Mrs Craig who, through what appears to be female solidarity, comes to visit and support them until the violence becomes a real hazard. When the barricades go up in the Bogside, Frieda is grounded by her authoritarian mother, who chooses not to join the street activities of the mainly male republicans.

The move to Donegal is another sign of Frieda's mother's strength of will. They return briefly for the funeral of Mr Craig who has been killed by the IRA. On this visit home, they discover that a family is squatting in their old home, but, far from offending the mother, she tells them that they are welcome to it as they leave again for Donegal. Leaving the house, she looks at the picture of her earlier days of campaigning for "one man – one vote". As the voice-over understates, for Frieda's mother and, in fact, for all the female protagonists in the films discussed in this chapter, "those days were gone".

Oppressive as the Roman Catholic Church and Irish republicanism may be for young women, they do provide structures against which the female protagonists here can define themselves. Yet, one comes away from these films feeling despondent, as these women have such a large inheritance of assumed inferiority and marginalisation to overcome that possibilities of rapprochement – only briefly glimpsed in *After '68* – with Protestant women are, at best, discordant and abortive. We learn next to nothing in these films about Protestant women, which reflects, unfortunately, on the ghettoisation of each community. Where would these Catholic characters meet Protestants?[7] In this sense, these films are studiously, if depressingly, realistic. The mode of "realism" (articulated unusually here by flashbacks) is a dominant one found in the productions discussed in this book, although its best-known adherents are in British film, examples of which are to be found in the next chapter.

Notes

[1]　Ron Hutchinson, *Rat in the Skull* (London: Methuen, 1984): 15. In the introduction to this play, Rob Ritchie provides a useful survey of "Troubles"-related theatre and television drama.

[2]　The same subject-matter as Sheridan's film was presented from the perspective of the mother in the television play, *Dear Sarah* (Frank Cvitanovich, RTE 1990), written by Tom McGurk.

[3]　The two most useful critical pieces on the film are Claire Johnston, "'Maeve'", *Screen* 22: 4 (1981): 54-71; and Luke Gibbons, "Lies that tell the Truth: *Maeve*, History and Irish Cinema", *The Crane Bag* 2 (1983): 148-155. Johnston's article includes a probing interview with the filmmaker which provides a good explanation of the feminist and political context of the film's genesis.

[4]　The film's unconventional narrative structure bemused many reviewers. See, for example, Mosk., "Maeve", *Variety* 21 October 1981: 17. To this reviewer's mind, the film "suffers from rather makeshift scripting and narrative", a comment revealing the unawareness of the goals of the filmmaker in rejecting "classic" cinematic conventions.

[5]　The Giant's Causeway folklore is that it was formed by a battle between two male giants, one Scottish, one Irish.

[6]　The RTE information was supplied by Margo Harkin in the package of press cuttings accompanying the film.

[7]　Interestingly, the new Northern Ireland Women's Coalition did succeed in 1996 in gaining a place at the Peace Forum. The success of this political group, although small, augurs well for feminists in Northern Ireland attempting to bridge the gap between Protestant and Catholic women.

6

The elephant at the kitchen sink: British social realists

I say tow that entire fucking wet island and its incomprehensible bleeding tribes into the Atlantic, pull the plug and give us all some fucking peace and quiet. (Naylor in Ron Hutchinson's *Rat in the Skull*)[1]

It would be misleading to suggest that the feminist issues raised in the previous chapter dominate the sheer volume of films on the "Troubles". In returning to the mainstream we inevitably return to the malestream, where numerous filmmakers appear to have a televisual aesthetic. Everyone who watches public television in North America knows its reliance on British television series. From the 1960s to the present, British television drama, whether made by the BBC or independent television companies, has almost always assured an impeccable cast, a refined and enviable production standard, plus a willingness to take on subject-matter which is difficult, challenging or painful. Since the British film industry was deflated in the 1960s and 1970s, it is understandable that many would-be filmmakers began in television, because, firstly, it allowed training in a wide variety of areas, and, secondly, creative work was not always confined to the studio. In short, it was an attractive medium for filmmakers and writers from a working-class background, and for those who sought to explore social issues while intent on reaching a wide audience. It must be remembered that Britain has been very slow to expand its channel offerings.

In the 1980s, there were only four nationally available terrestrial channels, so the ability and opportunity to affect a large group of people through drama have only been contested with the introduction of satellite television.

Another quality "tradition" with which British television drama and film are associated is "social realism". This is certainly a style, which may be traced from the 1930s documentaries of Basil Wright, Harry Watt and John Grierson to the "kitchen sink" films of the 1950s and 1960s by (rather middle-class) directors such as Tony Richardson, Karel Reisz and Jack Clayton.[2] Alan Clarke, Mike Leigh and Ken Loach are inheritors of this tradition; indeed, they have helped to ingrain it into British television drama and film practice. These three directors have a joint interest in the "everyday" and in realism as a style, although they appear to have different strategies to achieve their respective configurations. The most rigorously controlled of the three, and, in my view, the best filmmaker is Alan Clarke.

Alan Clarke (1935-90) made three feature films and over 30 television productions.[3] Two of these television productions deal specifically with Northern Ireland: *Contact* (1985) and *Elephant* (1989).[4] Both are taut and intense experiences. Following the lives of young men in a British regiment on patrol in "bandit country" of south Armagh, the former film poses a series of veiled questions which Clarke's unremitting observational style of fictional filmmaking avoids answering directly – Who are they fighting against? Why are they there? What do they think about their job?

Many of the images and sequences presented remain locked in one's mind after viewing: the platoon commander (Sean Chapman) in his bed considering the loss of one of his soldiers; the same commander, with an apparent death-wish mentality, methodically opening the doors to an abandoned car, while we watch, unsure if it will blow up; the extremely close but perilous relationship between the soldiers and the land: here nature is dangerous, for each broken branch may indicate a booby trap.

The sheer youthfulness of these soldiers is striking. They are "doing a job", albeit one of extreme danger. Their tiredness, fear, boredom and muted camaraderie are honestly portrayed. The commanding officer who gives the platoon its assignments is listened to with a listless deference, while the general lack of speech and dialogue draws us closer to the minutiae of the Army operation.

A catalogue of "events" suggests that a narrative can be tabulated, but no links are cemented. At the beginning of the film, an ambush occurs. The platoon commander stops a car, clinically kills one man, and threatens to kill the other by letting his rifle hover over the man's face as he lies spread-eagled on the ground. Another "event" includes the cornering of eight "terrorists" who are transferring rifles from one car to another. This ambush and chase lead to the stake-out of a house and the eventual capture of four men. Again the platoon commander "toys" with the idea of shooting one of his prisoners. At one point, the platoon exchanges fire with a sniper who remains unseen. At another point, a soldier is blown up and his body blackened. The commander rushes forward to the corpse and shouts at his men to stop staring at the dead man and get back to their job of surveillance. For the soldiers, the killing is, in a macabre way, "proof" of their vocation, one which is always close to sudden violence. The death-wish of the platoon commander seems unstoppable: when an arms cache is found, he decides to handle and search the ammunition himself. They arrest an Irish farmer who is nearby, and the commander orders his men to shoot him if the stockpile proves to be wired for explosion. The film ends with the noise of a booby-trap bomb going off. We are not sure who has succumbed to the blast.

Small incidents become highly significant in understanding these soldiers' lives. They chance upon what appears to be a deserted farmhouse and begin to surround it, only to find an old couple who come outside to watch, disbelievingly, as the soldiers point their weapons at them. The helicopter lands them nowhere distinct and, after their five-day "expedition", takes them out of "nowhere". Clarke's major technical innovation to convey this weird mental and physical landscape is the choice to observe the soldiers through greenish-hued "night glasses". It gives the impression that the soldiers are being observed by the "enemy", and yet also illustrates how their "night world" is both dangerous and beautiful. During one of these night patrols, the men come across a caravan with an adjoining tent in which small children are sleeping. One of the children awakes and stares back at the platoon leader. Both parties seem fascinated and appalled by this potentially violent intrusion of a peaceful scene. All this is captured in the greenish tint of the night glasses, suggesting that Clarke's camera and the audience have access to voyeuristic equipment, as well as its accompanying danger. It is a society predicated upon clandestine surveillance. It is also a world which is eerily quiet; the absence of dialogue for large parts of the film is engrossing, for only when it is absolutely necessary does the platoon leader speak.

In this silence, Clarke underlines the demoralisation of the men. Omnipresent is the fear that the enemy, whom they cannot even see most of the time, will kill them. The platoon leader is a burnt-out professional, who finds no power worth having, even in his arrest and torture of the terrorists. When he puts his gun into the mouth of one captive, he seems as equally disgusted or disillusioned by his action as viewers are encouraged to be. Part of this disillusion is that we are not told why the troops are in Northern Ireland. The fact that they are not shown any support from the local populace should not be overinterpreted because the film focuses on day-to-day operations. The routine is simply that, and, for Clarke, with his almost mathematical precision, to go beyond observation might appear to be a disservice to what an army actually does. In short, a soldier follows orders and tries not to get killed in the process. This tension is what the filmmaker captures.

Clarke's interest in precision is extended beyond belief in *Elephant*. Made under the auspices of BBC-NI, in its 37 minutes it comprises some eighteen murders. Very formalistically, each representation follows a specific structural pattern, what might be called Clarke's "Steadicam aesthetic". Initially, we accompany the murderers looking for their victims, most often on foot; we observe the shooting; we see the murderers march away, and sometimes the camera drifts away with them; then we return to a view of the murdered. Particularly disturbing is the way in which the silence (again no dialogue) seems to promote an affinity with the murderers, a feeling which is enhanced by the constant camera view from the murderers' perspective. No reverse-shots are made available to us. In this way, the characters seem distanced from us, and yet the sheer matter-of-factness of the killings is overwhelming. It as if the relentless sequence of murders has no end, and therefore no point. Certainly, this viewing experience is no elongated artistic structuralist joke, but it is unbearable in its own fashion. One must surmise that this unbearableness is exactly Clarke's point. The title is a suitable metaphor for the way in which people in Northern Ireland, the Republic of Ireland and Great Britain viewed the "Troubles" during the 1970s and 1980s. It was big, monstrous even, but possible to contain as long as it was ignored. The disjunction between the title of the film and its contents provokes the viewer, confuses, and forces the questioning of the "problem" of Northern Ireland in a more energised way.

This interpretation was also taken by the producer Danny Boyle when he appeared on a viewers' phone-in show after the film was broadcast.[5] Ludovic Kennedy, the host, held up a huge wad of letters from viewers and took three calls from Northern Ireland, all critical. The first caller wanted to know why Clarke was intent on "stylisation" when a documentary attitude seemed to be warranted. Boyle responded that they did not wish to travel the documentary route because that would be intrusive on specific people's private pain. It was simply an unfortunate occurrence that a number of killings similar to those depicted in the film had just happened prior to broadcast. A second caller wanted to know by what authority Boyle and Clarke had been able to make this film. The producer explained that there was a process within the BBC whenever Northern Ireland as a subject came up. Boyle remarked that "as long as it's not propaganda", a project is normally given the green light. The time constraints of the programme did not allow Boyle to be quizzed further on this point, which is a pity, for the BBC in particular has been a locus of many media censorship battles. A third caller argued that, although billed as a "chilling commentary" in the pre-publicity, there was no overt commentary, either verbal or visual. Boyle countered that their inspiration was to present material and leave it up to the viewer to make up his or her own mind. Most of all, Boyle and Clarke wanted to illustrate that individual murders were going on all the time, while the media tended to focus primarily on major events where many people were killed at once.

Mike Leigh's *Four Days in July* (1984) shares the interest of Clarke in detailing the everyday through long periods. Leigh's film contrasts a Protestant couple and a Catholic couple, both of whom are expecting a baby. The action takes place over four days, 10-13 July, at the height of the Protestant 12 July celebrations (commemorating the victory of William of Orange over James II in 1690). The Protestant man Billy (Charles Lawson) is a member of the locally recruited UDR, while the Catholic man Eugene (Des McAleer) is disabled from a British Army stray bullet wound received many years earlier.

For a war zone, surprisingly little happens in the external world of these characters, although both have histories with which to contend. The choice of Leigh to represent the Protestant community by a soldier is indicative of his implicit assumption that it is the Protestants who have the "big stick". Furthermore, by setting the film at the apex of Protestant triumphalism – the eleventh night bonfires, which are regularly followed by all-night parties and drinking, then on through the 12 July parades – the sense of oppression against the Catholic minority in the city of Belfast is strongly conveyed. What Leigh chose not to show is how liberal Catholics and Protestants also find the parades of both traditions very oppressive, down to the beat of their respective drums and the flute-playing. A small hint of this frustration is found in the character of Mr Roper (John Hewitt), who appears together with Billy and Eugene in the waiting-room at the hospital. He is nervous and angry, sounding off at both the Protestant parades and the "terrorists", but it is unclear what his political and religious affiliations are.[6]

In Mike Leigh's politically uneventful *Four Days in July*, the acting is so "authentic", or clearly "improvised", that one never knows what is going to happen next. When Billy's patrol stops a van in a routine search, the driver, Mr McCoy (John Keegan), proceeds to give a long recounting of a theory that the Protestant community are an ancient people who originated in Ireland, went to Scotland, and then came back. Historically, this is not as ridiculous as it sounds, although to talk about "Protestantism" before the Reformation is somewhat wide of the mark! The point, however, is that the man is articulating a narrative of the Protestant community, mythical or otherwise.[7] They may be inaccurate or unrealistic stories, but, just as the UDR soldiers feel that they are overtrained and underused (and betrayed) by the British, such narratives sustain their sense of identity and purpose.

In Colette (Brid Brennan) and Eugene's home, a series of narratives or shared experiences define their community: Eugene's three brushes with death during the "Troubles"; the songs that Colette sings to send her husband to sleep (an ironic rendition of the Protestant "The Sash My Father Wore", and then the republican song, "The Patriot Game"); the shared experience between Dixie (Stephen Rea) and Brendan (Shane Connaughton) when they were interned in the early 1970s: from setting up a poteen still to bad jokes, mathematical quizzes, and the general poverty of the neighbourhood.

In Billy and Lorraine's (Paula Hamilton) home, there is less warmth, which is perhaps common in a military subculture. Billy has to keep his firearms hidden in the house, and has to check underneath his car every morning in case terrorists have booby-trapped it. The anger and danger seem to go hand-in-hand. The personal relationship between Lorraine and Billy is much cooler than that between Colette and Eugene, and both get much less screen time than the Catholic couple. Billy seems to exhibit the signs of a person who is burdened by responsibility while insecure of his ability to live up to it. This burdensome insecurity leads to his reactive and somewhat bitter responses to his wife's emotional needs. Within Billy's working subculture – a job that often featured men going away for days and nights in the countryside and sleeping rough – a crude bravado has arisen. The most telling narrative among the soldiers is the one about how one night Billy killed a bullock, and his friend cut it up for camp-fire sustenance. It is presented as a Boy Scout prank with extreme violence, probably symptomatic of what Leigh thought of the UDR. Other readers may interpret the caricature which Leigh has created as racist and imperialist.

Stylistically, Leigh uses parallel montage between the Protestant couple and the Catholic couple to underscore that, although they share an forthcoming birth, small but significant differences exist. Both couples live in small houses, are clearly working-class, and regard their tribalism as natural. Hence, it is as normal for Eugene and Colette to have a picture of the Pope on their wall as it is for Billy and Lorraine to have an Ulster flag above their bed. The only occasion where they would indeed meet is in an institutional setting such as a hospital. Yet, even here, Leigh does not allow the two men to share the same frame for very long. In fact, it is telling that the film ends with a wide shot of the two young mothers with their babies. They share the same space and frame, the same experience, the same hospital ward, but they are miles apart. Colette's attempt to strike up a conversation with Lorraine is doomed to failure (and suspicion) when she tells her that her baby is called Magraid, the Irish for Margaret. Lorraine cannot understand why the baby cannot simply be called Margaret, and they both fall into silence, as if knowing that a cultural barrier has arisen. Through talk, through these mini-narratives and shaggy-dog stories, songs half-remembered, small domestic adventures, and so on, each community declares itself. Leigh's realism is enhanced by authentic dialect and accent, even if the "situations" which his characters discuss and act out have been rehearsed beforehand.

Leigh has begun to transfer his "authentic" and "improvised" or "devised" technique to the big screen with critical success. In contrast, Ken Loach's career has long concentrated on feature films. Loach's early work, however, was also in television, and he has always been deeply involved with social reform. From *Cathy Come Home* (1966) to such works as *Ladybird Ladybird* (1994), Loach has assembled a substantial body of work that relies upon telling stories in a gritty, realistic way. Loach has been tied strongly to the Left of the Labour Party in Great Britain.[8]

The limitations of Loach as a filmmaker, as distinct from a social realist and social rights activist, are shown up in *Hidden Agenda* (1990). It is a film that could easily have been shot on video and broadcast on television. Unfortunately, it is also very light on analysis. Whereas Clarke seemed to be able to get under our skin, and the skin of his characters, and whereas Leigh set out for a year of research, rehearsal and filming for *Four Days in July*, Loach appears to have made this film quickly, and, rather predictably, the results are very uneven.[9]

Before discussing the film itself, since it seems inspired by certain historical events some background information is necessary. On 12 December 1982 at a vehicle checkpoint, an undercover unit of the RUC killed Seamus Grew and Roddy Carroll, members of the INLA, an extremist offshoot of the left-leaning Official IRA. Both men were travelling home to Armagh city when a speeding car overtook and forced them off the road. At close range, Grew and Carroll were shot dead, although neither man was armed or wanted for a specific crime. Murders such as these by the undercover RUC unit led to a police inquiry into what became known as the "shoot-to-kill" policy in Northern Ireland. Deputy Chief Constable John Stalker of the Greater Manchester Constabulary headed an internal investigation authorised to present a report, one recommending what charges, if any, should be laid against police officers in Northern Ireland. Before Stalker could present his findings, he was "disgraced" back in Manchester by allegations that he kept company with criminals. Although proved false, these allegations removed Stalker from the Northern Ireland investigation.[10]

Commentators and authors put forth many theories to explain this bizarre turn of events, one of the most popular claiming that Stalker found connections between clandestine operations and their authorisation from within the higher levels of the British government. Also in the conspiracy vein – although a completely separate development – it later emerged that the former Labour Prime Minister Harold Wilson had allegedly been the target of a CIA-instigated plan to discredit him.[11] Hearing this, some quickly assumed that right-wing forces actively made conditions conducive for the rise of Margaret Thatcher and her Conservative policies. Loach attempts to combine these two theories in his film.

In *Hidden Agenda*, an American Civil Liberties Union lawyer Paul Sullivan (Brad Dourif) is killed while uncovering the story behind an ex-SAS soldier Harris (Maurice Roëves), involved in a conspiracy against Wilson's Labour government in the 1970s. Loach tries to tie the Conservative Party's supporters' shenanigans against the Labour Party government of the 1970s with the alleged "shoot-to-kill" policy in Northern Ireland many years later. He fails, however, to make this connection stick firmly, even in the context of his own film. Two separate issues are (half-)addressed here – one well (Conservative Party conspiracy) and one confusingly (the British policy within Northern Ireland). The director stacks the decks from the very beginning. We see policemen and soldiers make a violent house arrest; former detainees allege mistreatment inside police stations; a police/SAS/MI6 unit eliminate the lawyer and his companion with "efficiency"; and British undercover agents kidnap (and kill offscreen) Harris on Dublin's streets, thereby suggesting that England continues to "invade" the Republic of Ireland. Amidst these abuses of human rights, the Chief Constable of the RUC, Brodie (Jim Norton), resists the investigation of Kerrigan (Brian Cox) and Ingrid (Frances McDormand). Loach offers little in the way of explanation as to why Brodie believes in his cause, as if the Conservative and English grandees stand in for the Protestant community. In Loach's constellation, the almost one million Protestants of Northern Ireland are represented by a long shot from a high window during the 12 July celebrations. What other Protestants we see are involved in violence or implied bigotry. Loach's total acceptance of anti-imperialist rhetoric is nowhere more evident than in the absence of a Protestant and unionist voice.

It is precisely because the film has pretensions to "tell the truth" that it must be challenged. Loach opens with two quotations which again underscore, in their duality, the anti-imperialist stance. The first is from Margaret Thatcher, who states that Northern Ireland is as much part of the United Kingdom as her own constituency; the second is from James Lalor, a 19th-century Irish republican, who indicates the imperative of Irish independence. To imply that Thatcherism and Conservative Party "dirty tricks" in the 1970s remained part of an alleged "shoot-to kill" policy in Northern Ireland in the 1980s, without investigating IRA violence and murder, and the forces of nationalism and unionism behind the rhetoric, makes one question the ethics of Loach's intertwining of fictional filmmaking and politics. His film seems more an exercise in political correctness, a response to recent (and rushed) published material, than a real effort to lift the veil on mysterious events.[12]

In truth, Loach and screenwriter Jim Allen are not interested in Northern Ireland *per se*, only with how it might be used to consolidate their attack on British intelligence agencies and their alleged connections to the Conservative Party ideology. This cheap manœuvre by a leading Socialist filmmaker is both surprising and disappointing.[13] It leads Loach to force certain narrative structures which are difficult to achieve convincingly. For example, Allen's script would appear to copy the original events: two men are shot in a car by an undercover RUC unit. But, whereas Carroll and Grew were Irish republican sympathisers, Sullivan and particularly Malloy are much more ambiguous figures. Malloy is from a Catholic Belfast family, if the rosary beads draped over his sitting room mirror are an indication, but he is a man who worked for the Ministry of Defence in London before being posted back to Northern Ireland. When Malloy talks to Sullivan in the car, however, he becomes the quintessential nationalist soothsayer: "1169. 800 years. That's as long as we've been fighting for independence. Sword, famine, burning, hanging, shooting, transportation, we've had it all". Is Malloy a double agent? Is he someone blackmailed or placed by the IRA to provide information? Loach and Allen do not make it clear, suggesting that the ambiguity did not occur to them. Even when we meet Harris, protected by the IRA and Sinn Féin, he is adamant that he is concerned with upholding the validity of the British state, claiming that he has given the IRA nothing of use, except a promise to go public and denounce British imperialism.

The use of the American Sullivan and his assistant Ingrid is of interest, for it implies that what is going on in Northern Ireland needs American intervention. One could read this outright change from the Grew and Carroll story in a number of ways. Sullivan's death allows an English policeman and an American lawyer to work together much in the way in which the US and UK administrations have worked together on Northern Ireland. What the film seems to endorse, in fact, is congruent with the views of John Hume: that the Northern Ireland conflict cannot be resolved internally, and requires an external and possibly imposed framework for peace to occur.

Significantly, Loach's film ends with a quotation from an ex-MI5 officer, who claims that there are two laws in operation: one for the secret security forces, and one for everyone else. This is perhaps where Loach should have begun his film and set it in England, since his foray into Ulster amounts to background filler. What clearly interests Loach is Kerrigan's dilemma, a career officer in the police force who must turn a blind eye to conspiracy and subterfuge in order that a "greater evil" (terrorism and civil disobedience in the UK) be suppressed. But Loach does not need Northern Ireland to make his conspiracy allegations, and it ill-serves the conflict in that province to "muddy the waters" in the way in which he does.

Similarly to Leigh's work, Loach's film has a great deal of talk and "talking heads", but, whereas Leigh uses such conversation to build character, Loach is merely interested in dialogue for the sake of furthering his detective's investigation. His characters do not "flesh out" as in a Leigh film. The strength that Loach exhibits is his fervent critique of the status quo, while both Clarke and Leigh are subtler explorers of the psyche or state of mind which is manifest in Northern Ireland.

Social realism, therefore, among these three artists, varies in style and effect. They have produced sound small-screen fictions, reliant on character or a character's behaviour to carry their respective narratives. Such fidelity to outward signs, as narrative realism often demands, leaves us nevertheless strangely distant from the possibilities of explorations and demystifications for which

Northern Ireland cries out. As the next chapter shows, even local television drama is prone to contorted visions of Northern Ireland not unlike the choices made by Ken Loach.

Notes

1 Ron Hutchinson, *Rat in the Skull* (London: Methuen, 1984): 23.

2 The term "social realism" is admittedly vague, implying a distinction between it and "psychological realism" or "fantasy". The word "social" suggests subject-matter that deals with interactions between individuals and their work, and individuals and their families, lovers and friends. The term "realism" suggests, in this context, an attempt to transfer both the quotidian and remarkable experience of the "ordinary man" to the screen. An unobtrusive, observational (even possibly "documentary") style is favoured. This does not preclude narrative action and point, however, for this is how Loach, in particular, achieves his modulations on the human condition. An extended attempt to characterise the British realist films of the late-1950s and early 1960s is John Hill, *Sex, Class and Realism: British Cinema 1956-1963* (London: British Film Institute, 1986). Hill views these films as fundamentally conservative, hampered by a conventional style, despite their risqué subject-matter. While I agree with Hill's analysis, the larger unanswered question remains: why has this "conservative form" been so favoured until well into the 1980s and 1990s? One answer may well be that gradual change of opinion is best achieved through familiar forms, as many television writers with a Socialist agenda will attest. Another answer is that material realism is never pure, allowing sections of psychological realism to venture much further in formerly taboo areas without alienating the audience.

3 The three feature films are *Scum* (1979), *Billy the Kid and the Green Baize Vampire* (1985) and *Rita, Sue and Bob Too* (1987). David Thomson discusses some of the television plays in "Walkers in the World: Alan Clarke", *Film Comment* 29: 3 (May-June 1993): 78-83.

4 One might also include *Psy-Warriors* (1981), in which two men and a woman are interrogated by a special intelligence unit to establish their ability to be involved in counter-terrorism activities. This is an excellent programme to discuss the depths of violence and subversion to which a democratic state will stoop to sustain the status quo. For a discussion of this film, see Philip Elliott, Graham Murdock and Philip Schlesinger, "The State and 'Terrorism' on British Television", in Bill Rolston and David Miller (eds), *War and Words: The Northern Ireland Media Reader* (Belfast: Beyond the Pale Publications, 1996): 369-372.

5 "Right to Reply" hosted by Ludovic Kennedy, 26 January 1989 on Channel 4. This short programme may be viewed at the Film and Sound Resource Unit, University of Ulster at Coleraine.

6 In the only major article on the film, Paul Clements suggests that Mr Roper is a Protestant loyalist, but this is pure supposition, and Leigh gives no substantial visual or aural clue either way. Clements, however, provides a marvellous account of how Leigh works in "pre-rehearsing" and

"structuring" his stage and television plays. See Paul Clements, "*Four Days in July* (Mike Leigh)", in George W Brandt (ed), *British Television Drama in the 1980s* (Cambridge: Cambridge University Press, 1993): 162-177.

[7]   To a large extent, the contentious historical work of Ian Adamson is relevant here. See his *The Cruithin: A History of the Ulster Land and People* (Belfast: Pretani Press, 1974).

[8]   In 1995, Loach made *A Contemporary Case for Common Ownership*, a short film to lobby against Tony Blair, then Leader of the Opposition, because of his (ultimately successful) campaign to remove Clause IV from the Party's Constitution. Clause IV bound members to strive for ownership of the means of production in the hands of the people, and was regarded as the most avowedly Marxist ideology left in the Labour Party programme.

[9]   I am not alone in criticising the film. Even a sympathetic account by John Hill necessitates revealing its shortcomings. See his "*Hidden Agenda*: Politics and the Thriller", *Circa* 57 (May/June 1991): 36-41; and his "Finding a form: politics and aesthetics in *Fatherland, Hidden Agenda* and *Riff-Raff*", in George McKnight (ed), *Agent of Challenge and Defiance: The Films of Ken Loach* (Trowbridge: Flicks Books, 1997): 125-143. Surprisingly, the screenwriter Jim Allen, long-time collaborator with Loach, is supremely articulate about the complexities of Northern Ireland, which makes it all the stranger that his even-handedness does not transfer to the screen. Allen claims that the film is not about Stalker and more about the fate of Colin Wallace, a British operative who, like Harris in the film, found himself caught between legal and illegal government actions. See Paul Foot, *Who Framed Colin Wallace?* (London: Macmillan, 1989). However, reading Foot's book shows that it is important to underscore that Wallace was an Ulster Protestant betrayed, whereas Harris' origin in the film is simply collapsed into the British Army. This is to miss a complex point. See Allen's interview with Patsy Murphy and Johnny Gogan, "In the Name of the Law", *Film Base News* 19 (September/October 1990): 13-17. It would appear that the weakness lies with Loach and his choice of the thriller genre, with all its requisite ingredients.

[10]   Useful books on the Stalker mystery include: Frank Doherty, *The Stalker Affair* (Cork; Dublin: The Mercier Press, 1986); Peter Taylor, *Stalker: The Search for the Truth* (London; Boston: Faber and Faber, 1987); Committee on the Administration of Justice, *The Stalker Affair: More Questions Than Answers*, second edition (Belfast: CAJ, 1988); John Stalker, *Stalker* (London: Harrap, 1988); Kevin Taylor with Keith Mumby, *The Poisoned Tree* (London: Sidgwick and Jackson, 1990); and David Murphy, *The Stalker Affair and the Press* (London; Boston; Sydney; Wellington: Unwin Hyman, 1991).

[11]   David Leigh, *The Wilson Plot: The Intelligent Services and the Discrediting of a Prime Minister* (London: Heinemann, 1988).

[12]   One imagines that Loach read Doherty's book on Stalker (see note 10), which raises many of the theories upon which the filmmaker touches. Some of the issues are better traced in Chris Ryder, *The RUC: A Force Under Fire* (London: Methuen, 1989), but I doubt, even if the book came

out before the shooting of the film, that Loach would have thought much of it, given his Procrustean tendencies.

[13]   At the press conference at Cannes in 1990, Loach and Allen were attacked by British journalists, including Alexander Walker, who is from Northern Ireland, for "boasting about making a republican and nationalist film", and of sidelining the major issues in Northern Ireland. See Michael Dwyer, "Cannes hots up over new political thriller on North", *The Irish Times* 17 May 1990: 2.

7

"I want out of this bloody country": British television drama

> It was not until 1980, twelve years after the onset of the crisis, that a television play appeared that seriously examined the experience of a Catholic family in the North, Jennifer Johnston's *Shadows On Our Skin*. In the same period, there was not a single play from the point of view of a Loyalist family. (Rob Ritchie)[1]

There are many compelling arguments to consider television drama as a category apart from independent film and video production, and from the kind of work discussed in the previous chapter. One of the truisms that distinguishes television drama is that it is fundamentally a writer's medium.[2] For example, the official list of BBC-NI productions from 1980 to 1994 documents transmission date, title of production and writer. The director is not deemed important, assuming perhaps that he or she is "on assignment" and, perforce, does not have the same motivations and commitment as independent filmmakers and videographers. In other words, by nurturing certain writers, broadcast institutions have a habit of narrowly dictating what kinds of drama are commissioned, produced and broadcast.[3]

One crucial difference between early television drama and film/video production is the tendency to concentrate on indoor locations manufactured in the studio. While more evident in the 1970s than later, when lightweight equipment for shooting outdoors became more widely available, one suspects that this tradition helped enormously to perpetuate a realist style in subsequent years. The dominance of this aesthetic has rarely been the subject of much debate, as if television drama and "realism" are natural partners. To be sure, the "box"'s small dimension and the penetration it has into the households of Great Britain and Ireland have resulted in few dramas that take an unconventional attitude in set or production design and general concept. As a "talking heads" or talking medium, often at the expense of the visual, producers naturally limited budgets for location work. The reasons for this policy were undoubtedly institutionally based. At the time when the BBC did most work in-house in its own studios, there was a pressing need to ensure work for its camera operators, floor managers, set-builders and light-riggers. Some writers and directors intentionally waited years so that the "film slot" would come up for their project, rather than rush into studio production. With the arrival of Thatcher and the change in market forces, contracting out became much more the norm. This change led to a proliferation of outdoor location television drama, although not particularly to any major rethinking of the realist aesthetic.[4]

With regard to Northern Ireland as a subject area for British television production companies, the situation has always been prone to interference. To expect British television drama blatantly to undermine the presence of British soldiers on the streets of Northern Ireland is naïve, since, after all, television serves the public and/or its advertisers, and controversial programming liable to upset the audience (which both BBC and ITV stations need to keep) would be counterproductive. Northern Ireland also raises the problem of balance, largely seen as policy in the news media, but which cannot be successfully achieved in drama due to its individualist tenor, stemming ultimately from one commissioned writer. In a sense, it is hard to see how any truly original work on the conflict can be transmitted, given the complicated relationships cited above. Afraid to criticise the Army presence directly, but equally afraid to argue that their presence gives comfort to the majority in Northern Ireland, television drama producers have selected scripts that developed an ambivalent middle position or that followed an established genre: classical revenge, romantic thriller, detective story, and so on. While the majority of these writers whose work has been broadcast disliked the British presence in Northern Ireland, their productions often tried to mask this posture.

Examining this same BBC-NI list, one discovers that, of the 27 productions made between 1980 and 1987 inclusive, no fewer than eleven were written by Graham Reid, with Stewart Parker and Anne Devlin coming in next with three each.[5] This congregation around one particular writer is of interest less as evidence of an institution guilty of possible favouritism than because Reid's brand of television drama is locked in a working-class Belfast "realism". For many families in Northern Ireland, ardent watchers of *Coronation Street*, Reid's *Billy* plays – *Too Late to Talk to Billy* (1982), *A Matter of Choice for Billy* (1983), *A Coming to Terms for Billy* (1984), and *Lorna* (1987), starring Kenneth Branagh and Brid Brennan – typified to many a certain ethos of the "Troubles" in working-class Protestant Belfast.[6] The series touched on many contemporary issues such as broken families, unemployment, the effect of the "Troubles" on "ordinary" people, and "mixed religion" relationships. Subsequent productions utilising working-class Belfast or Derry tended to be judged against Reid's particular take on northern Irish reality. The main criticism that attentive viewers had of the Reid plays was that Northern Ireland's problems became hidebound to working-class issues and representations, and thereby limited an investigation of political and religious faultlines in the society as a whole.[7]

Television drama is thus clearly more than the "moving wallpaper" that some film and theatre purists dismiss it as, and it did offer, in the 1970s and 1980s, an incredible instant audience, often in the millions, because of the few national channels at that time.[8] It can also provide writers with fairly substantial payment. For the critic, however, it is very frustrating, since these programmes are only occasionally rebroadcast and are copyrighted to the institution, allowing very limited access for reviewing them. Only a few television dramas have made it to video, the most notable being *Harry's Game* (aka *Belfast Assassin,* 1982), a Yorkshire Television (YTV) production.[9] And, of course, the BBC, ITV and RTE stations have made numerous dramas about Northern Ireland in various formats, and no single chapter could do justice to the variety of work that has been broadcast since 1968. What follows, therefore, is, by necessity, a reading of selected television dramas made between 1985 and 1994, a period that fulfilled the hopes of which Rob Ritchie wrote. This reading reveals that the anti-imperialist myth was alive and well in television drama, closely followed by atavistic urges. We discover, too, that the ideological position of the nationalist and republican communities in Northern Ireland has been well-served.[10]

One of the few productions to be written and directed by the same person is Douglas Livingstone's *We'll Support You Evermore* (BBC-NI, 1985). This drama sets out to show the labyrinthine complexities of the British Army role in Northern Ireland focalised through a father of a murdered soldier. Geoff Hollins (John Thaw) travels to Belfast to see if he can find out anything about his son's death. Ostensibly, he is attending the trial of people suspected of killing his son David (Christopher Fulford). On the plane, he meets an English television news-reporter Su Friday (Sheila Ruskin), who is simply concerned about her own career and casually cynical about the "acceptable level of violence" which the British government settled for after the failure of various political experiments in the early 1970s. Once Hollins checks in at the Europa Hotel in Belfast (famous as the most bombed hotel in Europe), he discovers that he has been monitored by the security forces, and is met by Morden (Nicholas Le Prevost), the Army liaison officer. Morden tells Hollins that David died a soldier's death, but, since he was on "special operations" at the time, the Army cannot reveal the details of his death.

Hollins begins his own investigation, since at heart he is dissatisfied with the official explanation of his son's death, and Livingstone intersperses sequences of father and son in better times: from baby pictures, to father reading him a story when a young boy, to father and son attending a soccer match, and having a quiet drink together in a pub. These images serve to personalise the quest and to raise the question how such an eager and "moral" young man could be persuaded, as we eventually discover, to go undercover, to deliberately strike up a relationship with an Irish girl while abroad (with the express purpose of infiltrating the IRA, but he does have feelings for her), and appear to desert the Army in the process.

At the court, Hollins is barred from attending the trial, but notices Siobhán O'Hagan (Paula Hamilton), David's Irish girlfriend, also waiting. He follows her and, although he loses her, his pursuit allows him to see the world of West Belfast: the black taxis serving as buses; the walled Peace Line that separates Protestant and Catholic neighbourhoods; and the fear of strangers in local bars. At one point, Hollins rescues Siobhán from a crowd of screaming and stone-throwing Protestants after her brother is publicised as an IRA killer. True to the anti-imperialist rhetoric of the film, this is the only apparent depiction of the majority Protestant community in Northern Ireland. The latter does not count in Livingstone's universe, as if it can be equated with the British Army. His play sees the "Troubles" or "struggle" between the English and the nationalist community as the key tussle. This vision is to accept the nationalist terms of the debate. Furthermore, the fact that the drama highlights a perversion of the "natural" order – David Hollins, against his instincts, finding himself living a lie – only adds to the argument of England's illegitimacy in Ireland. Hollins' near final remark, "I'm getting out of this bloody country", is the seal on Livingstone's implicit rhetoric, for Hollins is the quintessential English everyman, and, the logic runs, if he, someone who has lost a son, can declare that it is time to leave, what is stopping our politicians and military?

The Europa Hotel figures largely in another production broadcast in 1985: *The Daily Woman* (BBC-1), written by Bernard Mac Laverty and directed by Martyn Friend.[11] Set in the early 1970s, it charts a remarkable day and evening in the life of one Elizabeth O'Pray (Brid Brennan) who works part-time for Mr and Mrs Henderson (Denys Hawthorne and Doreen Hepburn) in the affluent area of Belfast. Already from this brief description, readers, with antennae extended, will not be surprised to learn that Elizabeth hails from a working-class Catholic area, and Mr and Mrs Henderson are the stereotypical rich Protestant family who have bigoted views and bigoted friends for dinner. In one scene, where Elizabeth is helping to serve coffee and dessert to these apparently Protestant barons of industry, she overhears their blatant anti-Catholic views. The assembled company is surprised that their host, Mr Henderson, has more liberal views on the matter; he argues that industry must now be more welcoming to Catholics. This apparent liberalism must be seen against his real intention, which is to seduce Elizabeth (with money) for sexual favours. Since Elizabeth has inherited a wastrel and sometime abusive husband Eamon (Colum Convey), and is mother of two children, she is in constant need of money, and finally gives in to Mr Henderson's rather lugubrious approaches. Not content with stereotyping Mr Henderson as the deceitful and corrupt Protestant business patriarch, when the two do attempt to make love, it is suggested that he is, after all, impotent!

Taking the money, and leaving her children with her mother (Trudy Kelly), Elizabeth treats herself to new clothes, a hairdo, and a night in the Europa Hotel. Her past indignities are not ended, however, for, arriving without luggage and paying in cash, she is strip-searched in case she might be carrying a bomb. During the evening she meets an American journalist, Max Callister (Christopher Malcolm), who shares with her dinner and conversation. It seems that Elizabeth is seeking at least one night of romantic passion, but the American demurs. The final image of Elizabeth rocking an apparently abandoned baby in a nearby room returns her to "servitude".

Mac Laverty's script, as hinted above, has an intrinsic understanding of working-class Catholic Belfast. He is on less assured ground when he characterises the Protestant upper-middle classes, who seem to be outrageously stereotyped. His drama appears to be caught between the dreams of Elizabeth – of a rich, powerful American sweeping her off her feet – and the harsh reality of two children and a dissolute husband. One wonders what point is made by setting the 1985 production in the early 1970s, except perhaps to show that Protestants and Catholics then did meet often in a working environment as distinct from the increasing polarisation of the communities throughout the 1980s.

One provocative television production that sought to get underneath the "Europa Hotel" plays was *Naming the Names* (BBC-1, 1986), written by Anne Devlin and directed by Stuart Burge. In this drama, a young Catholic woman, Finn (Sylvestra Le Touzel) is arrested for luring a Protestant judge's son Henry (Michael Maloney) to a park where the IRA apprehends and murders him. Henry is studying Irish history at Oxford. While at home, he travels to the Catholic Falls Road Bookshop to look at its Irish collection in search of materials for his PhD thesis. Finn, the bookshop assistant, is steeped in Irish history but – given the *de facto* separate educational systems in Northern Ireland for Catholics and Protestants – from a purely republican perspective. Finn and Henry form a romantic attachment, even though both admit to having English partners. In this way, writer Anne Devlin emphasises the love-hate relationship both northern Irish Catholics and Protestants have with the English mainland.

Finn delivers the two volumes of R M Sibbert's *Orangeism in Ireland and Throughout the Empire* (1914-15) to Henry, and this history of Orangeism written by an Orangeman sparks a lively debate. In the midst of their discussion, Henry utters the Protestant unionist position rarely articulated verbally or visually in television or film narratives:

Finn: You think that's all not irrelevant now? Gladstone and home rule?

Henry: No, no. Gladstone tended to dismiss the Protestants as a bigoted minority. Successive British governments are making the same mistake.

Finn: What is your thesis, briefly, in a line?

Henry: The Protestant opposition to home rule was rational. Because at the time Ulster Protestant industries, linen, shipbuilding, were dependent on the British market. Home rule would have ruined Ulster financially.

Finn: But it wasn't just about money, was it?

Henry: No, no. The Protestants were also worried about being discriminated against in a largely Catholic state.

Finn: They were worried?

Henry: Yes, I think those fears were justified.

Given Henry's murder, his words concerning fears of discrimination against Protestants by Catholic republicans have a prophetic air to them. The Catholic community, shown to be frightened and vulnerable in the 1969-70 period, becomes totally radicalised and emboldened by the mid-1980s, as evidenced by the continuation of their argument in Belfast City Library:

Henry: Take Parnell, for example – Charles Stewart Parnell, a Protestant, a leader of the home rule, was destroyed by the Roman Catholic clergy over his divorce case.

Finn: He was destroyed by Gladstone, and the English nonconformists...And when has any Protestant movement had a Catholic leader?

Henry: Come on, they're not exactly queuing up at the door, are they?

Finn: How could they be? What of the wars of the constitution?

Henry: That's not relevant.

Finn: A Protestant parliament for a Protestant people. And it's not relevant! You think that's all right? It's economic, rational...

Henry: You get angry very quickly. Who's done that to you, Finn?

[They both run out into the street and face the large sign on the City Hall, "BELFAST SAYS NO", a reference to the unionist resistance to the Anglo-Irish Agreement]

Henry: Confirmed what they've [the unionists] always believed. The British government are the real republicans!

Finn: Welcome to Belfast.

These two exchanges are remarkable for their willingness to grapple with the standard "positions" taken by both unionists and nationalists. Henry tries to point out to Finn that the nationalist position, even with a Protestant leader, was undermined by the Roman Catholic Church. Finn refuses to accept that Roman Catholicism has anything substantial to do with it, preferring instead to blame English politics. Henry points to the "BELFAST SAYS NO" sign to illustrate that the Ulster Unionists are extremely wary of English politics as well, thereby creating two, not one, defensive communities in Northern Ireland.

The film evolves as an extended flashback, highlighting the critical event in Finn's life – the Protestant fire-bombing of her home in 1969. This action almost kills her guardian grandmother, and it occurs while Finn is making love in a hotel room to an English journalist. When her grandmother dies a few years later, an orphaned Finn depends on her English boyfriend to distract her from the IRA, although he remains unaware of her true predicament until the closing scenes. Their breakup seals her fate with the men of violence.

Naming the Names, as the title implies, suggests the way in which both Protestants and Catholics return in their speech to their cultural signposts. When quizzed by the police for her IRA contacts, Finn utters only the names of the streets in her neighbourhood. This behaviour not only shows her psychological distress, but also casts doubt on the very mantras which she has been brainwashed to repeat. She is trapped, and knowingly so, in debilitating nationalist and republican myths.

Every step forward in television drama depictions of Northern Ireland is often followed by two steps backward. Thaddeus O'Sullivan's *In the Border Country* (Channel 4, 1991), written by Daniel Mornin, is inspired by extracts from Aeschylus' *Oresteia*, and is stylised very much like a stage play. Set in what looks like parts of Donegal, all the characters wear black or dark attire, which proves to be striking against the chalk whitewalled cottages in which the local inhabitants live. Hugh Athey (Sean McGinley) is an IRA leader who coldly kills a man on a beach. He disappears from home days at a stretch, much to the distress of his wife Margaret (Juliet Stevenson), son David (J D Kelleher) and daughter Morna (Dervla Kirwan). The relationships among the four are only lightly sketched in, adding to the inexorable narrative movement towards a terrifying violent climax.

In a curious subplot, Helen (Saskia Reeves), Margaret's sister who is married to one of Hugh's henchmen, has an affair with Smith

(Sean Bean) who appears out of nowhere in this barren landscape, but who can instantly provide a seclusive room in a hotel for their lovemaking. Meanwhile, a neighbour of Athey's, McQuire (Ian McElhinney), who desires a relationship with Margaret, waits for the opportune moment to inform on Hugh. When Hugh is betrayed, it is Smith, now revealed as a British Army soldier, who kills him. David closes the tragedy by killing McQuire and, by accident, his mother.

It is easy to conclude from this utter mayhem that Nairn's "myth of atavism" of Irish predilections is powerfully reinscribed. One must ask for what purpose such a script is constructed. No political motivation is provided for any of the killings; we are meant to assume that it is natural for such murders to go on. Nevertheless, the myth of anti-imperialism is called upon by suggesting that the British, represented by Smith, invade "our land", seduce "our women", and kill "our patriots". In many ways, this play borders precariously on misogyny, and revels in its stereotyped mythology.[12]

Much more productive in stimulating debate, if not vitriol, was Pat O'Connor's *Force of Duty* (BBC-NI, 1992). Writers Bill Morrison and Chris Ryder produced one of the few scripts that actually gives voice to members of the RUC. In the drama, RUC Inspector Simpson Gabby (Donal McCann) attempts to deal with the killing of his colleague (Adrian Dunbar), but gradually deteriorates under the pressure. He drinks, becomes obsessed with his informants, discovers that his dog no longer finds his company desirable, and perfunctorily sleeps with an RUC widow as a feeble attempt to assuage his guilt over surviving the shooting.

Surrounded by neighbours and superiors far more bigoted than he, Gabby, the proverbial decent professional, goes out of his mind. One way of reading this film is to argue that it follows in the tradition of the depictions of the Northern Ireland "Troubles" as beyond the comprehension and ability of good people. A republican view is simply to blast the production, as Seamus Keenan does in a *Film Ireland* review, because it seeks to legitimatise the RUC:

> [T]he RUC is the most investigated and condemned police force in Europe. It has been involved in systematic torture, sanctioned shoot-to-kill, perversion of the course of justice, and widespread collusion with loyalist gangs. It has always been the armed defender of the six-county state and in recent times become a lucrative and legitimate alternative to the loyalist gangs at a time of increasing unemployment in traditional Unionist strongholds. And, whether people like it or not, that is not Republican propaganda, it is the simple truth. However, given Chris Ryder's background as an RUC apologist and journalistic laughing stock, it is hardly surprising that *Force of Duty* should seek to humanise and depoliticise the RUC.[13]

Northern unionists would point out to Keenan that a direct correlation exists between RUC abuses and IRA violence, a constant theme in many British productions, such as Peter Kominsky's *Shoot to Kill* (YTV, 1990). As a possible republican sympathiser, he cannot seem to understand that the RUC is perfectly acceptable to the majority Protestant population of Northern Ireland, and that this kind of drama strikes a chord with that besieged community. So concerned with giving the minority a voice of protest, Keenan must deny the sensibilities of the majority. He does not choose to probe beneath the IRA rhetoric of "legitimate targets". For the Protestant community, the killing of every policeman is an assault on their individual liberties, and reminds them of the fate awaiting them in a united Ireland influenced by Sinn Féin. This fear is the base upon which plays such as *Force of Duty* work. Nevertheless, Keenan and others have been correct to argue that certain genres of fiction can only investigate the "Troubles" up to a certain level, after which simplistic or banal clichés tend to be inserted.

Whereas Ryder and Morrison's script touches the deepest fears of the Protestant and unionist community, Ronan Bennett's *Love Lies Bleeding*, directed by Michael Winterbottom, actively tries to investigate conflicts within the nationalist community, and to suggest one way forward. As it happens, the events depicted in Bennett's play have a close resemblance to actual occurrences a year later, those leading up to the IRA cease fire on 31 August 1994. Bennett chooses to focus on the role of the republican prisoners in furthering the "struggle", and he is ingenious in invoking this particular aspect of Irish republicanism, since it has always relied upon the "prisoner issue" to force political concessions from British and unionist politicians.

Love Lies Bleeding is a heavily plotted drama, and viewers have to pay attention to an overwritten script to figure out the various complications. Republican prisoner Conn (Mark Rylance), incarcerated for twelve years when we meet him (for having killed two women), is let out on a day pass together with others of both political persuasions. Not long before, his girlfriend Leyla (Emma Jordan) was apparently murdered by loyalists. The drama traces Conn's search for the truth behind Leyla's death; he discovers that it was not the loyalists who had killed her, but supporters of Thomas Macken (Brendan Gleeson), a fellow republican prisoner who wants a cease fire and talks between Sinn Féin and the British government. For the latter to happen, the hardmen (and women) out on the streets must be neutralised, if not by ratiocination then by violence. This explains why we end, inevitably, with a bloodbath.

Bennett inserts one scene set inside a loyalist bar where, behind all the male bravado, he tries to suggest that the Protestant community is also looking for a way out. Since Conn is seeking revenge, the stories of other people's losses serve to put him on the defensive, to accept gradually that, as Macken remarks, "Death is not just a personal thing". Strangely, rather than twelve years of incarceration mollifying his anger, it is one day free in the "new" Northern Ireland that convinces Conn that to seek revenge is simplistic, however personal the loss. As he returns to prison, with Macken triumphant, Conn is reconciled to the death of his girlfriend, as perhaps he has accepted that she was not the woman he thought she was. One wonders what Bennett would say about the pressure of victims' families on the government to ensure that convicted killers serve out their sentences. This is a missing dynamic in the film, as is any serious consideration of the Protestant community beyond a threatening-looking pub at night and a mob of Neanderthal, tattooed "hard men". By closing the narrative on Sinn Féin meeting British government ministers, the anti-imperialist view of the "Troubles" is again reinscribed.

As the real cease fire came to be, the first productions of a joint Northern Ireland Film Council and BBC-NI programme came to fruition. For years, Northern Ireland was outside the remit of the British Film Institute, but, due to campaigning by various bodies, including elected BFI Governor Alexander Walker, who hails from the province, this inequity was finally resolved in the late-1980s, and the Northern Ireland Film Council was formed in 1989. To celebrate the fifth anniversary of the formation of the NIFC, John Forte's *Skin Tight* (1994) was shown. It provides an interesting insight into the kind of projects that find approval by this body in a heavily politicised culture.

Skin Tight opens with the overdetermined Orangeman symbolism of Terry (B J Hogg) beating his Lambeg drum on the roof of his house. The drumskin, however, keeps breaking, so Terry buys a goat, intending to fatten it up, kill it and skin it for a perfect drum. Meanwhile, his wife Norma (Marie Jones) hungers for a Greek or Spanish holiday, and is initially resentful of the goat's appearance. As time passes, she tries to save the goat from slaughter but is unsuccessful. She does, nevertheless, have the final word. She chances upon the dried and flattened goatskin and cuts out a small circle to make the traditional Irish one-sided drum, the bodhrán. It is a clever ending, suggesting that one culture/tradition, using similar materials, can transfer to the other. But it is even more interesting that it is the Lambeg drum which cannot be made now that the traditional bodhrán has been created. It may be pushing the symbolism too far, yet one can see how the material is bound to be interpreted: the bombastic (Protestant) Lambeg drum cut down to size and usurped by the traditional Irish (and mostly Catholic) musical instrument.[14]

Whenever considering television drama broadcast in the UK, one has to remember that, although a production may be made in a region, such as Northern Ireland, it has to be sufficiently broad in its scope to be transmitted throughout England, Scotland and Wales. While independent filmmakers and videographers may have a much larger commercial eye on their product, in-house television productions often reveal a cultural agenda. These economic (and political) determinants have led to many dramas about Northern Ireland revelling in inexplicable violence, and both simplistic and complex "troops out" anti-imperialist rhetoric. These determinants have also led to many dramas trying to walk into a "neutral zone" often unsupported by the (divisive) communities at large. Naturally, this utopianism raises the question as to what extent television stations and their drama producers envision their role as proactive, rather than reflective. With the proliferation of satellite channels coming on-line in recent years, and if the "Troubles" continue, this "liberal" balancing act will undoubtedly be more difficult to sustain and justify. Questions of balance and emphasis are part and parcel of documentary films as well, and over my remaining chapters I will concentrate on this related genre which – more than fiction – makes strong, although problematic, claims for truth.

Notes

[1] Rob Ritchie, "Out of the North", introduction to Ron Hutchinson, *Rat in the Skull* (London: Methuen, 1984): 3.

[2] A marvellous account of the writer's ambivalent feelings about television drama is given in *Ah! Mischief: The Writer and Television* (London: Faber and Faber, 1982). The seven contributors were prolific writers in the 1970s and 1980s: David Edgar, Trevor Griffiths, David Hare, Julian Mitchell, Peter Prince, Howard Schuman and Hugh Whitemore.

[3] This author-centred criticism of television drama is exhibited in two edited books of essays by George W Brandt (*British television drama* [Cambridge: Cambridge University Press, 1981] and *British Television Drama in the 1980s* [Cambridge: Cambridge University Press, 1993]). Brandt privileges the one-off play as a sign of "high art". As John Tulloch observes, there is a need to move between the one-off play and the popular series and serials to achieve a balanced understanding of television drama. Nevertheless, many viewers remember single dramas if they are "hard-hitting". Tulloch provides an excellent overview of the issues relevant to any theoretical or critical approach to television drama. See John Tulloch, *Television Drama: Agency, audience and myth* (London; New York: Routledge, 1990). I follow Brandt's methodological perspective in this chapter because a Northern Ireland series or serial that was highly popular did not really exist. There were a few mini-series, such as *Harry's Game, Shoot to Kill* (1990), *Crossfire* (1988) and *Lost Belongings* (1987). A useful account of the BBC's general relationship to Northern Ireland is Rex Cathcart, *The Most Contrary Region: The BBC in Northern Ireland 1924-1984* (Belfast: The Blackstaff Press, 1984).

[4] In effect, documentary realism or material realism is the structuring principle of British television drama. Film theorist Siegfried Kracauer, who argued for film to be utilised to "redeem" physical reality, would have

been proud of the development of this genre. See his *Theory of Film: The Redemption of Physical Reality* (New York: Oxford University Press, 1960). Much more simply, as Trevor Griffiths remarks, it is a question of audience expectations: "[W]hen you're trying to speak to large numbers of people who did not study literature at university, because they were getting on with productive work, and you're introducing fairly unfamiliar, dense and complex arguments into the fabric of the play, it's just an overwhelming imposition to present those arguments in unfamiliar forms". See *Ah! Mischief: The Writer and Television*: 39.

[5]   The list was kindly provided by Kevin Jackson at BBC-NI in January 1995. One must also bear in mind that other regions, including London, initiated separate dramas (and, later, films under BBC Films) concerning Northern Ireland. Richard Spence's *You, Me and Marley*, written by Graham Reid, is a good example of one feature-length project. The 1980-94 BBC-NI list (although not complete in all details) is as follows:

1980   *Catchpenny Twist* by Stewart Parker; *My Dear Palestrina* by Bernard Mac Laverty.

1981   *Iris in the Traffic, Ruby in the Rain* by Stewart Parker; BBC-1, *The Kamikazee Groundstaff Reunion Dinner* by Stewart Parker.

1982   BBC-1, *Phonefun Limited* by Bernard Mac Laverty; BBC-1, *Gates of Gold* by Maurice Leitch; BBC-1, *Easter 2016* by Graham Reid; 16/02/82 BBC-1, *Too Late to Talk to Billy* by Graham Reid.

1983   10/05/83 BBC-1, *A Matter of Choice for Billy* by Graham Reid.

1984   22/02/84 BBC-1, *A Coming to Terms for Billy* by Graham Reid; 04/01/84 BBC-2, *Aunt Suzanne* by Michael McLaverty (adapted by Stewart Love); 18/04/84 BBC-2, *A Woman Calling* by Anne Devlin; 09/05/84 BBC-2, *After You've Gone* by Frederick Aicken; 27/06/84 BBC-1, *Fire at Magilligan* by Harry Barton; 31/07/84 BBC-1, *The Cry* by Derek Mahon and Chris Menaul; 20/11/84 BBC-1, *The Long March* by Anne Devlin.

1985   14/07/85 BBC-1, *We'll Support You Evermore* by Douglas Livingstone; 12/11/85 BBC-2, *McCabe's Wall* by Graham Reid; 19/11/85 BBC-2, *Going Home* by Graham Reid; 26/11/85 BBC-2, *Out of Tune* by Graham Reid; 03/12/85 BBC-2, *Invitation to a Party* by Graham Reid; 10/12/85 BBC-2, *Attachments* by Graham Reid; 17/12/85 BBC-2, *The Military Wing* by Graham Reid.

1987   02/06/87 BBC-1, *Lorna* by Graham Reid; 11, 13, 15/07/87 BBC-1, the three *Billy* plays repeated; 08/09/87 BBC-2, *Scout* by Frank McGuinness; 09/09/87 BBC-2, *The Venus de Milo Instead* by Anne Devlin (repeated 18/03/88); 10/09/87 BBC-2, *The Rockingham Shoot* by John McGahern.

1989   25/01/89 BBC-2, *Elephant* by Bill Morrison and Alan Clarke; 01/02/89 BBC-2, *The Night Watch* by Ray Brennan; 08/02/89 BBC-2, *Monkeys* by Paul Muldoon; 02/08/89 BBC-2, *Chinese Whispers* by Maurice Leitch; 30/08/89 BBC-2, *Beyond the Pale* by William Trevor; 06/09/89 BBC-2, *The Hen House* by Frank McGuinness.

1990   01/08/90 BBC-2, *The Englishman's Wife* by Holly Chandler; 22/08/90 BBC-2, *A Safe House* by Bill Morrison; 29/12/90 BBC-2, *August Saturday* by William Trevor.

1991   17/07/91 BBC-2, *Events at Drimaghleen* by William Trevor; 19/07/91 BBC-1, *Murder in Eden* (ep. 1) by Shane Connaughton; 26/07/91

BBC-1, *Murder in Eden* (ep. 2) by Shane Connaughton; 02/08/91
BBC-1, *Murder in Eden* (ep. 3) by Shane Connaughton; 04/09/91
BBC-2, *Arise and Go Now* by Owen O'Neill (London production hosted by BBC-NI).

1992 08/07/92 BBC-2, *Force of Duty* by Bill Morrison and Chris Ryder.

1993 22/09/93 BBC-2, *Love Lies Bleeding* by Ronan Bennett.

1994 16/03/94 BBC-2, *All Things Bright and Beautiful* by Barry Devlin; 20/04/94 BBC-2, *Henri* by John Forte; 04/09/94 BBC-1, *A Breed of Heroes* by Charles Wood, based on a novel by Alan Judd.

[6] An indication of the significance of Reid's *Billy* plays is that they were rebroadcast (a rare phenomenon) in 1987.

[7] A curious report on television drama and northern Irish viewers is David Docherty and Alison Lyon's "Violent Culture, Violent Television", *Sight and Sound* 59: 4 (autumn 1990): 228-231. Their conclusion (231) that "[t]here *is* no simple story to tell about violent culture and violent television" is underwhelming, although the anecdotes of people's alienation from television drama's purported realism, including Reid's *Billy* plays, is indicative of the strange "middle position" adopted by broadcasters in general.

[8] The "moving wallpaper" description refers to the "flow" of television which further makes it difficult for discerning viewers to be critical participants. The argument here is that after a while, bombarded by continuous images, a drama is lost in the midst of earlier and later programmes and commercials. The fact of "flow" is what makes television criticism and practice so challenging.

[9] The video version is much shorter than the original series, which is 150 minutes in total. *Harry's Game* concerns the search for an IRA hitman who has murdered a British Cabinet Minister. YTV have supported various projects connected with Northern Ireland over the years, including independent film projects. One such is Dominic Lees' seventeen-minute *Borderland* (1993), made at the Northern School of Film and Television in Leeds. One synopsis of the film is typical of the working through of the anti-imperialist myth I have been discussing: "A young English squaddie and a raw IRA recruit are drawn inexorably to a face-to-face fight to the death in a lake on the Irish border. But there is no winner to this conflict..." Quoted in Bob Geoghegan (ed), *The Short Film Index 1990-1993* (Leeds: The Short Film Index, 1993): 17.

[10] While my examples are "serious dramas", there have been plays that take a more lighthearted or irreverent look at the conflict. Writer-director Barry Devlin's *All Things Bright and Beautiful* (BBC-2, 1994) takes us back to 1954 in County Tyrone where a ten-year-old altar boy believes he is experiencing visions (actually an IRA man on the run); and Owen O'Neill's *Arise and Go Now* (BBC-2, 1991), directed by Danny Boyle, takes a burlesque approach to local IRA politics in a rural community.

[11] The Europa Hotel in the centre of Belfast was one of the few hotels operating in Belfast in the 1970s and 1980s. It provided a space for liberal middle-class people of both persuasions to meet; mostly, however, the hotel housed all visiting journalists and political figures visiting Belfast. The hotel is utilised in many films, such as *Hidden Agenda* and John

Davies' *Acceptable Levels.*

¹² The play was not well-received in Ireland. Reviewer Brendan Glacken found it "just another glum piece of 'troubles' drama...this particular effort seemed weirdly, almost comically, dated". See Brendan Glacken, "Broody border drama", *The Irish Times* 5 March 1991: 10.

¹³ Seamus Keenan, "Force of Duty", *Film Ireland* 31 (September/October 1992): 20-21.

¹⁴ John Forte also was responsible for the hour-long *Henri* (1994), another humorous look at the two cultures, with a musical theme. Another short film which can be viewed at the Northern Ireland Film Council, although seemingly not directly funded by them, is Sean Hinds' *The Pan Loaf* (Channel 4, 1994). Set in Belfast, two Catholics Finbarr (Conor Grimes) and Gwen (Emma O'Neil) drift into a Protestant area looking for a loaf of bread. They wander into a threatening corner shop run by an officious Mr Stewart (Ian McElhinney). The suspicious nature of the clientele is not because of their dislike of Catholics, but because the Protestants are clandestinely watching a pornographic film in the shop! Here we see again a less than flattering depiction of the Protestant community masked under "humour". The first three NIFC and BBC-NI shorts, including *Skin Tight*, are eviscerated for their anti-Protestant bias by Stephen McKee. See his review, "Northern Lights: BBC NI", *Fortnight* 347 (February 1996): 41. In this same issue, McKee relates the problems which the close relationship between the NIFC and BBC-NI has raised for independent filmmakers and videographers seeking funding. See Stephen McKee, "It's grim up north", *Fortnight* 347 (February 1996): 29-32. Ironically, the major critique of this relationship comes from David Hyndman, whose work with Northern Visions has an intellectual vision of the Protestant community much in keeping with that found in the shorts produced.

8

Gorillas without lipstick: the documentaries of Northern Visions

> My separate claim for documentary is simply that in its use of the living article, there is *also* an opportunity to perform creative work. (John Grierson)[1]

> The supposition that any 'actuality' is left after 'creative treatment' can now be seen as being at best naive and at worst a mark of duplicity. (Brian Winston)[2]

Since 1968, Northern Ireland's "Troubles" have been the most photographed and documented "story" of the United Kingdom and Republic of Ireland's media. Regrettably, however, the opportunities for ordinary northern Irish folk to represent and analyse the "situation" have not been plentiful. Too often, the British and Irish state media machines have parachuted journalists and television crews in for short periods of time; satisfied with a few pictures and skin-deep analysis, they are then "lifted" out of the area, only to be replaced by another team the next time around. It has been compared to "putting lipstick on a gorilla".[3]

Faced with the inevitable propaganda war from the British and Sinn Féin publicity machines, the central social and political issues are too easily glossed in simplistic frameworks. Added to this is the general and understandable timidity by BBC-NI and UTV, for they are accountable every day to their divided audience; both stations try to cover the "Troubles" in a balanced, indirect or purely factual way. Probing analysis and risk-taking have not been these local stations' strongest suits (nor are they necessarily part of their mandate as providers of a *service* to the public).

It is hard sometimes to convey to people outside Northern Ireland the level of fear that can take hold in all types of social activity. Fear can produce quiescence, but it can also produce a passive-aggressive personality, where the tension building up inside an individual can only be expressed in sudden violent outbursts or excessively critical summations. In some senses, the work I discuss below, made under the aegis of Northern Visions, a company whose aim is to empower ordinary people's lives by the use of video, is indicative of this passive-aggressive personality. For large sections of these videos, an effort is made to build a comprehensible, logical case on a large number of social and political issues; yet equally, many sequences promote the pure desire to express raw emotions.

Nevertheless, these videos have an authenticity which the "classical" BBC, ITV or RTE documentary narrative sometimes fails to grasp. In addition, the financial necessity to use video (although many of the videos have been broadcast on Channel 4) circumscribes a particular aesthetic, a "poor cinema" or "poor video".[4] Video allows greater flexibility for those who seek to explore serious issues, since an elongated shooting period, so often a high cost factor in film production, can be managed relatively cheaply and cleanly.

One aspect that seems to be underscored in all these videos is the role of history, whether that of the relationship between Northern Ireland and Great Britain, or that of the relationship between the 1922-72 Stormont government and its governed people. Time and time again, history is pointed to for explanations, answers and problems. It might also be fruitfully argued that this launch backwards militates against solutions to some of the issues presented. It is one milestone to describe and understand an obstacle, and it is quite another to overcome it.

I think it sufficiently easy for a cultural critic simply to describe the issues discussed in these videos, important as they are, but this would be a disservice to those who conceived and made them. What they need is not only recognition, but also healthy criticism, so that – when shown – these works can be debated within at least one external frame of reference. Made by northern Irish people, they reflect that perspective. Part of their intention was to claim a wide audience in the UK and Ireland, and that they have done. These videos can now be seen in North America and beyond, and so, in certain respects, a counter or modified argument, on occasion, needs to be made to allow debate to flourish.

I believe it significant that one of the very first videos produced by Northern Visions focused on women's health. As Anne Crilly discusses as late as 1994 with Robert Cooper of BBC-NI, the perspective of women has been sadly missing from the Northern Ireland scene, with some notable exceptions, such as the media frenzy over the "Peace People" of the 1970s.[5] *Under the Health Surface As Told By Belfast Women* (1986) begins – after a montage of fast-motion shots of the city – with a man seated writing at his desk, elaborating on the poor health conditions of the people of Belfast. The year is 1850. We see old photographs of the slums of the city, reinforcing this allusion to poverty. Thus, a sad tradition of inequity is established.

On a similarly historical note, the link between ill health and working conditions in the 1940s is created by an interview with a former linen worker. Her information, prompted by a mainly offscreen questioner, reveals the damp and cold conditions experienced both at home and at work by a large number of female workers. Black-and-white footage of one of Northern Ireland's former major industries leaves no doubt as to the terrible atmosphere, full of flax particles, and the incessant dripping of water from the frames of the machines. A female voice-over tells us the depressing statistics: women in Northern Ireland are more likely to die before the age of 60 due to respiratory problems, heart disease or cancer than in most other places in Europe; Northern Ireland has one of the highest incidences of spina bifida in the world. The reason for the latter statistic seems to be the reluctance of doctors to test for the condition, which can be detected in England where, unlike Ireland, abortion is legal (one of the possible choices for parents after detection).

Instead of simply taking these statistics and pulling the focus to immediate "contemporary" remedies, such as diet and lifestyle changes, videographers Marilyn Hyndman and Frances Bowyer attempt to give concrete reasons for their occurrence and for reasons why there are no quick solutions. To begin with, the reluctance or inability of Catholics in West Belfast to move to alternate housing in the city led to extreme and unhealthy overcrowding which, in tandem with the high unemployment and low wages of those who did have jobs, made a large group of people susceptible to contagious disease. In 1982, for example, the video records that a polio outbreak in West Belfast killed one child and necessitated a vaccination programme.

In order to explain why people are unhealthy, the videographers must turn not only to the lack of job opportunities, but also to the poor housing conditions. In this analysis, criticism of the old Stormont government is central. The narrator/voice-over claims that the unionists voted against a national health service. This claim is not well-substantiated in the video, and, in any case, needs to be understood more fully against the historical backdrop that both videographers seem keen to incorporate. One general argument that should be considered is that the unionist government did not regard itself as a stable entity, given the possibility of English "perfidy" and the southern government's unhidden desire for a united Ireland, at least in its constitutional framework which was to rise in 1937 and to be cemented in 1949.

I know that it is a tired and problematic explanation, but it still needs to be voiced: for the unionists, the Catholic population could not be fully trusted, since they were more than likely to be supporters of, or sympathetic to, the nationalist cause. Once an élite group in any society distrusts another group, it is only a matter of time and circumstance before some form of discrimination occurs. From the unionist perspective, the issues over the introduction of a national health service came down to those of regional autonomy and political advantage. As we already know, Westminster's laws do not equally apply to Scotland and Northern Ireland as to England

and Wales. Differences of law and precedent exist. It is, I think, inaccurate to argue or imply that unionists wished to deny their citizens, both Protestants and Catholics, a national health service *per se*. They wanted to be financially stable first of all, and the Clement Attlee Labour government differed with the Conservative Basil Brooke Stormont government on such a social and economic programme. As it turned out, and this is missing from the historical overview of the video on health, the unionist government eventually supported the "welfare state" proposal because it was more important to show certain kinds of equality (and benefits) accorded by UK citizenship over the Republic of Ireland's health provisions than to torpedo a social programme which forced an élite subgroup – doctors – to be removed from the private enterprise sector. Bew, Gibbon and Patterson actually argue that it was the relative strength of the Protestant working-class support for the Northern Ireland Labour Party that ensured a smooth passage for welfare and health reform on the lines of that in Great Britain.[6] This perspective is absent from the video.

Under the Health Surface brings us to the 1960s when we find appalling housing programmes embarked upon by the Stormont government – cheap flats and maisonettes which inevitably led to quick disrepair and problems with rodents and disease. The critique of government-controlled housing programmes and their administration, including the later Northern Ireland Housing Executive (effectively run by Westminster) is sharp, although little or no comparison, verbal or visual, is given to weigh the evidence. Parts of northern England, Scotland, Wales and the Republic of Ireland were equally or more disadvantaged than Northern Ireland, however unlikely this may seem.

Nevertheless, the political and social points which this video makes are also the most empowering ones. When women surveyed the health of their own areas, they realised the link between damp conditions and speech defects in children. They realised the need for peer group therapy; for doctors to live in the neighbourhood that they service; and for the medical Establishment to rethink the low priority given to social or environmental diagnosis and treatment in medical training.

If the role and fate of women in Northern Ireland have been downplayed, the role and fate of young children and youths have been virtually ignored. Northern Visions' award-winning *Our Words Jump to Life* (1988), directed and produced by David and Marilyn Hyndman, seeks to redress this shortcoming. The video opens abruptly with a stereotypical English "drinking lout" couch potato turning on the television only to see predictable Belfast images of bombs going off and soldiers running around the streets. He turns the television off. This reaction of boredom is the problem with any ongoing media violence story; after a while, the reportage simply becomes a body count. As the video progresses, young children are utilised to sing and shout the "real story" behind the violent images. Most immediately apparent is the lack of facilities: one song rings out the lines, "The chippie is gone and we're not alright" and "It's boring in Belfast".

Extremely strong throughout this video is how children and youths see the educational system in Northern Ireland. Most secular observers view the entrenched *de facto* separate education systems as one of the major causes for the crisis continuing. Cardboard cut-outs worn by boys and girls, indicating their social roles in society, satirise the lack of choice which children face in their upbringing. For a lengthy segment of the video, we are thrust into a surreal classroom with a series of caricatures. A grotesquely-masked teacher forces students to drink medicine from a bottle entitled "bullshit". It is a Belfast version of a Pink Floyd music video on the theme of disenchanted youth.

Again, as in *Under the Health Surface*, the premise of the production is to empower ordinary, largely working-class people. Two sequences achieve this by handing the reins of visual power to affected individuals. One, with a stills camera in hand, takes pictures of "classic" Belfast sites – the Andersontown DHSS office which services an area with over 80% unemployed; the sign "BELFAST SAYS NO" which was draped over the Belfast City Hall during and after the resistance to the Anglo-Irish Agreement signed in 1985; and Gloucester House Job Market which, as the onscreen narrator points out, rarely seems to find anyone a job! The apparently passive attitude which the state adopts to such youth unemployment is severely criticised.

Another individual, this time a visual artist, uses his ebullient paintings as background to depict and explain how, as a sixteen-year-old emigré in London, he discovered that escape to England was not the answer to his problems. His painful experiences in London included being homeless, picked up by the Moonies and rejected, forced to be deloused at hostels, and contracting various diseases such as scabies and hepatitis. As a punk, he was ostracised not only in Northern Ireland, but also in England. This experience raised his awareness that, no matter where you travel, some issues stubbornly remain to be fought and argued over. His descent into a personal hell is magnificently illustrated by his own art, dissolving from one image to the next as his narrative progresses.

As a series of visual sketches and essays, *Our Words Jump to Life* allows for some telling jabs at the forces of authority in these young people's lives. Most memorable is the same young man donning the requisite teeshirt when attending and marching in both an Orange and an Hibernian parade. Both traditions are seen as inadequate to the actual needs of these young people. But my personal favourite is the satire of the "do-gooders" who may be found in Ireland and abroad, where various schemes to integrate Protestants and Catholics are attempted. We see a journalist explaining that kids from both communities are in Donegal to play and talk together. In this particular forced marriage, every act that is "politically incorrect" is committed. Protestant Billy says that he has had a great time – mostly throwing stones "at the Taigs". He has discovered that the "Prods" can throw further than the Catholics, and aims to act upon this information when they return to their homes. Catholic Paddy says that he is really glad to have met people from the "other side". Before he knew any Protestants, he did not know why he hated them; after meeting these Protestants, he now knows why! The satire's point, that such schemes, however worthy, cannot deal with the underlying problems, is well-constructed.

After this very obvious satire, the six or seven young individuals take off their paramilitary masks and have a serious, honest discussion about their experience of Northern Ireland. The viewer greets this sequence with some relief because it helps to contextualise the over-the-top satire that preceded it. Many issues are discussed: the timidity of schools to develop truly inter-religious contacts; the stranglehold of living within an "ethnically pure" state or area; and the sad fact that none of these enlightened youths lives any longer in the area in which they were brought up. While these youths pinpoint numerous injustices – the use of plastic bullets; biased policing; Church interference – there is little in the way of possible remedies. One is left with an overwhelming sense of how difficult it is to see through the hegemonic or ideological state apparatuses. These youths have made the first step in searching for some theory to explain their suffering, and they all believe it important to reject the status quo.

It is perhaps too much to ask teenagers and young adults to be particularly acute in their analysis of the problem. We should ask more of their elders, and this can be found in *Moving Myths* (1989). One of the enduring myths is that the Northern Ireland conflict is a religious war. This assumption is investigated by Cahal McLaughlin, and he finds an absence of space for those who refuse the Protestant and Catholic Christian traditions. To some extent, McLaughlin fights a straw-man. Statistics showing that only a minority of both communities are *practising* Christians should not come as a surprise, not because of the amount of un-Christian activity witnessed since 1968, but because religion reaches beyond institutional affiliation. Of course, the assumption that Christianity equals non-violence is not unquestioned in general cultural discourse, particularly when we consider the history of the Roman Catholic Church and the Crusades. The Protestant Church has also done its share of supporting violence around the globe.

Unashamedly, the video's narrator remarks that "atheists provide the clearest response". Unlike the previous two videos which generally erase the identity of specific individuals and their views (as a form of protection?), McLaughlin seeks out men and women

Dust on the Bible

Hush-A-Bye Baby

Moving Myths

Irish Ways

Redeeming History: Protestant Nationalism in Ireland

Hidden Agenda

The Visit

Force of Duty

The Crying Game

In the Name of the Father

Between Ourselves: Songs, Satire and Some Sense

Skin Tight

After '68

Nothing Personal

Some Mother's Son

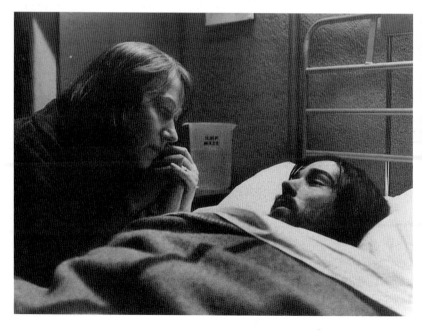

who are not afraid to tell their stories, both common and uncommon in nature. The strategy here is to critique institutions through the lives and experiences of strong individuals who have made a leap away from the ideologies that were inherited by dint of upbringing. Although the political issues are always near the surface, the main interrogation is social: demographics, health (abortion), prejudice and discrimination (homosexuality).

These individuals have a Catholic or Protestant "background" from which they have sought to rebel or to redefine themselves. Susan McKay was brought up in a Protestant area of Derry, attending a grammar school for girls. She remembers her liberal parents making clear to her that Catholics were assigned housing up on the poorer mountainside. McKay associates, as do other voices in the video, sectarianism with sexism, for both employ subtle forms of discrimination. Yet ultimately, Susan McKay experienced discrimination from a Roman Catholic nun, a Sister of Mercy, who disapproved of this liberal, progressive director of a Sligo youth centre. Although fired, and later compensated and reinstated for wrongful dismissal, McKay's autonomy as a "Protestant atheist", however absurd that sounds, in small-town Republic of Ireland was far less than she expected. Every community event in Sligo appeared to McKay as in need of Church approval.

When McKay, a feminist, went to Donegal to distribute leaflets for a campaign to legalise abortion in Ireland, the local response was extremely reactionary and, in some cases, threatening. It has to be said, however, that abortion is an issue that enflames people in countries other than Ireland. The purpose that the abortion issue serves in this video is to highlight the similarity of opinion between the Catholic and Protestant Churches. Even the relatively "minor" subject of contraception, as a matter of choice, helped to force Paddy Logue, a former priest, out of the Church. He faced an immovable brick wall both in Rome and in his old parish in Strabane, where the local Bishop was wont to read Rome's encyclicals as "Gospel".

Another dissatisfied and frustrated person featured, this time from a Protestant background, is Robert Bell, a single parent living on the Suffolk estate, which is an isolated Protestant enclave. Bell clearly disagrees with the intolerance and tribalism that he sees around him, yet he is sufficiently honest to point out that, if the estate were attacked, he would have to be counted together with people with whom he has next to no political sympathy. In contrast, the southern Irish Protestant man featured, Brian Trench, represents the liberal role which a minority community can play within a majority culture. Trench's family live in Drogheda, a mainly Catholic city with a small Protestant community. Trench's stories of his family's history make the point that accommodations and mutual benefit can accrue from a society with divergent beliefs.

The most enlightening and moving critique is the analysis of Frank McCallum, whose brother was killed by a loyalist gunman in a random sectarian murder. His brother was an atheist, and yet his death was described in religious terms, down to the humane desire of the family for no retaliation, which was characterised in the media, inaccurately, as the McCallum family's "basic Christianity". McCallum's support network was not the Church nor any political party, but simply his friends, with whom he could share his suffering. His orientation is primarily that of a working-class trades unionist. If only trades unions would take a stronger profile in the workplace, he argues, much of the sectarian discrimination would decrease. The weakness of the trades union movement in Northern Ireland speaks of the power of vested interests, whether Protestant or Catholic. McCallum, like most of the individuals interviewed in the video, is photographed in his own home, which adds to the sense of authenticity and to the sense that these ideas are "home-grown".

Sonya Murray, who had an abortion, and who since has had two children, speaks of the rightness of her choice, and the personal (as distinct from Church-influenced) therapy she adopted in dealing with the consequences of that decision. As mentioned earlier, the abortion debate is often palpably muted in Ireland, both north and south, which is indicative of a generally conservative society. But in addition, since more liberal laws exist in England, each year some 6000 women from Ireland travel there for abortions. This relative ease of access allows Ireland to avoid the issue, although there have been numerous occasions recently when personal tragedies have forced the subject into the public limelight.

Although the video does not interview any Irish homosexuals, we are told how the law pertaining to sexual orientation has been changed, or at least modified, by individual (not governmental) court actions north and south. Following on the theme of sexuality and sex education, interviewee Eddie Conlon raises, even with an embarrassed and humorous air, the sorry state of sex education in Ireland. Young Irish males and females can easily fall prey to misinformation, which can seriously stunt their emotional development. Conlon's remark, that it came as a great revelation to him in his late teens or early twenties to learn that women actually have orgasms, speaks volumes.

Whereas *Moving Myths* actively endeavours to avoid labelling – as in favour of a particular political analysis – David Hyndman's *Schizophrenic City* (1990) is primarily a republican or "neo-united Irishman" interpretation of the divided city of Belfast. The city is schizophrenic in a number of ways, not only Protestant and Catholic, but also loyalist and republican, unionist and nationalist, Orangeman and Hibernian, rich and poor. The onscreen narrator and his band of followers re-enact Henry Joy McCracken's and Wolfe Tone's Cave Hill oath of 1796. The abortive 1798 Rebellion, which led to McCracken's execution, is viewed here as a missed opportunity to unite Protestant and Catholic against established interests in Ireland.

We see John Gray, librarian of the Linen Hall Library (which was founded by the same movement espoused by McCracken) speaking at Clifton Street cemetery where the United Irishman is buried. Gray is portrayed as the "expert" speaking to the ordinary folk, presenting (by default) the nationalist dream interpretation: that Protestant and Catholic worked well together in the past for similar goals, and this rapprochement can and must be carved out again. However, Gray does make the point that Protestant nationalism was only *one* part or stream of opinion within the Irish Protestant community. The video provides us with images and discussion of Orange "artefacts" and "culture". Some of the Linen Hall Library's large collection of the current "Troubles" is put on show, and Gray speaks wisely when he refers to each tradition's sensitivity to criticism from the other tradition, particularly when it is added to the lack of real debate *within* each tradition.

Other notable aspects of the video include the long sequence spoken in Irish, underlining the point that BBC-NI and UTV have no Irish-language programming. The problem with this sequence, apart from the isolationism it presents in a primarily English-language video (there are no subtitles), is that insufficient consideration is given to facing the reality that the majority of Protestants in Northern Ireland, by happenstance of schooling, have no Irish and, furthermore, see it as a *political* "football", often used by Sinn Féin. Secondly, the discussion of murals leads us down a rather slippery path, linking republican violence with all manner of "freedom movements" around the world – the PLO and ANC, for example. The Protestant muralists celebrate mainly the 1690 victory of William of Orange over James II, and thereby appear "stuck" in history. This "muralism" is shown to be an essential part of the parading of a culture or tradition, whether static or dynamic.[7] For the republicans, it means that every IRA "victory" can be immortalised and co-opted via imprinting on the walls of nationalist areas. This gives the impression of a constantly evolving "modern tradition" to which a neutral viewer would more likely agree. While the 1916 Rising is the key date for traditional republicans – the ultimate blood sacrifice – the northern republicans appear to have actively sought to build self-esteem in their own communities by focusing on more local heroes, such as Bobby Sands and the Gibraltar Three.

The rhetoric that the unionist and British Establishment has failed to incorporate "history" from 1968 onwards is best achieved by the sequence in the video when the group of young people visit the Ulster Museum. In such a museum, one would expect to find artefacts connected to the "Troubles", but the group do not. Instead, and very ironically, the main event is a dinosaur exhibit! Together with the absence of information on contemporary Ulster, few women are featured. In its desire not to offend, the Ulster Museum thereby pleases no one.

David Hyndman's subsequent video, *Unfinished Business* (1993), is a series of interviews with academics and American politicians on fair employment legislation and the (American) McBride Principles. Strangely, in some senses, the thesis of the video that "job discrimination lies at the heart of the ongoing conflict in Northern Ireland" would not receive a difficult hearing from the British administration. Since 1972, the British have thrown money at the province in the hope of improving the economic climate sufficiently to reduce support for the IRA. In actuality, such infusion of money, particularly for social security payments, has "kept the lid on" the job discrimination issue by ensuring that financial assistance is higher than that available in the Republic of Ireland.

Hyndman's video provides widely agreed-upon statistics – that Catholics are over twice as likely to be unemployed than Protestants. Given *Moving Myths'* attempt to destabilise the notion of "Protestant" and "Catholic", we seem to be moving backwards here in providing new frameworks for understanding. In addition, unlike *Our Words Jump to Life*, there is insufficient acknowledgment that the "Troubles" have created a demographically divided city where both Protestants and Catholics will not travel to each other's neighbourhoods, even in the day. This divisiveness places extraordinary pressure on firms and services in the centre of the city, a generally neutral zone, to balance their workforces. Hence, *Unfinished Business* reveals an Equality Working Group targeting for boycott the Northern Bank for the low ratio of Catholics in its workforce. Everyone agrees that one of the answers must be for jobs to be created in Catholic nationalist-dominated areas, yet, while there is political instability, few investors – apart from the government – will intervene.

The British government's fair employment legislation has certainly not been a success for the Catholic unemployed, but a few qualifying statements need to be placed against the video's strong rhetoric that – effectively – the British have actively discriminated against the Catholic population. Firstly, the Conservative government's credo is free enterprise, and, apart from overseeing the civil service and police, there are those who regard interference in recruitment policy in "service" industries, such as banks, as unethical. Secondly, the flow of emigration is still statistically unknown, a "solution" of sorts for both Protestant and Catholic unemployed. It is desirable to be able to work and live in the neighbourhood or province of one's birth, but in post-1968 society the opportunity for young people, whether educated or not, to do so is severely limited (and, one ventures to say, unrealistic). Protestants as well as Catholics accept that they have to leave Northern Ireland for work and careers. The dependency culture created by an economy based primarily on the British Treasury, which in turn is perpetuated by political instability, leads only to skirmishing on the edge of the problem. Forcing the Bombardier company and the

Northern Bank to the equity table is only common sense and indicative of respect for human dignity. But, as with affirmative action programmes in North America and elsewhere, such "quotas" can be counterproductive in the social sphere. To a northern Protestant viewer, Hyndman's video is good at detailing the problem of fair employment; the usual, albeit problematic unionist rejoinder is to argue that once northern nationalists commit themselves to the state of Northern Ireland they will not be treated as less reliable workers by mainly Protestant industry. Since they cannot – by political conviction – be committed to the same values as their Protestant workers, nothing short of a political solution will improve the job situation dramatically. The fact that there has been little change in the ratio of Catholic to Protestant unemployed, despite the McBride Principles and British and international awareness, suggests that the solution lies at a political level, not in labour legislation.

Between Ourselves: Songs, Satire and Some Sense (1993), together with *Moving Myths* and *Our Words Jump to Life*, is a provocative and challenging visual satire and social commentary. This group project opens with the sounds of drums beating on the soundtrack and a triple split-screen. From left to right, image (a) is of young girls brandishing painted bin lids promoting IRA ideology, which changes into an image of masked IRA men walking the streets; (b) is an image of a police "STOP THE KILLING" poster which changes to another sign of the security forces: "BLAME THE TERRORISTS"; but the most interesting image is (c), which starts with the loyalist poster "SUPPORT ULSTER'S DEFIANT RESISTANCE" and "HAUGHEY IRA PROTECTOR". This image turns into a parked vehicle blowing up. So, from the very opening seconds of the video, the anti-imperialist argument has been thrust front and centre. Subliminally, the loyalist cause has been deflated, rejected and finally blown apart. It leaves the (a) and (b) images in the viewer's mind: the IRA vs. the militarism of the British state.

Following these initial images, we have at least 25 different sketches which move from simple outrage at specific events to more philosophical moments when black British and Indian poets are interviewed in an effort to internationalise the conflict into a postcolonial struggle. Unquestionably, the most powerful visual images are those recording a demonstration in London over the Birmingham Six (six Irish men wrongly imprisoned by the British justice system subsequent to the Birmingham pub bombings in 1974). It is a well-orchestrated demonstration, befitting the egregious act of injustice perpetrated by the British legal apparatus. Six gondola-shaped boats drag enormous portrait pictures of the six men along the River Thames. Later, a firework display and march are wedded to a poetic and impassioned score.

Near the end of the video, black British poet Abdul Malik and Indian poet Mahmoud Jamal argue that the basic ongoing problem of colonialism is often not what the colonising power did in the past, but how the previously colonised people continue to behave as colonised, and, worse, accept neocolonialism in its stead. Both poets discuss the stereotypical image of Northern Ireland (street rioting) as evidence that it is not part of Great Britain or the United Kingdom; however, neither man conveys any real knowledge of the inhabitants of Northern Ireland and their wishes. More effective is the testimony of a former British soldier who had been wounded in Northern Ireland. His analysis bears listening to not just because "he was there" and "suffered", but because he could see that, as a poor northerner (from England), he was simply a pawn in a complex chess game.

Many of the satires in *Between Ourselves*, as in all the videos discussed here, are full of colour, and assault the visual and auditory senses. A concerted effort is made to link Thatcherite capitalism, religious intolerance and unionist hegemony. Unemployment, discrimination and sexism also become targets. The video ends, leaving us in no doubt as to the nationalist/republican desiderium, as an onscreen narrator asserts: "Always a minority turning the rudder of change against the dead-weight of the majority". The same onscreen commentator finally concludes, "800 Year War. I'm Celt." It is a mantra that could stand for most of the work of Northern Visions. The "dead-weight" in these videographers' eyes is, for the most part, a euphemism for the Protestant community and its wishes.[8] As the next chapter on another video workshop reveals, this exclusionary attitude is common in Northern Ireland.

Notes

[1]   John Grierson, "First Principles of Documentary", in Forsyth Hardy (ed), *Grierson on Documentary* (London; Boston: Faber and Faber, 1966): 37. Emphasis in original.

[2]   Brian Winston, *Claiming the Real: The Griersonian Documentary and Its Legitimations* (London: British Film Institute, 1995): 11.

[3]   See Marilyn Hyndman, "Resisting cultural arrest", *Film Ireland* 32 (November/December 1992): 16-17. Hyndman's article gives an excellent overview of the context in which Northern Visions works, and the difficulties of making meaningful documentaries in Northern Ireland for broadcast.

[4]   The term "Poor Cinema" is considered at length by Colin McArthur in "The Cultural Necessity of a Poor Celtic Cinema", in John Hill, Martin McLoone and Paul Hainsworth (eds), *Border Crossing: Film in Ireland, Britain and Europe* (Belfast and London: Institute of Irish Studies in association with the University of Ulster and the British Film Institute, 1994): 112-125. See also his earlier article, "In Praise of a Poor Cinema", *Sight and Sound* 3: 8 (August 1993): 30-32. Sean Cubitt's *Timeshift: On video culture* (London; New York: Routledge, 1991) provides a more

controversial and challenging characterisation of the video medium. In particular, he focuses on "community video" as one way of resisting the mainstream "balance" positions taken by the professional media. Although not mentioned by Cubitt, Northern Visions is one such community video outlet.

[5] See Anne Crilly, "Stories for Television", *Film Ireland* 42 (August/ September 1994): 20-22.

[6] See Paul Bew, Peter Gibbon and Henry Patterson, *Northern Ireland 1921-1994: Political Forces and Social Classes* (London: Serif, 1995): 81-144.

[7] See Bill Rolston, *Politics and Painting: Murals and Conflict in Northern Ireland* (Rutherford; Madison; Teaneck: Fairleigh Dickinson University Press; London; Toronto: Associated University Presses; 1991); and his *Drawing Support: Murals in the North of Ireland* (Belfast: Beyond the Pale Publications, 1992).

[8] At a very basic level, people talk about the supposition that, in 25 years' time, Catholics may well outnumber Protestants in Northern Ireland. If so, one wonders, with a fair degree of irony, if the minority Protestants will be embraced by Northern Visions' videographers as the minority turning the rudder of change against the dead-weight of the Catholic majority.

9

The feminist historical and political documentary reconsidered: Anne Crilly's Mother Ireland

Over time, seeing oneself as the seen rather than the seer, as the desired or repudiated object or victim rather than the subject, may not have been empowering, and might have fostered an interior colonization. We have learned more about male desire than women's lives. It's time to change our focus, to let what Virginia Woolf called 'the bright eyes that reign influence' look elsewhere. (Patricia Mellencamp)[1]

Irish women in post-revolutionary Ireland did not make the political traditions: they inherited them from fathers, husbands and brothers. (Margaret Mac Curtain)[2]

Derry Film and Video Workshop came to public attention in the early 1980s, due in large part to the liberal policies of Channel 4 in the United Kingdom. The channel's brief to give preference to diverse production companies was seen in most quarters as innovative. Ironically, this massive decentralisation as the organising principle for a major television broadcaster was directly linked to the competitive, capitalistic ideology heralded by Thatcherism, yet it also paved the way for the empowerment of previously marginalised groups. With reference to the latter, the workshop's use of broadcast and non-broadcast quality video not only brought in many former technophobes, but also raised awareness that serious issues could be tackled and productions disseminated. One of the central thrusts of the workshop was to examine women's experiences within a political framework.[3] The workshop's own press release in 1989 described itself as follows:

Derry Film and Video was set up in 1984 in the desire that people in the north of Ireland should and could make an indigenous contribution to media presentation of their own lives after being the focus of external media coverage over the preceding fifteen years. Channel Four T.V. provided the Workshop with development funding for three years during which time members were developing video and film skills, researching their programme ideas and offering training and assistance with local community video projects. In addition to its other work in the field of education Derry Film and Video was involved in setting up the first Foyle Film Festival which has now become an annual event with continued involvement from the Workshop. In 1987 Derry Film and Video became a fully franchised Workshop receiving funding from Channel 4 to make a documentary called *Mother Ireland* which was completed in February 1988 and became the first programme to be banned from broadcast in Britain under the new government censorship legislation imposed in October, 1988. *Mother Ireland* was directed by Anne Crilly and it explores the development and use of images and music which personify Ireland as a woman in Irish culture and nationalism.

In 1990, the workshop closed down because of the withdrawal of Channel 4 funding, but not before the production of Margo Harkin's *Hush-A-Bye Baby* which is discussed in chapter 5.

Since the late-1960s, what we have seen happen in Ireland – socially a deeply conservative country – is an attempt to begin the long and necessary process of building alternative images of Irish women, while also calling into question the dominant images of women in the popular psyche. Crilly's *Mother Ireland*, a video documentary censored in Britain and Ireland, sets out to demythologise images of Irish women in the hope of energising a female audience and of educating a male audience. Crilly's video is an important intervention into Irish visual history, and I make no apology for devoting a chapter to the theoretical, historical and political issues it raises.

If one were to ask what two central issues Crilly sets herself to question, one would probably come up with the tenability of the phrase "Mother Ireland", and the ideology behind feminism and violence. I think the latter is Crilly's real agenda: to give credibility to the women who have chosen support of the armed struggle in Ireland. What the director is able to do is to set up an alternate history of Ireland's violent struggles through the lens of women's struggles. We are meant to see connections between Warrior Queen Maeve who invaded Ulster in pre-Christian times, the women of Cumann na mBan, and present-day IRA activists such as Mairéad Farrell.

A series of interlocking issues presents itself whenever considering approaches to an Irish feminist historical documentary. Firstly, sensitive viewers are aware of the long history of women's oppression and of the need that this history be dealt with visually. Secondly, the subject-matter of Ireland itself (a "national history") brings an array of confused and certainly complicated signifiers, given the present crisis in Northern Ireland. Thirdly, the connection between the women's movement and the use of violence in the "national struggle" must be addressed. Fourthly, the formal strategies applied in this work interact inevitably with previous practical and theoretical moves by other documentarists and their critics. Finally, the choice/necessity to shoot this kind of programme on video and not on film deserves comment as a corollary of the expected distribution and reception envisioned by the collective.

For some of these points, there are basic glosses. The history of women's oppression/devaluation in the political arena is almost a given. Video is cheaper than film, and can be distributed quickly and widely. *Mother Ireland* at 52 minutes was conceived as a good candidate for a Channel 4 hour-long programme, as well as for all kinds of community situations. Much more difficult to confront is the overlapping of women's history with national history within an Irish perspective, and, furthermore, the utility and appropriateness of the documentary strategies employed. The "official" impetus behind the censoring in Britain and Ireland was motivated less by a denial of women's history than by a refusal to give credence to women devoted to the armed struggle. This distinction is deeply problematic and cannot be well-defended intellectually within a democracy. It can only be understood in the context of broadcast restrictions in both countries *vis-à-vis* the reporting of Sinn Féin and/or the IRA.

Before examining *Mother Ireland*, I want to contextualise my comments by surveying salient points in feminist film theory, feminist documentary and images of Irish women. By working from theory to a specific practice, from "abstraction" to "criticism", I hope to avoid the more egregious errors associated with overemphasising either the general or the particular.

As I mentioned in chapter 1, much of the theoretical work in feminist film theory has been applied to classical Hollywood film texts. This focus is not surprising, given the dominance of this paradigm throughout the world, and the dominance by sheer numbers of Americans (although many of European origin and inspiration) working in the related field of psychoanalysis. The efforts to reclaim a female spectatorship in these films seem to me less important politically than investigating various forms of counter-cinema and documentary with the latter's greater "appeal to the real". It is in these areas that feminist theory has vital work still to do.

In its simplest sense, feminist documentary attempts to make clear to viewers the reality of women's experiences and their hopes for change. The formal strategies involved have led to much debate, but first the "straightforward telling" of these experiences is important. Theoretically speaking, the standard thinking on this subject was sparked by Julia Lesage,[4] who points out that the feminist documentaries of the 1970s were typified by "[b]iography, simplicity, trust between woman filmmaker and woman subject, a linear narrative structure, little self-consciousness about the flexibility of the cinematic medium".[5] Lesage qualifies her approval of this approach by asking for a balance between the experiential and the analytical, so that what is created is a "collective process leading to social change".[6]

Noel King takes Lesage's qualification much further, considering the mini-narratives of biography, autobiography and popular narrative history as seductive and often misleading.[7] He sees these three intersecting discourses as static, since, while they appear to give the impression of a causal chain of events, they are so overdetermined that "[t]he effect of employing such a familiar narrative system is that the origin always already contains the end".[8] King favours a more problematic approach to knowledge/reality, revealing his attachment (and *Screen*'s at this time) to Brechtian contradiction.

Soon after King, Ann Kaplan reviewed the debate over realism and the then-popular acceptance of semiological inquiry towards feminist filmmaking.[9] Kaplan steers a middle course, uneasy at the abrupt shifts from "realism" to "anti-realism" as the best means to address feminist concerns. The central weakness of semiology is the tendency to distance the experience of live human beings from their "history". As Kaplan puts it, "[i]f semiologists were wrong in denying that realism can produce an effect leading to change, then leftist-activists were wrong in assuming that merely showing something is an argument in its own right".[10] For Kaplan, counter-cinema could also find a place in feminist documentary by emphasising illusion-breaking, an unfixed spectatorship, a denial of simple visual pleasure, and a mixing of documentary and fiction (since the two are so indivisible theoretically). One could see Pat Murphy's *Maeve* as one counter-cinema example. To my mind, *Mother Ireland* fits into Kaplan's own taxonomy of "theory films", a film about women's history that attempts to "take on Ireland" in a much more specific and provocative way than previous television histories.[11] It does so, moreover, within the realist mode.

One of the central difficulties facing the documentarist intent on revising images of Irish women is the extensive mythology that has built up over the centuries. In Ireland, the connection between the land and the image of woman is a solidified one. In Irish mythology, the woman is most often a goddess who must be worshipped because she reigns over the land, determining if a Chieftain's crop will be bountiful or poor. Thus, it is easy to see the origin of the appellation "Mother Ireland". Certain landscapes were sacred: the "secular" hill of Tara, for example, was where many of the ceremonies between Goddess and Chieftain or King were carried out, much to the disdain and discouragement of the Christian Church.

The image of woman in Irish mythology has taken a number of forms. Often an allegorical naming was necessary to circumvent British penal laws which, as Nina Witoszek reveals, forbade written reference to Ireland[12] – hence the interchangeable names of Dark

Rosaleen, Hag of Beare, Kathleen ni Houlihan and Shan van Vocht that connoted a *free* Ireland through femininity. Proinsias Mac Cana reminds us how these archetypal figures were transformational agents in simple narratives, such as "the Hag" who guards the well from which men must drink to survive.[13] To be granted water, they must first kiss the woman and be willing to sleep with her. The one brave man who submits is "rewarded" with wealth, prestige and the transformation of the old woman into a beautiful young bride-to-be. A modern homage or parody of this particular myth is to be found in Neil Jordan's *High Spirits* (1988).

If we examine Irish historiography with specific regard to the representations and the status of women, we are faced with a poverty of reliable written materials. The standard work is a collection of essays published originally by a women's press.[14] In the introductory essay to this collection, Donncha Ó Corráin surveys the much-misunderstood period of early Irish society in the sixth and seventh centuries, and this research has helped to clarify that early Irish law and society were decidedly patriarchal.

Ó Corráin outlines how, up to the 12th century, in the sole area of marriage, women began to have their rights defined and defended in law. An erosion of women's rights in medieval times began with the Norman invasion, and reached its acme with the wars and subsequent plantations in the 16th and 17th centuries. The famine, of course, devastated any hope of improving the lot of women in the mid-19th century; however, in the wake of the 1867 Reform Act in the British Parliament, wherein women were officially denied the vote, women mobilised to oppose the status quo. Charles Stewart Parnell's sisters Fanny and Anna, for example, founded the Ladies' Land League. Historian Margaret Mac Curtain observes, somewhat ironically, that this organisation was dissolved by Parnell because it seemed to undermine his control of the Home Rule Party.[15] Clearly, a gap existed for the intellectual and moral pursuance of women's rights, and this gap was finally filled not only by suffragettes and the Irish Women Workers' Union, but also by Cumann na mBan, a woman's organisation formed in April 1914 to help the Irish Citizen Army and Irish Volunteers in the national struggle.

Nationalism, feminism and working conditions were all deemed important, but the former took precedence over the latter two in the Easter Rising. Mac Curtain argues that Cumann na mBan's contribution has been undervalued, although she reveals a frustration with the organisation since the losing republican side in the Irish Civil War contained the most eloquent women representatives in Ireland; therefore, the newly formed Irish Free State was effectively defeminised.

In returning to *Mother Ireland*, I want to revisit four of my five points stated earlier, and, in doing so, consider how Crilly's approach has interacted with the feminist issues so far discussed. Crilly presents an overview of Irish women in history; she details pre-Christian Ireland much in the same way as described by Donncha Ó Corráin and Proinsias Mac Cana. She seeks out and documents various cultural signifiers: an oil painting of a naked woman shaped like an Irish harp; songs/ballads which show women as objects (to be sung *about*); and political cartoons which present women in submissive or romanticised positions. The traditional line of such oppression is the detailing of the suffragette movement in both Britain and Ireland, but perhaps the most telling image is from post-revolutionary Ireland: a Miss Ireland beauty contest in 1942. We see uniformed males acting as judges who, with pens and noteboards in hand, motion the bathing-suit-clad women to stop, turn, and walk at their pleasure.

More problematic for Crilly is the power of religion in Ireland, since the image of the Virgin Mary is very real for believers. We see at different points film footage of the pilgrimage to Knock in 1937 and a video recording of the pilgrimage in 1987. Religion's hold over the Irish woman was in part written into the Irish Constitution, which validated a special position for "women in the home". In a very slippery and calculated way, therefore, "Mother Ireland" refers both to the land and to the image of a pure woman. Having determined and revealed that "Mother Ireland" is a historical and political construct, Crilly goes on to test its ongoing "historicity" in the lives of "concrete" women. The result of such empirical testing is fascinatingly varied. All women interviewed are agreed on the need to confront the appellation, but alternatives to it lead along different paths.

For the Peppard sisters, who seem to be representatives of the ordinary rural Irish women, a conflict exists between the romanticised image of women and the land (in this case, the image of one of the women carrying peat on the cover of *Ireland of the Welcomes*, an Irish Tourist Board publication), and the reality of what their lives are about. Here we have a typical Irish antagonism between word and image.[16] The women both remember being told at school to "produce for God" as many children as possible. They laugh at this stricture, as we see their children playing in the background. It is not for the Catholic Church that these women had their children, but the tact with which they treat the teachings of the Catholic Church tells us much about the power of that upbringing. Their main desire is for women to be accepted within the Church as equals, particularly through the ordination of women priests.

The "Mother Ireland" label is regarded as a site of controversy, even by the feminist republican activists who dominate the "talking heads" in Crilly's video: Bernadette McAliskey (née Devlin), Pat Murphy, Nell McCafferty, Sighle Humphries and Miriam James, Mairéad Farrell and Rita O'Hare. Socialist activist McAliskey sees herself as a child of "Mother Ireland", arguing that imperialist countries are often viewed as male (she cites the German fatherland as an example), while countries which have experienced oppression are often viewed as female. *Republican News/An Phoblacht* editor Rita O'Hare also finds the label useful, pointing to the connotations of nurturing, caring and devotion attached to it. In contrast, filmmaker Pat Murphy sees it as pernicious to compare a woman to a country, with all the suggestions of penetration and rape; equally, IRA activist Mairéad Farrell is cynical in her response, revealing that while in prison she and her comrades would chant: "Mother Ireland: Get off our backs!". Journalist Nell McCafferty, always acerbic and to the point, would far prefer a sheela-na-gig as an emblem. This is a stone or wooden carving of a naked woman seemingly intended to celebrate fertility, and often found in ruined churches (but now mostly hidden away in Irish museums!).[17] Women's sexuality should be celebrated in its own right, McCafferty believes, and not restricted to the confines of marriage. So, even here, the questioning of "Mother Ireland" as a label invites Crilly to produce contradiction and confusion in the viewer; she avoids the temptation of editing to erase such conflicts.

The testimonies of Sighle Humphries and Miriam James reveal that there were republican women who saw themselves as feminist activists, and who took up the gun for their political beliefs. One of the interesting contradictions in the video is the difference between Margaret Mac Curtain's academic response to Cumann na mBan and that of Sighle Humphries, whose own personal memory of the events resists strongly any suspicion that the woman's organisation was a glorified tea-serving activity. The images of women on hunger strike in the 1920s and the reinforcement by the interviewees' personal experiences as hunger strikers are extremely powerful. I want to emphasise this contradiction between Mac Curtain's academic overview and the sense of personal injustice that this overview causes among the surviving members of Cumann na mBan: it strikes at the core of what I have indicated above is sterile in the current academic debates over psychoanalytical categories and critical orthodoxies. This very "inconsistency" or "roughness" gives *Mother Ireland* a special place in documenting Ireland's troubles.

We notice how Mac Curtain tries to broaden the empowerment of women away from "narrow" violent concerns; she sees the modern woman in trades union activities, ecological battles, nuclear disarmament and other global issues. In the context of this video, she seems strangely reticent about the violence in the North which directly concerns Pat Murphy, Bernadette McAliskey, Nell McCafferty, Rita O'Hare and Mairéad Farrell.

Pat Murphy's contribution as filmmaker is well-documented. I wish here only to mention what Crilly decides to show: a critique of "Mother Ireland" already discussed, an extract from *Anne Devlin* (1984), and Murphy's own assessment of the history behind the film. Anne Devlin supported Robert Emmet's Rebellion against the British in 1803. It was ill-fated, but the right of women to advance a political cause through violence was upheld, and, in the extract shown, it is clear that Devlin suffers the pain of interrogation in silence not for her lover *per se*, but for the political cause he and she championed.[18]

Bernadette McAliskey's final comment, that women must organise and fight for their rights, and sometimes physically have to take them, resounds with the authority of one who has been in the wars (behind the barricades, on soapboxes with megaphones, and as the survivor of a major assassination attempt). Her serenity and sureness of purpose are remarkable for their "naturalness". Rita O'Hare also lends a committed sense to the debate, understanding the historical debt which the present republicans owe to those women of Cumann na mBan who took a principled but ultimately losing position in the Civil War.

Nell McCafferty's change of views within the women's movement in Ireland is of great interest. At first, she agreed to fight for general "neutral" issues such as pay equity and birth control, but now she sees that the national question is inextricably bound up with women's issues. For McCafferty, the writing is on the wall for the British rule of Northern Ireland, and she wants women to be represented strongly when the "last green field" of Ireland comes back into the fold. McCafferty ruminates that no great text has been written about women and violence, the absence of which she finds symptomatic of the quiet suppression of women's political voices.

When we turn to Mairéad Farrell's testimony, it is now impossible to watch as originally intended, because of the knowledge that she was subsequently murdered by the British SAS while on "active duty" in Gibraltar. Her murder serves, in a sense, as an extratextual exemplar of the issues Crilly has been addressing in the video. Farrell's revulsion at the "occupation" of the British troops, her desire for training in firearms (and presumably explosives), her imprisonment in Armagh Jail followed by the "dirty protest" for political category status are all presented as personal and principled decisions. Farrell and her female compatriots connect to the women of Cumann na mBan, unpopular in their time and often written out of history.

Crilly has adopted a carefully crafted and edited response to the subject of Irish women and their struggles. She decides to *exclude* both men and Irish Protestant women. The former is understandable; the latter is, in my view, the Achilles' heel of Crilly's project: how can she raise women's consciousness by denying or "writing out" the history of a quarter of Ireland's women? Having said that, Crilly's aim to make known Irish republican women is indeed satisfied. *Mother Ireland* is both a "string of interviews" documentary with female authority figures set against suitable backgrounds, *and* an analytical documentary in that Crilly is to be heard in voice-over, contextualising the material shown (except for the comments by the interviewees whose opinions are sometimes given visual support as they talk). Only on a couple of occasions does Crilly feel she must prompt Sighle Humphries: to speak about Cumann na mBan members' anger at De Valera, who felt women should not be fully involved in the armed struggle.

As with most Direct Cinema documentaries, the absence of probing direct questions by the documentarian makes the viewer impatient on occasions where questions would seem necessary. One such moment is Mac Curtain's point that for middle-class women to smash windows during the days of the suffragettes was a "radical" move. Here was needed a pertinent question, only implied by Crilly's montage editing: do not those such as Mairéad Farrell develop as they do because they too have been radicalised by the same issues and grievances?

On the other side of this "arrested" *cinéma-vérité* technique is the problem of representing Farrell herself. As viewers, we want to know more about the involvement of Farrell in the three explosions which (at her own admission) caused her to be sent to Armagh Jail for ten years. Were people killed in these explosions? Did she intend to kill for her political beliefs? Gaining information from Farrell is one side of the coin; the other side has to do with the viewer's relationship with Crilly's "position". Our spectatorship is structured here less by masculinity or femininity, as psychoanalytical theorists would claim, than by a political perspective. We are encouraged to favour the republican cause: we are witness to footage of a civil rights march in 1968 clumsily resisted by the RUC. The use of slow-motion here seems to confirm to Crilly the inevitability and perhaps necessity of confrontation. Other conflicts are paraded: we see footage of a house search by British soldiers (also in slow-motion with a "rebellious" song on the soundtrack) with women trying to beat the intruders back with bin lids; we also see footage of the horrible results of a rubber bullet hitting a young mother. These sequences operate at the manipulative level of "emotional truth". As viewers, we are meant to feel outraged at such indiscriminate and "unnatural" acts. In this way also, Crilly deliberately taps into our sense of political and intellectual rage. Unsurprisingly, in order for the video to be broadcast, the filmmakers had to omit Mairéad Farrell, a rebel song, a dissolve from *Anne Devlin* to a poster of a masked IRA female volunteer, and the "rubber bullet" incident. [19]

Most students of committed documentary will know of Thomas Waugh's definition that it must believe in social change and that it must reveal openly its political position, [20] and of Chuck Kleinhans' excellent recipe for the ideal committed documentarian: one aware of the pitfalls of extreme formalism, the political compromises effected by smooth visualisation, the prejudices of his/her own political position, and the historical context in which the production will be made and distributed. [21] Kleinhans argues for political analysis in tandem with emotional commitment. The right balance must be found to draw out the audience's political, intellectual and emotional rage, if political documentaries are to be worthwhile.

As Bill Nichols says, "[i]n documentary, an event recounted is history reclaimed".[22] Crilly's task in *Mother Ireland* is to reclaim as many "events" of women's history as possible within the Irish context. Foremost among these are the recognition of real gender asymmetry, and the need to accept that such inequality will inevitably lead to violence. In response, the power-brokers will attempt to make invisible that struggle for equality (for example, the ploy of granting political status to male, but not to female, prisoners). With such a gendered asymmetry, "historical reality" is always up for question, and Crilly steers into this whirlpool by privileging subjective discourses of republican women, thereby forcing an already fractured sense of Irish history to be rethought. Formally speaking, *Mother Ireland* may not have the artistic play of a film by Errol Morris, Michael Moore or Trinh T Minh-ha (and it has its own blind spots, as mentioned earlier), but what it does have is true about the best political studies as well, and that is a basic "moral critique" of established practices and views. It is a film that seeks to answer the bold political questions we are often so unwilling even to ask.

Notes

[1]   Patricia Mellencamp, "Female Bodies and Women's Past-times, 1890-1920", *East-West Film Journal* 6: 1 (January 1992): 23. Much of what Mellencamp and I find limiting but dominant in feminist film criticism can be usefully surveyed in Patricia Erens (ed), *Issues in Feminist Film Criticism* (Bloomington: Indiana University Press, 1990).

[2]   Margaret Mac Curtain and Donncha Ó Corráin (eds), *Women in Irish Society: The Historical Dimension* (Dublin: Arlen Press, 1978): 55.

[3]   A brief description of the workshop and its work can be found in Annette Kuhn (ed), with Susannah Radstone, *The Women's Companion to International Film* (London: Virago, 1990): 118. I also wish to acknowledge a related unpublished paper by Jeffrey Chown, whose work started me thinking about *Mother Ireland*: "Representing the Unrepresentable: The IRA and Sinn Féin in British/Irish Documentary", delivered at the 12th Annual Ohio University Film Conference in Athens, OH, 1990.

[4]   Julia Lesage, "The Political Aesthetics of the Feminist Documentary Film", in Erens (ed): 222-237.

[5]   Ibid: 223.

[6]   Ibid: 224.

[7]   Noel King, "Recent 'Political' Documentary: Notes on 'Union Maids' and 'Harlan County USA'", *Screen* 22: 2 (1981): 7-18.

[8]   Ibid: 12.

[9]   E Ann Kaplan, "Theories and Strategies of the Feminist Documentary",

Millennium Film Journal 12 (autumn/winter 1981/82): 44-67.

[10] Ibid: 58.

[11] For a discussion of some of these television histories, see John Pym, "Ireland – Two Nations", in Alan Rosenthal (ed), *New Challenges for Documentary* (Berkeley; Los Angeles; London: University of California Press, 1988): 480-487. Women in the Irish media and film are considered in two notable articles: Margaret Ward and Marie-Therese McGivern, "Images of Women in Northern Ireland", in M Hederman and R Kearney (eds), *The Crane Bag Book of Irish Studies* (Dublin: Blackwater Press, 1982): 579-585; and Barbara O'Connor, "Aspects of Representation of Women in Irish Film", *The Crane Bag* 8: 2 (1984): 79-83.

[12] See Nina Witoszek, "Ireland: A Funerary Culture?", *Studies* 76: 302 (summer 1987): 206-215.

[13] Proinsias Mac Cana, "Women in Irish Mythology", in Hederman and Kearney (eds): 520-524.

[14] Mac Curtain and Ó Corráin (eds). See also Margaret Mac Curtain, "The Historical Image", in Eilean Ni Chuilleanain (ed), *Irish Women: Image and Achievement. Women in Irish Culture from earliest times* (Dublin: Arlen House, 1985): 37-50; Roger Sawyer, *'We Are But Women': Women in Ireland's History* (London: Routledge, 1993); and Margaret Ward, *In Their Own Voice: Women and Irish Nationalism* (Dublin: Attic Press, 1995).

[15] Mac Curtain: 46.

[16] See Luke Gibbons, "Word and Image: The Resistance to Vision", *Graph: Irish Literary Review* 2 (spring 1987): 2-3.

[17] For an in-depth discussion of sheela-na-gigs, see Bob Quinn, *Atlantean* (London: Quartet Books, 1986).

[18] For information on this film, see Luke Gibbons, "The Politics of Silence: *Anne Devlin*, Women and Irish Cinema", *Framework* 30/31 (1986): 2-15.

[19] For discussion by Irish critics of the travails of *Mother Ireland*, see Sheila MacDowell and Johnny Gogan, "*Mother Ireland*", *Film Base News* 10 (December 1988/January 1989): 10-11; and Belinda Loftus, "*Mother Ireland*", *Circa* 44 (March/April 1989): 33-34. Loftus has considered the resonance of "Mother Ireland" within nationalist and unionist traditions. See her "Mother Ireland & Loyalist Ladies", *Circa* 51 (May/June 1990): 20-23; and *Mirrors: Orange and Green* (Dundrum: Picture Press, 1994).

[20] Thomas Waugh (ed), *"Show Us Life": Toward a History and Aesthetics of the Committed Documentary* (Metuchen, NJ; London: The Scarecrow Press, 1984): xiv.

[21] See Chuck Kleinhans, "Forms, Politics, Makers, and Contexts: Basic Issues For a Theory of Radical Political Documentary", in ibid: 318-342.

[22] Bill Nichols, *Representing Reality: Issues and Concepts in Documentary* (Bloomington and Indianapolis: Indiana University Press, 1991): 21.

10
Unacceptable levels: losses and games

> I remember once, in the early days of the troubles, the local
> RUC received a call one wintry night from a Protestant
> farmer reporting intruders on his property. As the patrol car
> turned into his drive, they saw a colour television plonked
> smack in the middle of the road. One constable got out to
> remove it – and was blown to kingdom-come. In Ulster, the
> medium really is the message. (John Naughton)[1]

The British Minister fully responsible for Northern Ireland at the
beginning of the "Troubles", Reginald Maudling, was once quoted as
saying that one of his main tasks was to reduce the violence to
"acceptable levels".[2] To many, this *realpolitik* has characterised the
whole direct rule period, from the fall of Stormont in March 1972 to
the present. The argument here is that Britain has no idea
whatsoever of how to create conditions for an overall settlement, and
therefore, in the hope that "something might come along", security
matters take pride of place. Giving back effective municipal and
regional government may be desirable, but only if it is clear that
opening such a Pandora's box will bear results. Hence the British
hesitation and the endless "talks about talks" processes, which
nearly every Secretary of State before Mo Mowlam had pursued with
no tangible political success.

In the absence of real political dialogue, documentary films in
particular became lightning-rods for speaking the unspeakable, for
raising issues which people in Northern Ireland were reluctant to
bring up outside the confines of their closest family and friends. A
number of these documentaries came from England, but also from
continental Europe. This chapter looks at a few of these films, three
of which are feature-length: Marcel Ophüls' *A Sense of Loss*, Arthur
Mac Caig's *The Patriot Game* (1979) and John Davies' *Acceptable
Levels*.

A Sense of Loss is the major early feature documentary on the
"Troubles", certainly the most significant one made before
Stormont's demise. What is captured by this film is very valuable
from a sociological and historical perspective, since it demarcates a

great number of the established points of view emanating from the various political and interested parties which have not shifted appreciably in 25 years. The role that Ophüls plays throughout, however, is complicated. He offers himself as the disinterested investigative journalist who will simply ask the direct questions which he considers the most pertinent. On occasion, we see Ophüls asking questions, and we often hear his voice offscreen. In this respect, Ophüls' documentary belongs to the category of *cinéma-vérité* so much in vogue in the late-1960s and early 1970s. It is a form which has some advantages in raising immediate issues to be answered by leading questions, yet it also draws attention, sometimes unfortunately, to the nature of the questioning. This drawback is linked to the technique applied, for, as the filmmaker puts it: "The idea is that you rush around to thirty or forty people in different towns, trying to create epic frescoes on the basis of straight interviewing".[3]

Ophüls' strategy is thus delineated: he pushes himself headlong into as many aspects of the problem as he can. Hence, we witness interviews with political figures; people on the street in London (although, strangely, not in Belfast or Derry), former IRA activists; internees' wives; spouses of murder victims; the British Army; IRA sympathisers; Protestant extremists; moderates; two Roman Catholic priests (although no Protestant ministers); and teachers from a Roman Catholic school. Cleverly, Ophüls begins the film with St Patrick's Day in New York in March 1972, where the romantic notion of Ireland, "united and free" is arguably strongest. At the parade, there are many anti-English signs and the occasional rowdy disturbance. Here Ophüls zeroes in at the base of the anti-imperialist myth: if only the British military and political machinery would leave Ireland, a natural and organic solution would result.

This interest in militarism naturally recurs throughout the film with numerous shots of young children playing with toy guns, and even – as in one Protestant family – a child wearing full Army uniform. The Queen's Christmas message is visually contrasted with young street urchins on a pile of rubble where cheap housing once stood. As Gerry O'Hare of the "People's Democracy" remarks in the surroundings of his kitchen with his children and recently hospitalised wife Rita: "All the children are political now". It is a society for children where, as one Catholic school caretaker puts it, "a riot is better than saving stamps". As Ophüls wanders around a school art class, he sees one boy drawing the British Army as Nazis. Given Ophüls' own background and his previous film, *Le Chagrin et la pitié* (*The Sorrow and the Pity*, 1971), he is particularly sensitive to any Nazi parallels, and naturally includes Michael Farrell's comment that Ian Paisley's Party, the DUP, published material on Catholics which, Farrell claims, resembled that of the attitude of the Nazis to Jews. Generally, however, Ophüls takes an empirical approach:

Our aim was to catch death while it was still there. The system, then, was to wait for a few weeks. Then Anna Carrigan – because she's Irish – would contact the family, and I would go in a few weeks after the funeral and talk with the members of the family, asking them who were these people that had died, what were they trying to do in their lives...One death is missing, and that's a British soldier. We tried for weeks, but the Ministry of Defence said no. I think it was very foolish on their part. It would have given balance.[4]

Within the methodology quoted above, it has to be said that Ophüls' sympathies lie foremost with the victims, but the emphasis is on the Catholic community. Apart from the death of Protestant Colin Nicholl, aged seventeen months, in an IRA bomb explosion, Ophüls concentrates on Catholic IRA member Gerald McDade, killed by the British Army, Anne-Marie Caldwell, a Catholic schoolgirl killed in a road accident involving the security forces, and John Lavery, a Catholic barman who was killed by an IRA bomb when he attempted to render it harmless. The filmmaker does interview UDA Protestant activist John McKeague, whose mother died in an arson attack on his bookshop, but makes it clear by his hard questioning that he believes this man has helped to fan the flames of violence in Northern Ireland.[5] This approach would be fine if it were consistent. No questions are asked about McKeague's mother's views and her life, unlike in the cases of the three Catholic victims. Ophüls also strangely allows Gerry O'Hare to avoid the issue, by saying: "Whether or not you are a member of the IRA is none of our business". One wonders, therefore, what Ophüls views as his documentary "business"?

Apart from the extremism of McKeague, the defensive inarticulateness of one Shankill Road Protestant family, the political posturings of two unionist political figures – William Craig and John Taylor – and Billy Hull, a trades unionist, Ophüls does not address Protestant fears and aspirations. He does not, in short, fulfil General Sir Harry Tuzo's (Commander of British forces, Northern Ireland) request in the film: "Don't forget those Protestants, will you?". Instead, he goes to the south of Ireland to Noel Browne and Conor Cruise O'Brien, both of the Labour Party in the Republic of Ireland, to address the weakness in the cause of an united Ireland. Browne points out that the 1916 Rising, which the IRA and Sinn Féin hold so dear, can easily be regarded as a disaster for the country, for its legacy of blood sacrifice and martyrdom has only served to encourage violent acts. Browne also raises the problem of the position of the Roman Catholic Church in the Republic of Ireland, with its Catholic population of at least 95%. As Minister of Health, Browne could not bring legislation to fruition that did not have the consent of the Church. Ophüls follows this lead quite ingeniously by interviewing both Catholic priests on the one hand and Official IRA members on the other. The debate within the nationalist tradition is therefore touched upon. Ironically, Charles Haughey, who was later to become the Prime Minister of the Republic, is pilloried as a conservative rabble-rouser who hated the Socialists and Marxists, including the Official IRA. Although it is not mentioned forcefully, Ophüls begins to prize open the south of Ireland's fear that, if the British leave the North, the Republic would face insurrection not only from recalcitrant Protestants, but also from militant republicans. It would be as divisive as the 1922-23 Civil War period. Nairn's phrase, "relic or portent?", his title summary of his essay on Northern Ireland, could not be more apt in assessing the uncertainties of the Republic of Ireland's policy towards the North.

By interviewing Father Desmond Wilson and Father Dennis Faul, Ophüls shows us the Socialist and Conservative nationalists within the Roman Catholic Church. Faul represents the standard line on Church practices and attitudes: he believes that the Protestants are oppressive but moral, and takes comfort in the fact that laws regarding homosexuality and abortion do not apply in Ireland as they do in Great Britain. This fact makes the Protestants in Faul's eye more Irish than they know. Wilson strikes a different note; echoing Noel Browne, he seems concerned that the mythology of revolution is so engrossing for many Catholics, although he concedes that revolution may be necessary in certain cases.

Ophüls spends a great deal of the latter half of the film with Bernadette Devlin, who at that time was the youngest member of the British Parliament. Her campaign for civil rights, and the irony of her British state-supported upbringing (reliant on child and widow allowances, more generous than in the Republic of Ireland) are typical of the complex situation in Northern Ireland. This "ingratitude" and "lack of common sense" are what most Protestants found hard to stomach at the time. Devlin is consistent, however, since her Socialist, even Marxist leanings put her at war not only with the British state, but also with the mainstream political parties of the Republic of Ireland.

Unlike *A Sense of Loss*, *Acceptable Levels* is not a documentary, but a fiction film about the process of making a documentary. It centres around a BBC film crew whose job it is to make a programme on the "children of the 'Troubles'", one of a series on children in the UK.[6] John Davies' film also serves as a dramatic critique of the practices of filmmakers such as Marcel Ophüls. The director Simon (Andy Rashleigh), personal assistant Jill (Frances Barber), researcher Sue (Kay Adshead) and two English technicians join up with the local sound-recordist Ricky (Derek Halligan) and cameraman Andy (Ian McElhinney) in Belfast. Sue has made contact with the McAteer family whose nine-year-old daughter Roisin (Tracey Lynch) they succeed in interviewing. As the interview proceeds inside her home, Roisin's friend is killed outside by a plastic bullet shot by the Army. In the final editing of the programme, this murder is referred to, but nearly all the visible emotional anger of the community against the presence of the British Army is removed.

We assume that this is a standard half-hour or one-hour programme with, as the director explains at one point, contributions from both sides. In fact, we do not see this other side at all: no Protestant children are shown interviewed. *Acceptable Levels* therefore concentrates on how a sequence, lasting less than a minute of screen time, is put together. That minute involves a study of the working-class Catholic Divis Flats area.

In bringing this story to television, Simon and Sue walk very thin ethical lines. Initially, Sue runs into resistance from Mrs McAteer (Sally McCaffrey) who doubts that these English people, parachuted in, will tell anything like the truth. Of course, by the time of broadcast, her instincts are proven correct. The researcher's perseverance and clear liberal sympathies for the Catholic working class enable the interview to go ahead. We watch unsurprised at the ruses that Simon, the director, must indulge in: he pays one small boy a pound to vacate a swing so that Roisin can be photographed on it; he asks quiet, emotionally-laden questions to the young girl; he perfunctorily visits the Army media relations officer after the shooting incident; he encourages his cameraman to take "cheap" shots of a burning car and an irate woman; he bows to the editorial authority of the producer who subtly steers the programme away from controversial material by his measured feedback; and he manipulates Sue to try to get a post-shooting interview with Roisin.

We enjoy the conflicts among the group of filmmakers. The two Irish crew are just out for a good time, clocking up as much overtime as possible together with prepaid meals in the Europa Hotel, and looking out for sexual adventure. All this is contrasted with the unemployed Mr McAteer, whose only occasional joys are a bet on the horses and the odd pint. The only ethical conflict that the crew feel is when the director goes back in to interview Roisin after the shooting. The crew discuss it among themselves, but decide to accede despite the exploitative nature of this tactic.

Spectators tend to associate with Sue who appears earnestly to wish to get the story of the Divis Flats area out into the public consciousness. She is only the researcher, however, and does not have the final cut. Her anger at the Army media relations officer, her conviction that the Army and police are biased, and her belief that Simon is gutting controversy from his film are all very well, but, at the end of the day, she needs another contract and is only too glad not to ruffle feathers with the all-powerful BBC producer of the series. The interesting fact is that, while the cutting out of the emotional material, most of it anti-British, is consciously done, it is also presented as quite natural. Anyone who has been involved in editing video will know of the need to create a "proper" consistency and rhythm for the piece, which often necessitates excising important material which is not aesthetically pleasing, however authentic. It is precisely this situation that allows the director Simon to instruct his obedient editor to take out the "offending" footage. It is the argument that certain kinds of footage belong in another, more politically aggressive film – one which, in the world of the BBC, would not be transmitted.

The Patriot Game is one such politically aggressive film. Whereas Marcel Ophüls was naïvely bemused that Provisional IRA supporters attended his film screenings to lobby viewers,[7] no one could be left in doubt after watching *The Patriot Game* as to why mainstream distributors in Britain did not wish to handle it.[8] The film is anti-British and pro-IRA in its approach, but at least there is a solid, albeit limited analysis of the Northern Ireland situation. Mac Caig works often with street-level images of British troops, which naturally conjure up the words "occupation" and "oppression".

In the film, Mac Caig develops the standard Sinn Féin/IRA thesis that the present "Troubles" are due to the unfinished decolonisation of Ireland. He also taps into the assumption that this "incomplete narrative" leads to an united Ireland, preferably one with secular Socialist leanings. Archive television footage of many of the benchmarks of the "struggle" – the Falls Road curfew, internment, "Bloody Sunday", and so on – are utilised to create the misleading overall impression that the majority in Northern Ireland seek the overthrow of the British. A low-key female voice-over narration adds *gravitas* and inevitability to this historical continuum. No Protestants appear in the programme to give their perspective, so this is very much a ghettoised film about Catholic ghettos.

The communal struggle is often successfully communicated visually by the filmmaker's good fortune. For example, in one republican club where a band is playing, an Army patrol enters, only to be treated to the singer's sarcastic "I drove my Saracen through your garden last night" to the tune of "I've got a brand new pair of roller-skates". He also seems to be right on the spot for various demonstrations. Completed in 1978, the major critique of the "Peace People" appears central to the republicans at this time: they were threatened, although it is denied, by the ability of the "Peace People" to bridge sectarian lines, and also to harness the general revulsion of women to the violence mostly perpetrated by men. It is trite but understandable that the republicans would belittle this movement, since it was an appeal to the humanitarian *present*, rather than to the republican *past*.

Working again for French Television ten years later, Arthur Mac Caig made *Irish Ways* (1989), effectively an update of his previous Irish film. In this hour-long piece, Mac Caig interviews Sinn Féin and IRA activists, recounts the hunger strikers story of the early 1980s, and follows up on a number of 1988 events – the shooting of the Gibraltar Three, the Milltown cemetery killings at the burial of these three, and one of the few extraditions of an IRA man to Northern Ireland from the Republic of Ireland. A nice sense of irony exists in listening to Gerry Doherty, Sinn Féin councillor in Derry, who now sits as an elected member in the Guildhall, a building he helped to bomb in the early 1970s. The twin-prong republican strategy of the ballot-box and the Armalite is therefore encapsulated in one individual's life.

Nevertheless, this is a very "lazy" film by Mac Caig. The cheap sensationalism of showing IRA commandos wandering around streets with guns held high is faintly ridiculous when, in fact, most IRA operations take place undercover. Curiously, the only serious conversation that the film unit has with a policeman is with one who has what sounds like a South African accent. The only interview in a Protestant loyalist area is with Gusty Spence, the UVF man who served eighteen years in jail for murder. His status as a former British Army man helps to imply that the IRA is fighting a militaristic loyalist group and not a civilian ideology. Behind all the surface republican slogans, one does, however, sense the conviction of these people and their unwillingness to be part of the British state. They see no contradiction in taking full advantage of the British social system while refusing to take responsibility for it. Hence ripping up the roads with pneumatic drills to stockpile stones for throwing at the British Army, or burning buses or milk lorries leaves this community with little burden of guilt.

While Mac Caig's films, and videos such as Frank Martin's *Behind the Mask* look at the problem from the inside of the republican community,[9] the work of David Fox's Faction Films tries to broaden the debate without jumping to easy conclusions. This approach is very clear in Fox's *Trouble the Calm* (1989), a meditation on the role which the Republic of Ireland has played while purportedly at peace and a non-combatant. It is generally recognised that the modern era hit Ireland in the late-1950s when foreign investment was encouraged. Now, in the 1980s of the film, Fox discovers a new spurt of business activity with multinationals. Irish ministers and government advertising promote the Republic as a haven for European and American businesses looking for low taxes and low labour costs.

As Fox points out, however, the spectre of the Civil War (1922-23) still hovers, whether in the diktat to teachers to explain to children that the period was a great tragedy, or in the emergency legislation still in force which allows harassment of the families of the 100 or so "political prisoners" in southern Irish jails. Fox's class analysis leans on the writings of Irish Socialist James Connolly, who would indeed not be surprised, although undoubtedly disappointed, that the "new" Ireland pays only lip-service to the notion of economic liberty. This business "calm" does not erase the after-effects of the Civil War which, after all, created the two mainstream political parties, Fianna Fáil and Fine Gael. In searching for this radical republican past, Fox does not have to look far: two women give Premier Charles Haughey a letter pleading not to sanction extradition of republicans to the North. Fox brings the memory of the spirit of the War of Independence period to the fore with extracts from Tom Cooper's *The Dawn* (1936), the classic romantic nationalist film produced independently in Ireland. Its concluding title, "The fight must go on", refers indirectly to Ulster. To Fox, the southern Irish have embraced global capitalism to help remedy an unemployment problem, and the past, with all its republican principles, has been reduced to the status of necessary ritual.

Ever-interested in media representation, Fox's *Irish News, British Stories* (1984) and *Picturing Derry* (1985) focus on the perceived struggle for the nationalist community to have its images accepted over those of the British media. In the former film, Fox utilises many clips from British television drama to illustrate that the predominant British conception of the "Troubles" is linked inextricably to some genetic compulsion to violence, a "curse" which cannot be lifted (Nairn's "myth of atavism"). He also takes to task a 1983 Granada Television *World in Action* programme which sought to denigrate Gerry Adams and Sinn Féin, while photographing Adams at a British Labour Party Conference fringe meeting. Fox makes the usual (incorrect) assumption that the British media reflect what northern Irish Protestants think. As he interviews no Protestants, he leaves himself in the dark. Instead, we have the invisible "expert" voice-over of Philip Schlesinger ruminating on the strategies of the British government in dealing with the "Troubles" and the IRA in particular.

Picturing Derry is less ambitious than other works described here, yet more stimulating in the sense that it confronts the very real problem of how photographers frame historical and political events. On the one hand, we listen to community activists involved in a young people's exhibition of their photographs which deliberately "frame out" the "Troubles", while, on the other hand, we are presented with the Fleet Street and international freelance photographic core who take pictures for profit, and therefore seek to capture an image that will tell an immediate story, however blunt and unaesthetic. Apart from these photographers, there is the prosaic police photographer who must take close-ups of shell casings after a shooting incident, as well as aerial or landscape photographs, to help in any investigation; the local amateur photographers who happened to record the street disturbances of the 1969-72 period; and the local artists who use photographs of the landscape with text to emphasise that Derry is constantly under some kind of surveillance. To Derry people's eyes, the countryside may be beautiful but can contain instruments of violence, unseen at first glance.

As a whole, Ophüls, Davies, Mac Caig, Fox and others attack the British position in Northern Ireland, but commit sins of omission time and time again. The Protestant voice is either deliberately made absent or reduced to a minor role, or collapsed simply into the views of the mandarins at the British Northern Ireland Office. It is not a question of "balance" that I am arguing for here, but rather for an element of realism and self-criticism while profiling the nationalist position. The unionist case is not put and, ironically, cannot be trusted to be put by Protestants themselves, as the next chapter illustrates.

Notes

[1]   John Naughton, "The good spies come back", *The Listener* 113: 2891 (10 January 1985): 33-34.

[2]   Jonathan Bardon, *A History of Ulster* (Belfast: The Blackstaff Press, 1992): 679.

[3]   "Politics and Autobiography: An Interview with Marcel Ophuls by Daniel Yergin", *Sight and Sound* 43: 1 (winter 1973/74): 20.

[4]   Ibid: 21.

[5]   John McKeague was murdered by the INLA in January 1982.

[6]   Frontroom Productions of London coordinated *Acceptable Levels* with Belfast Film Workshop. This was one of the films made under the ACTT/BFI/Channel 4 Film Workshop franchises. Local talent Alastair Herron and Kate McManus were assistant directors and credited with helping on the script.

[7]   "Politics and Autobiography": 22.

[8]   The British première took place at the Royal Court Theatre in June 1979, sponsored by the United Troops Out Movement and The Other Cinema. A publicity leaflet at the time indicated: "The Other Cinema is a non-commercial organisation, for the distribution of independent films to film societies, independent cinemas, trade-union and community groups up and down the country...The library of films is particularly strong in Latin-American cinema, left wing documentaries and films for the women's movement".

[9]   *Behind the Mask* profiles Brendan Hughes and Gerry Adams among other IRA/Sinn Féin members. Hughes relates a remarkable story of his escape from prison. A collaborative work by the "'68 Committee", written and narrated by Bernadette McAliskey (née Devlin), is *Off Our Knees* (1988), which covers the "twenty-year history of mass struggle in the north of Ireland". Lin Solomon and Cahal McLaughlin's *Pack Up the Troubles* (1991), broadcast on British television, argues for the withdrawal of British troops from Northern Ireland.

11

"We'll fight and no surrender": Protestant visions

It's important to make a film about your own country and find out where you stand in relation to all this. (John T Davis)[1]

The vast majority of Irish films and videos made on the Northern Ireland "Troubles" have been conceived and executed by Roman Catholics. Very few Protestants have been either sufficiently successful or interested to delve into this well of poisoned water. However, Protestants have been more present in the BBC and UTV, providing news coverage, and many would-be filmmakers and videographers did become part of the 1970s and 1980s "brain drain" from the province. Furthermore, it may be generally accepted that a community which wishes the status quo to remain has the appearance of less to say, and certainly less to be motivated by than the radical republican tradition. A community under siege by the IRA on one hand and by British reluctance on the other will see any change as a destabilising ploy in the precarious short term. What I am suggesting is that the concentrated depictions of Protestantism emerge from writers and directors who earnestly want change. I might go further to argue that film production is only really worth doing if change is the motivating factor. This ideological framework explains the video documentaries of Desmond Bell and John T Davis whose work I discuss below. Firstly, however, I want to consider a narrative feature film made by a Roman Catholic director, Thaddeus O'Sullivan, from a Protestant's script (Daniel Mornin).

O'Sullivan's *Nothing Personal* interrogates the "cease fire" period of 1975, when for a few weeks in Belfast there was a modicum of peace. This cannot be detected from the film, which reeks of crude violence. At the film's screening at the Vancouver International Film Festival in 1995, Ian Hart, who plays the psychopath Protestant gunman Ginger, explained that his character was based on the so-called "Shankill butchers", one of whom, he argued, was Britain's largest serial killer, who hid under the guise of the "Troubles".[2]

In the film, Kenny (James Frain) and Ginger are the "hard men" of the Protestant paramilitaries. They are armed defenders of their own community and run a drinking club for the leading loyalist godfather Leonard Wilson (Michael Gambon). Both leaders of the Catholic and Protestant paramilitaries appear to want to give peace a chance, and they meet to clear up logistical matters, such as punishment of petty criminals, similar to what we saw at the beginning of *In the Name of the Father*. An early shooting shows mad Ginger kill or maim someone, and then mutilate him with a knife. For most of the film, Ginger appears to be in a frenzy, constantly seeking to wreak havoc and violence. It is Kenny's job to settle him down, and then finally to kill him in case he disrupts the cease fire.

The results of the violence have divided families: Kenny has a wife and two children, but he is separated from them, presumably because of his murderous activities, although this is not explained. On the other side of the divide, there is Liam (John Lynch), a Catholic and single father with two children. The narrative really gets going when Liam, out protecting his community, ends up on the wrong side of the barricades and is beaten up. He is taken in by Kenny's wife Ann (Maria Doyle-Kennedy) who patches him up, and both take the opportunity to share their feelings concerning marriage, children and relationships. Liam, however, is picked up by Kenny and Ginger, roughed up, and subjected to Ginger's Russian roulette gun games. Depositing Liam near his home, Ginger prepares to kill him, but Kenny intercedes and shoots Ginger in the leg. As they scramble to safety, a young Catholic boy takes out a gun and attempts to shoot Kenny. Liam's daughter (Jennifer Courtney) tries to stop him, and is killed by accident in the scuffle. Seemingly disgusted by his actions, Kenny murders Ginger, knowing that the British Army, who have been directed to his location by Wilson, will kill him.

Four levels of discourse are at work in this film: (1) the interactions of the IRA and UDA/UVF leaderships; (2) the discussions among the foot-soldiers of the Protestant paramilitaries; (3) the views of the non-combatants Liam and Kenny's wife Ann; and (4) the children of the "Troubles". Of these, perhaps of most importance are the actions and suffering of the children, both Protestant and Catholic. In the loyalist drinking den, Tommy, a teenager (Ruaidhri Conroy), drinks and dreams of courting a blond girl dancing on the floor. Eventually, he goes over to dance with her, beating up a rowdy lout into the bargain. This earnest behaviour is rewarded by Kenny, who gives him a gun and a brief to search people at the door of the club. Feeling like a "real man" with a gun in his pocket and having used his "fists" gallantly for his girl, he plucks up enough courage to kiss her. Interestingly, she puts the gun down on the road as he attempts to kiss her, but he picks it up again. Gunplay is obviously a substitute in some measure for repressed sexuality. Carried along by the promotion to Kenny and Ginger's side, the boy is party to Liam's abduction and ill-treatment (even forced by Ginger to press the gun against Liam's head in the

Russian roulette sequence). These events traumatise the boy who clearly is having second thoughts about being a "hard man". The reason for Ginger's extreme violence is never fully explored. By implication, he represents the vicious side of loyalism which, the film seems to suggest, is an ideology most likely to support ethnic cleansing.

On the Catholic side, Liam's daughter has a suitor. This young boy tries to help her look for her father. He even goes as far as to steal a gun from one of the IRA men's coats. It is his desire to shoot Kenny at the end that precipitates the young girl's death in the ensuing struggle. Children and youth in general suffer at the barricades, where Kenny kills a Catholic boy who has been engulfed in flames.

Throughout the film, various (admittedly rather stilted) conversations among the Protestant paramilitaries try to articulate what their overall purpose is: killing the "enemy"; defending and patrolling their own neighbourhoods, and fighting for their "country". But this is as far as such "intellectualising" goes. The film does little to displace the moral vacuum of these characters. Very strangely, the film begins with an IRA bombing of a pub. The attempt to kill members of the RUC fails, as we see them leave the pub just as young female and male civilians enter, who are then killed or maimed. In the aftermath of the bombing, as the security forces and the rescue services pick their way through the rubble, we see Liam making his way through the devastation in a way intended to emphasise his sympathy for the victims. The reason why this is curious is because the bombing has gone off in a Protestant area, and here is Liam, a Catholic, blithely walking around at a time when sectarian feelings would be very high. It would make more local sense to have Kenny walking around the bomb site, as a visual way of making sense of the Protestant paramilitaries' motivations: that of a community which feels itself under siege and subject to random attacks by the IRA. The bombing campaign of the 1970s was the IRA's "total war" against the Northern Ireland state and (although they officially denied it) against the Protestant loyalist community.

One area of the film that is unfortunately not developed is the relationship between Liam and Kenny. A reference is made to Liam's father having taken Kenny's family to the hills for safety during the Second World War's German bombing raids on Belfast. This reference, added to their previous and presumably pre-1968-69 fights, gives them a connection which the present "war" seems to have almost completely eradicated. Hints at a more complicated relationship between Protestant and Catholic are no more than that in this film, which tends to return to naked violence for its "resolution" of conflict. Of course, Kenny's "nothing personal" comment to Liam as he is tortured and nearly killed is far less than the truth, although it is true in the sense of an ideological war between Irish and British nationalism. O'Sullivan knew that the film would cause controversy, since it shows the loyalists as aggressors and the nationalists as victims: "I guess it was a political decision [to show the loyalist guerrillas] but that was what the book was about, and it was written by a Protestant".[3] One could have wished for at least some self-criticism on O'Sullivan's part. That critical pose is plentiful in the work of John T Davis and Desmond Bell.

Davis' films may be regarded as documentaries, although he is not sure himself whether they should be so categorised: "I don't know what my films are. I don't think of them as documentaries and they're not fiction, but there's drama in them of some description even though they're not acted."[4] By his own admission, Davis is a lapsed Protestant, but he has retained an ethnographical interest in Northern Ireland's local and religious inhabitants. An independent filmmaker of some repute, Davis has made many startling American-themed films, such as *Hobo* (1991) and *Route 66* (1985), which succeed partly because they capitalise on the fascination Europeans have for the wide expanses of North America. His Irish films are more directly focused. *Shell Shock Rock* (1978) and the "doublet", *Dust on the Bible* (1989) and *Power in the Blood* (1989), comprise an unusual body of northern Irish work. The first film seemed to have emerged out of sheer serendipity. In the mid-1970s, at the height of the bombings and shootings, punk arrived in Northern Ireland as a refreshing and subversive counterblast to the prevailing gloom. (It did, however, channel and reinforce at some concerts the legitimacy of latent and not so latent violence.) Shaky, handheld camerawork, rapid editing and pulsating music are matched to loose and fast interviews with – and performance footage of – bands such as Stiff Little Fingers, Protex, The Undertones, The Outcasts and Rhesus Negative. It is easy to see the liberatory power of such songs as Stiff Little Fingers' "Alternative Ulster" and "Wasted Life", even to the great majority of youth who did not want to adopt the "revolutionary" punk attire. Together with David Bowie's apocalyptic song narratives at that time, the punk explosion promised a possible way of bridging various divides that had widened in the youth community. Davis uses extracts from Protex's "Strange Obsession", The Outcasts' "You're a Disease" and "Teenage Rebel", The Undertones' "Here Comes the Summer" and "Teenage Kicks", and The Parasites' "Society" to herald the punk invasion, but amidst all these "incursions" Davis inserts snippets of more conventional music: the sounds of a Salvation Army band over the image of the city of Belfast, the country style of Hank Williams' "I'll Be a Bachelor Till I Die", the home-grown ironic balladeer James Young singing "The Glentoran Supporter", and the more conventional pop of The Cascades' "Rhythm of the Rain".

To Davis, the fact that punk was happening at all in Northern Ireland was a blessing, a suggestion that cultural forces can change political and social feelings, if not action. Rather in the fashion of the 1960s Beatles films, Davis employs or stage-manages "streeter" interviews with ordinary people about the nature of punk. The inconclusive answers, although typical of this methodological approach, suggest that the adult population were indeed unmoved by the "beat" of their children. Of course, they may have been right, as the punk explosion subsided in the 1980s and more tribal bands reasserted themselves. Later in this chapter, this reassertion will be confirmed by Desmond Bell's work.

Punk was a form of secularised religion for young people for a short time. More commonly, the casual tourist to Northern Ireland's cities and towns will see a wide assortment of evangelical preachers parading the streets and lambasting walkers-by with warnings of sin and the need for redemption, outward signs of a Protestant fundamentalist culture. Davis captures aspects of this religious phenomenon in *Dust on the Bible* and *Power in the Blood*. The former opens with a shot of a bible with its pages flicking back, a voice-over of a bible reading, the sound of an electric guitar, and disparate voices relating that they have been "saved". One would expect from this beginning that a conventional, although perhaps overly subjective view of religion is to be presented. Yet, this proves not to be the case.

Thrusting the audience into the Cornmarket in Belfast at Christmas time, Davis indulges in a rather long-winded visual scrutiny of one evangelical preacher – he utilises many lugubrious close-ups of the preacher's face and eyes – who goes on at length about professors and teachers with their false "pet theories". Davis is obviously fascinated by the oratorical Protestant tradition, and makes a link between the rigidity of religious fundamentalism and Ulster Unionism – he contrasts the "BELFAST SAYS NO" political sign on the City Hall to "ULSTER'S NEED FOR JESUS" signs nearby. Amidst this "street analysis", we see shots of the Salvation Army, ambulances racing across the city, sirens blaring, soldiers running, Saracens moving quickly, and a robot defusing a suspected bomb before Davis returns to a biblical voice-over on top of a peaceful snowy night landscape. It seems that during the day the world is all akimbo and the end of the world may well be nigh, but night and quiet do return.

After the curious sea baptisms we witness, the filmmaker attempts to provide a basic narrative structure of a man (Martin Donnelly) driving in his car to various evangelical meetings. Here, as elsewhere, an apocalyptic energy is suggested by Davis' camerawork. He loves blazing red sunsets, and capitalises on this image, and the memory of it, by having Damian Gorman read extracts from Revelations. In a sense, Davis' film is an exploration of issues dealt with tangentially in Pat O'Connor's *Cal*, whose hero is surrounded by Protestant religious fundamentalist signs. In *Dust on the Bible*, even the rocks at the seaside are painted with religious warnings – "Prepare to Meet Thy God". And the beating of small drums which the evangelists use to gain attention leads visually to the more politically charged beating of the Lambeg drum.

The blood-red sunsets occur again in *Power in the Blood,* where Davis focuses on country and western singer Vernon Oxford, who gave up the high life in Nashville to "follow the Lord" and sing for him. (There is an element of this in Jordan's *Angel,* when Danny listens to a Salvation Army Band-member who tells him that he once played all the major halls, but now plays "for the Lord".) The film traces the journey around Northern Ireland by the Tennessee evangelist. Davis begins the film in the United States, as Oxford telephones Northern Ireland in preparation for his "mission" to Ulster. The filmmaker cleverly and evocatively ties together images of telegraph poles and small towns in the US Bible Belt with similar images in Northern Ireland, where the fundamentalist streak is also strong. Officially, Oxford's visit is occasioned by his communication with Wilfie Cummings, a Long Kesh/Maze prisoner who has apparently seen the error of his ways and seeks the Lord (Cummings has also made the preacher a music box). Oxford is interviewed by Davis, and is recorded playing and speaking in bars and halls in the Protestant community. The film ends humorously at the prison where Vernon Oxford sings "Redneck" to the Prison Officers' Country Music Society. Notably, Oxford visits Darkley, the scene of a terrible shooting where fundamentalist worshippers were gunned down inside their small church by the INLA. As Davis has remarked in an interview, while one may not agree with the religious position of Oxford and his northern Irish "sisters and brothers", they completely believe in what they are doing, and that has to be respected, whether at mission halls on the Shankill Road in Belfast or in small rural village churches.[5]

Desmond Bell is also an ethnographer. Whereas Davis dwells on the adult and religious formations in the Protestant community, Bell is interested in Protestant youth culture. Since the mid-1980s, Bell, a sociologist by training, has been concerned with redeeming Protestant history in Ireland. He rightly believes – and his academic research has supported him – that young working-class Protestant males have had little opportunity to question their culture of unionism and their subculture of marching band loyalism.[6] In at least three video productions – *We'll Fight and No Surrender: Ulster Loyalism and the Protestant Sense of History, Redeeming History: Protestant Nationalism in Ireland* (1990) and *Facing the Future* (1991) – Bell explores and questions the tribalism evident in many of the current Protestant demonstrations, with his home city of Derry as his focus.

Bell argues that Protestant marching bands have emerged rapidly since direct rule was enforced in 1972, because of the increasing residential segregation of the two communities, the drop in attendance at churches, and the withering of the UUP and the

Orange Order control over the working-class community. The increasing problem of unemployment has left thousands of Protestant youths with few other avenues than such bands for entertainment and teenage social bonding.[7] Significantly, Bell links the rise of the marching bands to an effort by the Protestant working class – at a time of political and economic crisis, and under the duress of often thinking that their culture is somehow inferior to that of the republican tradition – to reassert a form of Ulster identity. Bell is a Protestant Socialist who does not believe in unionism, since he sees it as intrinsically sectarian and a form of imperialism (which needs to be contested), and we suspect that he would prefer to see Northern Ireland become part of a united Ireland.[8] This view is never starkly imposed, but implied in his choice of subjects and the way in which he analyses the Protestant subculture of militant loyalism.

We'll Fight and No Surrender casts the spotlight on the working-class loyalist culture of Derry. The danger in taking Derry as the centre of any research project or video is of falling into general assumptions about unionism, Protestantism and loyalism that are not necessarily true in other parts of the province. The major difference between the Protestant community in Derry and Belfast, for example, is one of demographics. Whereas some 60% of Belfast is Protestant, only 30% of Derry is. This numerical question makes the Protestants in Derry more insecure, and is partly responsible for their apparent extreme militancy. The border with the Republic of Ireland is almost an actual stone's throw away from Derry, whereas living in Belfast you would have to traverse many miles to reach the other Ireland.

As I refer rather critically to *We'll Fight and No Surrender* in chapter 1, I will attempt here to redress the balance by pointing out a few of its major contributions to the overall debate. Perhaps the most beneficial aspect of Bell's video is his analysis of the myths surrounding the siege and Relief of Derry in 1688-89. From December to August the citizens of the walled city held out against the army of James II, which was mostly Catholic, but which also contained numerous mercenaries from Scotland and elsewhere. The English commandant of the city, Robert Lundy, desired not to defy the King's authority, even if that King was Catholic and hated in England. The closing of the city's gates by the Apprentice Boys, the local youth of the city (beautifully captured in the shot of the stained-glass window depiction from the city's Guildhall) provides Bell with the necessary link to his study of contemporary loyalist youth. To Bell, the actions of the untutored but loyal young, both rash and brave, explain in part the Protestant love of stubborn resistance – "ULSTER SAYS NO" and so on. The videographer makes a strong argument that it is the defiance of the siege, rather than the relief by the English fleet, which is the dominant myth. One may see this psychological imprimatur in another way, however.

Certainly, the siege is important, and the ritual burning of Lundy (shown in the film) points to the Protestant inability to rely upon the British to "do the right thing". Yet, the relief is an important myth, too, since it justifies the act of sacrifice in the minds of the Ulster Protestants. The relief tells him or her that if one is stubborn in standing for certain principles, fickle Albion will come round to the "proper" way of thinking and action in due course. In this respect, the Relief of Derry justifies all future acts of Protestant resistance whether against the 19th-century penal laws or against the 20th-century attempt to achieve a united Ireland.

One of Bell's utopian ventures is to suggest, by interviewing the chief of the Relief of Derry project, that an inclusive history and celebration of the siege and relief can be achieved. To this organiser, "the message is that the siege is over". At a time when the IRA was killing members of the mostly Protestant security forces, this is wishful thinking of the highest order, however laudable its aims. Yet, Bell hits on a key point: how are Protestants and Catholics going to share the history of the past? The simple answer is to say that they will not; that two versions will always sit side-by-side to mirror the residential segregation now evident in the city – the Catholics on the western side, the Protestants on the eastern side, and the British troops ironically patrolling the city walls looking down on both communities. Bell's placement of the Catholic "Sanctus" over the images of burning bonfires may indeed remind us, as Mary Holland observes, of the fact that the Pope blessed William's *coup d'état*, but to most Protestant ears it serves only to take away from the belief structure of those who are celebrating the Relief of Derry.[9]

In *Redeeming History: Protestant Nationalism in Ireland*, Bell turns his attention to the well-educated Protestant youth, those taking 'A' levels and heading for university. He follows a group of sixth formers as they discover the radical history of the United Irishmen and the efforts of Bishop Harvey of Derry, later Lord Bristol, in the 18th century to achieve Catholic emancipation. One has the awkward feeling of Bell as the arch manipulator of staged conversations. Many times we see the group of young Protestant men and women arguing over the constitutional future of Northern Ireland, giving the clear impression that women are more flexible towards an eventual united Ireland than men are.

The focus on the United Irishmen resembles that of the work of Northern Visions discussed in chapter 8. Yet here, too, the video is blind to the fact that unionism was always a stronger force among Protestants as a group than the republican tradition. As historian Roy Foster points out, "Antrim and Down, with very few Catholics and a strong New Light Presbyterian tradition, were radical; the rest of Ulster was not".[10] To his credit, Bell does point out that the utopian hopes of Bishop Harvey underestimated the power of Establishment interests, and the awareness of the new mercantile and bourgeois Presbyterian class that winning rights for themselves would have little meaning if they were to share them with Catholics. In other words, it is doubtful whether Bell's overall historical project with these young people can do much more than place selective material on the table for discussion. In a strange way, "discovering" that the majority of Protestants rejected republicanism in the 18th century only reinforces the "resistance" mentality which Bell wishes to undermine. Nevertheless, one of the video's strengths is the continual confrontation with the "other". The trip to Dublin and the attendance at a Roman Catholic Church Mass (for most of these simultaneously curious and suspicious Protestant teenagers, for the first time) add a wonderful surreal and absurd tone to the production. The trip south successfully captures the ghettoised world and associated thinking of present-day Ulster youth.

Some of these same teenagers are "rediscovered" two years later in *Facing the Future*. In this video, Bell has an implicit thesis: that those who leave Northern Ireland often question their inheritance more quickly than those who stay, which may go a long way to explaining why over half of Protestant school-leavers move away from the province for post-secondary education. Less than a third of those who do leave will return. Naturally, as these individuals are interviewed, they seem at times bewildered in their new habitat where they are constantly referred to as Irish, while back in Ireland they are used to seeing themselves as British. Bell finds grist for his mill, with one woman studying at a London polytechnic who discovers how small the religious conflict in Ireland is compared to the other religious conflicts around the world. Nevertheless, Bell finds one teenager who remained in the North whose views have changed. In the former film, this teenager appeared to be the most dogmatically loyalist, but in this video he even apologises for his previous behaviour! Bell has "redeemed" an apparently immovable loyalist, and rescued him from the "false consciousness" of loyalism. This political videographer can rest his case.

Notes

[1]   John T Davis in John O'Regan (ed), *John T Davis* (Dublin: Gandon Editions, 1993): 17.

[2]   See Martin Dillon, *The Shankill Butchers: A Case Study of Mass Murder* (London; Sydney; Auckland; Johannesburg: Hutchinson, 1989), which details the murderous escapades of Lenny Murphy. In 1998, Welsh director Marc Evans released *Resurrection Man*, adapted from the novel by Eoin MacNamee, which also highlights the "Shankill butchers".

[3]   Quoted by Claudia Parsons for Reuters, reporting from the Venice Film Festival and published on the Internet, 4 September 1995. The novel by Daniel Mornin is *All Our Fault* (London: Hutchinson, 1991). O'Sullivan has seemingly been long-interested in the Protestant community. His

previous feature film was *December Bride* (1990), another adaptation of a novel written by an Ulster Protestant, Sam Hanna Bell, which concerned a small rural Protestant community in the North. Even O'Sullivan's short, *The Woman Who Married Clark Gable* (1985), casts Bob Hoskins as a Protestant man married to a Catholic woman (Brenda Fricker). The incredibleness of *Nothing Personal's* story-line is well-observed by Shane Barry when the film was provisionally entitled "Fanatic Heart". See his review in *Film Ireland* 48 (August/September 1995): 30.

4   O'Regan (ed): 25. This short monograph contains an interview and a filmography.

5   Other useful material on Davis and his work include the following: Dermot Lavery, "Power in the Lens", *Film Ireland* 32 (November/ December 1992): 18-21; Ted Sheehy, "Northern Skyline", *Film Base News* 12 (April/May 1989): 16; and Kevin Smith, "Real documentaries: why the outlaw shot the preacher", *The Irish Times* 21 February 1989: 10.

6   Bell's fieldwork is written up in his book, *Acts of Union: Youth Culture and Sectarianism in Northern Ireland* (London: Macmillan, 1990). An incisive work on the Protestant paramilitaries and their views in the early 1970s is Sarah Nelson, *Ulster's Uncertain Defenders: Protestant Political, Paramilitary and Community Groups and the Northern Ireland Conflict* (Belfast: Appletree Press, 1984).

7   Apart from Bell's book, a succinct article which clarifies the same issues is his "Marching for Identity", *The Irish Times* 14 August 1985: 11.

8   See Desmond Bell's revealing letter in *Film Ireland* 39 (February/ March 1994): 36-37. Bell responds to a highly critical review of Joe Comerford's *High Boot Benny* and a report on the Imagining Ireland Conference which singled out criticism of his work by myself. Another Protestant Socialist is Geoffrey Bell who, with Chris Reeves, Lin Solomon and John Underhay, made *The Cause of Ireland* (1983), a documentary exploring links between James Connolly's ideas and Irish republicanism. They also explore the fragmentation in the Protestant unionist community. See "'Those Other Voices': An Interview with Platform Films by Sylvia Harvey", *Screen* 25: 6 (November-December 1984): 31-48.

9   Mary Holland, "Examining Roots of Ulster loyalism", *The Irish Times* 17 May 1989: 10; see also Jennifer Todd, "A Loyalist Video", *The Irish Review* 6 (spring 1989): 123-124.

10   R F Foster, *Modern Ireland 1600-1972* (Harmondsworth: Penguin Books, 1989): 266.

12
Epilogue: Where do we go from here?

It's not an American story, it's an Irish one. (Frankie McGuire in *The Devil's Own* [1997])

As this book has amply shown, the "Troubles" have provided stimulus for cultural production as much as for weapon sales and rapid increases in security-related employment.[1] The main thesis of this book – that the vast majority of films, television dramas and videos on the conflict are predicated upon either a "hard" or "soft" nationalist/republican stance – suggests that the cultural position of Irish nationalism is secure, while that of Ulster Unionism and the Protestant community is weak, incoherent or non-existent. But the suggestion does not necessarily follow the thesis in real terms.

Behind this state of affairs is the romantic appeal to the "unfinished narrative" of Irish unity.[2] This imagining is much more direct and straightforward (aided by the anti-imperialist myth) than agreeing to a more pluralist and revisionist history of the country favoured by the likes of Roy Foster, and certainly clearer than the reliance on an ambivalent British government, which is the lot of the Ulster Unionists and the Protestant community. British and Irish filmmakers and videographers have had difficulty in detaching themselves from creating stereotypical representations, and one suspects that this maximalist tendency tells us more about these cultural workers' distaste for the British involvement in Northern Ireland than about any real attempt on their part to suggest a realistic way forward. It also tells us about their unwillingness to face the fact that no basis for Irish unity (by consent) currently exists.

Edward Said has argued that the ability to produce narratives and to ensure other, less palatable or politically incorrect narratives from forming is important to imperialism, but I daresay that he would agree that they are as equally important to anti-imperialist movements which privilege nativism. As Said remarks in *Culture and Imperialism*: "To leave the historical world for the metaphysics of essences like negritude, Irishness, Islam or Catholicism is to abandon history for essentialisations that have the power to turn human beings against each other; often this abandonment of the secular world has led to...unthinking acceptance of stereotypes, myths, animosities, and traditions encouraged by imperialism".[3]

A better description of the ideology behind the IRA and the loyalist paramilitaries could not be found. It is tempting to go further and say that the visual representations of the "Troubles" have so underplayed the Protestant community that a major cultural dislocation has occurred: instead of cultural products, hybrid or impure as Said would say, allied to inventive possibilities of transformation and transcendence, the reverse is the case. These visual representations have, in fact, assisted in the building of Catholic nationalist and republican self-esteem at the expense of the link to actual historical and present realities.

While Said accurately vilifies the continuing acts of imperialism in the world today (the United States' relationship to Iran and Iraq, in particular), he is sufficiently astute to criticise the nativist reaction of previously dominated peoples. His point is that for us to get beyond these debilitating binary oppositions, we have to accept the history of colonialism, and that the coloniser and colonised must communicate with each other in this postcolonial era; the two are interdependent. This communication demands sensitivity from the former coloniser and realism from the former colonised. Ethnic nationalists will find this apologia unacceptable, of course, but Said's story of the Arab Christian Protestants who refuse to return (to the bewilderment and embarrassment of both Western Christianity and Eastern Orthodoxy) to their unconverted "original form" has a striking resemblance to the Ulster Protestants who appear habitually to disappoint both the British government and Irish nationalists with their claims of Britishness. In both cases, the Arab and Ulster Protestants' experiences are real and rooted, and finally must be respected.

The question beckons: where do we go from here? Some may argue that it is too late to ask such a question, since the animosities and traditions encouraged by imperialism have prevented – and will prevent – any reasonable solution. After all, the moderate nationalist SDLP position – that it will no longer consider an internal settlement of power-sharing within Northern Ireland – only goes to show that distrust and anti-imperialist rhetoric travel far, deep and wide. Others may argue that the visual onslaught of nationalist and republican images in the works I have been discussing is an inextricable part of a British "psychological withdrawal" from Northern Ireland.[4]

I tend to think that this onslaught is rather more due to the fact that artists who work with images love profiling minorities, particularly ones bearing arms. Such profiling is sensational and dramatic, and can always have a tragic structure, usually with a violent conclusion. These traits explain many narrative films. Harder to account for is the spate of documentaries implicitly favouring Irish nationalism, many of which emerge from British television stations. I believe this trend has mainly to do with a crisis of confidence in Great Britain itself, for it will have to face stronger nationalist movements in Scotland, if not Wales, in the years ahead. The discussions over devolution which rose to prominence in the early 1970s have never really gone away. If anything, Northern Ireland's apparent antiquarian backwoodsman labelling has turned out in the 1990s to be prescient: what is the relationship between our identity and the land in which we live? Northern Ireland certainly remains one very unfinished television and film narrative. Let us hope that future filmmakers and videographers will not so easily think that they can finish it by recourse to nativism.[5]

Notes

[1] I do not want to give the impression that all Irish film is obsessed with northern issues. Many writers have rightly complained that the filmmakers of the 1990s, particularly those working in the short fiction and documentary categories, have yet to be given their due. These filmmakers are a sign of a vibrant postnationalist Ireland, and they deserve a separate study. An excellent source of the debates over these films is the journal *Film Ireland*.

[2] Gerry Smyth provides an excellent digest of the main "critical narratives" on the "Troubles" from the various shades of nationalism. See his "The Past, the Post, and the Utterly Changed: Intellectual Responsibility and Irish Cultural Criticism", *Irish Studies Review* 10 (spring 1995): 25-29.

[3] Edward W Said, *Culture & Imperialism* (New York: Vintage, 1994): 228-229.

[4] See Jennifer Cornell's "Different Countries, Different Worlds: the Representation of Northern Ireland in Stewart Parker's *Lost Belongings*", in James MacKillop (ed), *Envisioning Ireland: Essays in Irish Cinema* (Syracuse: Syracuse University Press, forthcoming).

[5] We now have the post-cease fire films – Neil Jordan's *Michael Collins*, Mary McGuckian's *This Is the Sea* (1996) and Jim Sheridan's *The Boxer* – written and made at a time of continual ups and downs in the euphemistically named "peace process". It remains to be seen whether the change in nomenclature from "Troubles" to "Peace Process" will have tangible results. If the film and video representations discussed in this book are a marker, the future of Northern Ireland is bleak.

Film and video resources

Below are listed addresses to which enquiries can be made regarding the works discussed in this book. As the distribution and availability of films and videos may change rapidly, the interested reader may wish to contact the Information officer, Film Institute of Ireland, 6 Eustace Street, Dublin 2. *Email* filmbase@iol.ie *Website* http://www.iftn.ie/filmeire.html

(a) Television drama and documentary programmes rarely make it to accessible video. However, one can contact and view some programmes at the following institutions: Film Institute of Ireland Archive, 6 Eustace Street, Dublin 2; Northern Ireland Film Council, 21 Ormeau Avenue, Belfast BT2 8HD; Northern Ireland Political Collection, Linen Hall Library, 17 Donegal Square North, Belfast BT1 5GD; Film and Sound Resource Unit, University of Ulster at Coleraine, Cromore Road, Coleraine, BT52 1SA; Irish Studies Centre, University of North London, Faculty of Humanities and Teacher Education, 166-220 Holloway Road, London N7 8DB.

(b) The following films are available from video stores to hire or purchase: *Angel* (aka *Danny Boy*), *The Boxer*, *Cal*, *The Crying Game*, *The Devil's Own*, *Four Days in July*, *Harry's Game* (aka *Belfast Assassin*), *Hidden Agenda*, *Hush-A-Bye Baby*, *In the Name of the Father*, *The Long Good Friday*, *No Surrender*, *Nothing Personal*, *Odd Man Out*, *Patriot Games*, *A Prayer for the Dying*, *A Quiet Day in Belfast*, *The Railway Station Man*, *A Sense of Loss*, *Some Mother's Son*.

(c) For other films and videos, please contact: *Mother Ireland*: (UK) Anne Crilly, c/o 19 Magazine Street, Derry, Co Derry BT48 6HH; (North America) Celtic Video Inc., 141 E 33rd Street, New York NY 10016; Celtic Video also distribute *Pack Up the Troubles*, *Off Our Knees* and *Behind the Mask*; *The Patriot Game* and *Irish Ways*: First Run Icarus Films, 153 Waverley Place. Sixth Floor, New York, NY 10014; *Maeve* and *Ascendancy*: British Film Institute, 21 Stephen Street, London W1P 1PL; *Irish News, British Stories, Picturing*

Derry and *Trouble the Calm*: Faction Films, 28-29 Great Sutton Street, London EC1 ODU; *Acceptable Levels*: Jane Balfour Films, Burghley House, 35 Fortress Road, London NW5 1AD; *Dragon's Teeth*: De Facto Films, 30 Chamberlain Street, Derry, Co Derry BT48 6LR; *We'll Fight and No Surrender, Redeeming History* and *Facing the Future*: Glass Machine North, 14 Seaview Drive North, Portstewart, Co Derry; enquiries about *Shell Shock Rock, Dust on the Bible*, and *Power in the Blood*: Holywood Films, Ben-Edar, 14 Seapark Road, Holywood, Co Down, BT18 OLH; *Under the Health Surface, Our Words Jump to Life, Moving Myths, Schizophrenic City, Unfinished Business, Between Ourselves: Songs, Satire and Some Sense*: Northern Visions, 4 Donegal Street Place, Belfast, Co Antrim, BT1 2FN; *The Kickhams*: Hot Shot Films, 4-8 Donegal Street Place, Lower Donegal Street, Belfast BT1 2FN; *The Last Colony* and *No Simple Choice*: Straight Forward Productions, Crescent Studios, 18 High Street, Holywood, Co Down BT18 9AD; *The Visit*: Paul Donovan, Roisin Rua Films, c/o Film Base, Film Institute of Ireland, 6 Eustace Street, Dublin 2; *Borderland*: Northern School of Film and Television, 2-8 Merrion Way, Leeds LS2 8BT; *After '68* and *81*: Stephen Burke, Mammoth Films, c/o Film Base, Film Institute of Ireland, 6 Eustace Street, Dublin 2.

Selected list of films, television dramas and videos on Northern Ireland

The following list covers those works mentioned or discussed in the text and notes, together with the director's name. For television drama, I have also included the writer's name. For more credit information, see Matthew Stevens, *Directory of Irish and Irish-Related Films* (Trowbridge: Flicks Books, 1989), and Kevin Rockett (ed), *The Irish Filmography: Fiction Films 1896-1996* (Dublin: Red Mountain Media, 1996). For accessibility from 1989 onwards, the best resource is *Film Base News*, renamed later as *Film Ireland* (1992-), published from the Irish Film Centre.

Feature-length narrative films

Acceptable Levels (1984) John Davies
Angel [USA title: *Danny Boy*] (1982) Neil Jordan
Ascendancy (1982) Edward Bennett
Blarney (1938) Harry O'Donovan
Bossanova Blues (1991) Kieron Walsh
The Boxer (1997) Jim Sheridan
Boy Soldier (1986) Karl Francis
Branwen (1995) Ceri Sherlock
Cal (1984) Pat O'Connor
Children in the Crossfire (1985) George Schaefer
The Crying Game (1992) Neil Jordan
December Bride (1990) Thaddeus O'Sullivan
The Devil's Own (1997) Alan Pakula
Devil's Rock (1938) Germain Burger and Richard Hayward
The Early Bird (1936) Donovan Pedelty
The End of the World Man (1985) Bill Miskelly and Marie Jones
Four Days in July (1984) Mike Leigh
Hennessy (1975) Don Sharp
Hidden Agenda (1990) Ken Loach
High Boot Benny (1993) Joe Comerford
Hush-A-Bye Baby (1989) Margo Harkin
In the Name of the Father (1993) Jim Sheridan
Irish and Proud of It (1936) Donovan Pedelty

Jacqueline (1956) Roy Baker
The Long Good Friday (1979) John MacKenzie
The Luck of the Irish (1935) Donovan Pedelty
Maeve (1981) John Davies and Pat Murphy
No Surrender (1985) Peter Smith
Nothing Personal (1995) Thaddeus O'Sullivan
Odd Man Out (1946) Carol Reed
The Outsider (1979) Tony Luraschi
Patriot Games (1992) Phillip Noyce
A Prayer for the Dying (1987) Mike Hodges
A Quiet Day in Belfast (1973) Milad Bessada
The Railway Station Man (1992) Michael Whyte
Resurrection Man (1998) Marc Evans
Some Mother's Son (1996) Terry George
This Is the Sea (1996) Mary McGuckian
The Writing on the Wall (1981) Armand Gatti
You, Me and Marley (1992) Richard Spence

Short narrative films (under 60 minutes)

After '68 (1994) Stephen Burke
Attracta (1983) Kieran Hickey
Borderland (1993) Dominic Lees
Contact (1985) Alan Clarke
81 (1996) Stephen Burke
Elephant (1989) Alan Clarke
Henri (1994) John Forte
A Letter from Ulster (1944) Brian Desmond Hurst
Skin Tight (1994) John Forte
The Visit (1992) Orla Walsh

Television drama

All Things Bright and Beautiful (1994) writer/director Barry
    Devlin
Arise and Go Now (1991) writer Owen O'Neill, director Danny
    Boyle
Crossfire (1988) writer John McNeil, director Ken Hannan
The Daily Woman (1985) writer Bernard Mac Laverty, director
    Martyn Friend
Dear Sarah (1990) writer Tom McGurk, director Frank
    Cvitanovich
Force of Duty (1992) writers Bill Morrison and Chris Ryder,
    director Pat O'Connor
Harry's Game [aka *Belfast Assassin*] (1982) novelist Gerald
    Seymour director Lawrence Clark

In the Border Country (1991) writer Daniel Mornin, director
  Thaddeus O'Sullivan
Love Lies Bleeding (1993) writer Ronan Bennett, director Michael
  Winterbottom
Naming the Names (1986) writer Anne Devlin, director Stuart
  Burge
Shoot to Kill (1990) writer Michael Eaton, director Peter
  Kominsky
We'll Support You Evermore (1985) writer/director Douglas
  Livingstone

Feature-length documentary films

The Cause of Ireland (1983) Geoffrey Bell, Chris Reeves, Lin
  Solomon, John Underhay
The Patriot Game (1979) Arthur Mac Caig
A Sense of Loss (1972) Marcel Ophüls

Short documentary films (under 60 minutes)

At the Edge of the Union (1985) Paul Hamann
Behind the Mask (1989) Frank Martin
Between Ourselves: Songs, Satire and Some Sense (1993) Marilyn
  Hyndman and David Hyndman
Creggan (1979) Michael Whyte and Mary Holland
Dragon's Teeth (1990) Tom Collins
Dust on the Bible (1989) John T Davis
Facing the Future (1991) Desmond Bell
Fintona: A Study of Housing Discrimination (1954) Republic of
  Ireland Government Information film
Irish News, British Stories (1984) David Fox
Irish Ways (1989) Arthur Mac Caig
The Kickhams (1994) Brendan Byrne
The Last Colony (1994) Martin Dillon
Mother Ireland (1988) Anne Crilly
Moving Myths (1989) Cahal McLaughlin
No Simple Choice (1993) Siobhán O'Gorman
Off Our Knees (1988) Bernadette McAliskey ('68 Committee)
Our Words Jump to Life (1988) David Hyndman and Marilyn
  Hyndman
Pack Up the Troubles (1991) Cahal McLaughlin and Lin Solomon
Picturing Derry (1985) David Fox
Power in the Blood (1989) John T Davis
Redeeming History: Protestant Nationalism in Ireland (1990)
  Desmond Bell
Schizophrenic City (1990) David Hyndman

Shankill (1994) Mary Holland and Michael Whyte
Shell Shock Rock (1978) John T Davis
The Silent War (1990) Michael Grigsby
Steelchest, Nail in the Boot, and the Barking Dog (1987) David
    Hammond
Too Long a Sacrifice (1984) Michael Grigsby
Trouble the Calm (1989) David Fox
Under the Health Surface As Told By Belfast Women (1986)
    Marilyn Hyndman and Frances Bowyer
Unfinished Business (1993) David Hyndman
*We'll Fight and No Surrender: Ulster Loyalism and the Protestant
    Sense of History* (1987) Desmond Bell

Selected bibliography

Given that the subject of Northern Ireland has attracted more than its fair share of scholarship, this bibliography is restricted to books of note and of related interest. Pertinent journal articles may be found in the notes to each chapter. The bibliography is divided into two general sections: history and politics; and criticism and culture.

History and politics

Adamson, Ian. *The Cruithin: A History of the Ulster Land and People* (Belfast: Pretani Press, 1974).

Akenson, Donald Harman. *God's Peoples: Covenant and Land in South Africa, Israel, and Ulster* (Ithaca; London: Cornell University Press, 1992).

Anderson, Benedict. *Imagined Communities: Reflections on the Origin and Spread of Nationalism* (London; New York: Verso, 1991).

Aughey, Arthur. *Under Siege: Ulster Unionism and the Anglo-Irish Agreement* (London: Hurst & Company; New York: St. Martin's Press; 1989).

Bardon, Jonathan. *A History of Ulster* (Belfast: The Blackstaff Press, 1992).

Bew, Paul, Peter Gibbon and Henry Patterson. *Northern Ireland 1921-1994: Political Forces and Social Classes* (London: Serif, 1995).

Bloomfield, Ken. *Stormont in Crisis: A Memoir* (Belfast: The Blackstaff Press, 1994).

Boyce, D George and Alan O'Day (eds). *The Making of Modern Irish History: Revisionism and the revisionist controversy* (London; New York: Routledge, 1996).

Boyle, Kevin and Tom Hadden. *Northern Ireland: The Choice* (London: Penguin, 1994).

Brady, Ciaran (ed). *Interpreting Irish History: The Debate on Historical Revisionism 1938-1994* (Blackrock: Irish Academic Press, 1994).

Bruce, Steve. *The Red Hand: Protestant Paramilitaries in Northern Ireland* (Oxford; New York: Oxford University Press, 1992).

——————. *The Edge of the Union: The Ulster Loyalist Political Vision* (Oxford: Oxford University Press, 1994).

The Cadogan Group. *Northern Limits: Boundaries of the Attainable in Northern Ireland Politics* (Belfast: The Cadogan Group, 1992).

——————. *Lost Accord: The 1995 Frameworks and the Search for a Settlement in Northern Ireland* (Belfast: The Cadogan Group, 1995).

Coogan, Tim Pat. *The IRA* (London: HarperCollinsPublishers, 1995).

Darby, John (ed). *Northern Ireland: The Background To The Conflict* (Belfast: Appletree Press, 1983).

Doherty, Frank. *The Stalker Affair* (Cork; Dublin: The Mercier Press, 1986).

Farrell, Michael. *Northern Ireland: the Orange State*, second edition (London: Pluto Press, 1980).

Foster, R F. *Modern Ireland 1600-1972* (Harmondsworth: Penguin Books, 1989).

—————— (ed). *The Oxford Illustrated History of Ireland* (Oxford; New York: Oxford University Press, 1989).

Fukuyama, Francis. *The End of History and the Last Man* (New York: Avon Books, 1992).

Galliher, John F and Jerry L Degregary. *Violence in Northern Ireland: Understanding Protestant Perspectives* (Dublin: Gill and Macmillan, 1985).

Hamill, Desmond. *Pig in the Middle: The Army in Northern Ireland 1969-1985* (London: Methuen, 1986).

Ignatieff, Michael. *Blood and Belonging: Journeys into the New Nationalism* (London: Vintage, 1994).

Keena, Colm. *Gerry Adams – A Biography* (Cork: Mercier Press, 1990).

Lee, J J. *Ireland 1912-1985: Politics and Society* (Cambridge: Cambridge University Press, 1989).

Loughlin, James. *Ulster Unionism and British National Identity Since 1885* (New York: St. Martin's Press, 1995).

McGarry, John and Brendan O'Leary. *Explaining Northern Ireland: Broken Images* (Oxford, UK; Cambridge, MA: Blackwell, 1995).

Mac Curtain, Margaret and Donncha Ó Corráin (eds). *Women in Irish Society: The Historical Dimension* (Dublin: Arlen Press, 1978).

Miller, David W. *Queen's Rebels: Ulster Loyalism in Historical Perspective* (Dublin: Gill and Macmillan; New York: Barnes & Noble Books; 1978).

——————————. *On Nationality* (Oxford: Clarendon Press, 1995).

Moody, T W, F X Martin and F J Byrne (eds). *A New History of Ireland vol. 8. A Chronology of Irish History to 1976. A Companion to Irish History Part 1* (Oxford: Clarendon Press, 1982).

Nairn, Tom. *The Break-Up of Britain: Crisis and Neo-Nationalism*, second expanded edition (London: Verso, 1981).

Nelson, Sarah. *Ulster's Uncertain Defenders: Protestant Political, Paramilitary and Community Groups and the Northern Ireland Conflict* (Belfast: Appletree Press, 1984).

O Connor, Fionnuala. *In Search of a State: Catholics in Northern Ireland* (Belfast: The Blackstaff Press, 1993).

O'Brien, Conor Cruise. *States of Ireland* (London: Hutchinson, 1972).

O'Malley, Padraig. *Biting at the Grave: The Irish Hunger Strikes and the Politics of Despair* (Boston: Beacon Press, 1990).

Porter, Norman. *Rethinking Unionism: An Alternative Vision for Northern Ireland* (Belfast: The Blackstaff Press, 1996).

Rose, Richard. *Governing Without Consensus: An Irish Perspective* (London: Faber and Faber, 1971).

Ryder, Chris. *The RUC: A Force Under Fire* (London: Methuen, 1989).

Sutton, Malcolm (compiler). *Bear in mind these dead...: An Index of Deaths from the Conflict in Ireland 1969-1993* (Belfast: Beyond the Pale Publications, 1994).

Townshend, Charles (ed). *Consensus in Ireland: Approaches and Recessions* (Oxford: Clarendon Press, 1988).

Ward, Margaret. *In Their Own Voice: Women and Irish Nationalism* (Dublin: Attic Press, 1995).

Whyte, John. *Interpreting Northern Ireland* (Oxford: Clarendon Press, 1990).

Wichert, Sabine. *Northern Ireland since 1945* (London; New York: Longman, 1991).

Criticism and culture

Ah! Mischief: The Writer and Television (London: Faber and Faber, 1982).

Bell, Desmond. *Acts of Union: Youth Culture and Sectarianism in Northern Ireland* (London: Macmillan, 1990).

Bell, Geoffrey. *The Protestants of Ulster* (London: Pluto Press, 1976).

Bleasdale, Alan. *No Surrender: A Deadpan Farce* (London; Boston: Faber and Faber, 1986).

Brandt, George W. *British Television Drama in the 1980s* (Cambridge: Cambridge University Press, 1993).

———————————— (ed). *British television drama* (Cambridge: Cambridge University Press, 1981).

Butler, David. *The Trouble With Reporting Northern Ireland: The British State, the Broadcast Media and Nonfictional Representation of the Conflict* (Aldershot; Brookfield USA; Hong Kong; Singapore; Sydney: Avebury, 1995).

Cairns, David and Shaun Richards. *Writing Ireland: colonialism, nationalism and culture* (Manchester: Manchester University Press, 1988).

Cathcart, Rex. *The Most Contrary Region: The BBC in Northern Ireland 1924-1984* (Belfast: The Blackstaff Press, 1984).

Crozier, Maurna (ed). *Cultural Traditions in Northern Ireland: 'Varieties of Irishness'* (Belfast: Institute of Irish Studies The Queen's University of Belfast, 1989).

——————————— (ed). *Cultural Traditions in Northern Ireland: 'Varieties of Britishness'* (Belfast: Institute of Irish Studies The Queen's University of Belfast, 1990).

Cubitt, Sean. *Timeshift: On video culture* (London; New York: Routledge, 1991).

Curtis, Liz. *Ireland: The propaganda war: The media and the 'battle for hearts and minds'* (London; Sydney: Pluto Press, 1984).

Dawe, Gerald and Edna Longley (eds). *Across a Roaring Hill: The Protestant imagination in modern Ireland. Essays in Honour of John Hewitt* (Belfast; Dover, NH: The Blackstaff Press, 1985).

Dawe, Gerald, Edna Longley and John Wilson Foster (eds). *The Poet's Place: Ulster literature and society. Essays in honour of John Hewitt, 1907-87* (Belfast: Institute of Irish Studies, 1991).

——————————————————————————————. *Against Piety: Essays in Irish Poetry* (Belfast: Lagan Press, 1995).

Deane, Seamus. *Celtic Revivals: Essays in Modern Irish Literature 1880-1980* (London: Faber and Faber, 1985).

——————————— (ed). *Ireland's Field Day* (London: Hutchinson, 1985).

———————————, Andrew Carpenter and Jonathan Williams (eds). *The Field Day Anthology of Irish Writing*, volume III (Derry: Field Day Publications, 1991).

DeFelice, James. *Filmguide to Odd Man Out* (Bloomington; London: Indiana University Press, 1975).

Fennell, Desmond. *Heresy: The Battle of Ideas in Modern Ireland* (Belfast: The Blackstaff Press, 1993).

Foster, John Wilson. *Forces and Themes in Ulster Fiction* (Dublin: Gill and Macmillan, 1974).

——————————. *Colonial Consequences: Essays in Irish Literature and Culture* (Dublin: The Lilliput Press, 1991).

—————————— (ed). *The Idea of the Union: Statements and Critiques in Support of the Union of Great Britain and Northern Ireland* (Belfast; Vancouver: Belcouver Press, 1995).

Friedberg, Anne. *Window Shopping: Cinema and the Postmodern* (Berkeley; Los Angeles; Oxford: University of California Press, 1993).

George, Terry and Jim Sheridan. *Some Mother's Son: The Screenplay* (New York: Grove, 1996).

Gibbons, Luke. *Transformations in Irish Culture* (Cork: Cork University Press, 1996).

Green, F L. *Odd Man Out* (London: The Book Club, 1946).

Hayes, Maurice. *Whither Cultural Diversity?*, second edition (Belfast: Community Relations Council, 1993).

Hill, John, Martin McLoone and Paul Hainsworth (eds). *Border Crossing: Film in Ireland, Britain and Europe* (Belfast and London: Institute of Irish Studies in association with the University of Ulster and the British Film Institute, 1994).

Hughes, Eamonn (ed). *Culture and politics in Northern Ireland 1960-1990* (Milton Keynes; Philadelphia: Open University Press, 1991).

Hutchinson, Ron. *Rat in the Skull* (London: Methuen, 1984).

Jordan, Neil. *Angel* (London; Boston: Faber and Faber, 1989).

——————————. *A Neil Jordan Reader* (New York: Viking, 1993).

——————————. *The Crying Game* (London: Vintage, 1993).

——————————. *Michael Collins: Screenplay and Film Diary* (London: Vintage, 1996).

Kearney, Richard. *Transitions: Narratives in Modern Irish Culture* (Manchester: Manchester University Press, 1988).

Kilroy, James. *The 'Playboy' Riots* (Dublin: The Dolmen Press, 1971).

Lloyd, David. *Nationalism and Minor Literature: James Clarence Mangan and the Emergence of Irish Cultural Nationalism* (Berkeley,

CA: University of California Press, 1987).

—————. *Anomalous States: Irish Writing and the Post-Colonial Moment* (Dublin: The Lilliput Press, 1993).

Loftus, Belinda. *Mirrors: Orange and Green* (Dundrum: Picture Press, 1994).

Lundy, Jean and Aodán Mac Póilin (eds). *Styles of Belonging: The Cultural Identities of Ulster* (Belfast: Lagan Press, 1992).

McIlroy, Brian. *World Cinema 4: Ireland* (Trowbridge: Flicks Books, 1989).

McLoone, Martin (ed), *Culture, Identity and Broadcasting in Ireland: Local Issues, Global Perspectives. Proceedings of the Cultural Traditions Group/Media Studies UUC Symposium, 21 February, 1991* (Belfast: Institute of Irish Studies, The Queen's University of Belfast, 1991).

Manvell, Roger (ed). *Three British Screen Plays* (London: Methuen & Co., 1950).

Moss, Robert F. *The Films of Carol Reed* (London: Macmillan, 1987).

Nichols, Bill. Ideology and the Image: Social Representation in the *Cinema and Other Media* (Bloomington: Indiana University Press, 1981).

—————. *Representing Reality: Issues and Concepts in Documentary* (Bloomington and Indianapolis: Indiana University Press, 1991).

O'Regan, John (ed). John T Davis (Dublin: Gandon Editions, 1993).

Renov, Michael. *Theorizing Documentary* (New York: Routledge, 1993).

Richtarik, Marilynn J. *Acting Between the Lines: The Field Day Theatre Company and Irish Cultural Politics 1980-1984* (Oxford: Clarendon Press, 1994).

Roche, Anthony. *Contemporary Irish Drama: From Beckett to McGuinness* (New York: St Martin's Press, 1995).

Rockett, Kevin (ed). *The Irish Filmography: Fiction Films 1896-1996* (Dublin: Red Mountain Media, 1996).

——————, Luke Gibbons and John Hill. *Cinema and Ireland* (London; Sydney: Croom Helm, 1987).

Rolston, Bill. *Politics and Painting: Murals and Conflict in Northern Ireland* (Rutherford; Madison; Teaneck: Fairleigh Dickinson University Press; London; Toronto: Associated University Presses; 1991).

——————. *Drawing Support: Murals in the North of Ireland* (Belfast: Beyond the Pale Publications, 1992).

Rosenthal, Alan (ed). *New Challenges for Documentary* (Berkeley; Los Angeles; London: University of California Press, 1988).

Said, Edward W. *Culture & Imperialism* (New York: Vintage, 1994).

——————. *Orientalism* (New York: Vintage Books, 1994).

Stevens, Matthew. *Directory of Irish and Irish-Related Films* (Trowbridge: Flicks Books, 1989).

Tóibín, Colm. *Bad Blood: A Walk Along The Irish Border* (London: Vintage, 1994).

Tulloch, John. *Television Drama: Agency, audience and myth* (London; New York: Routledge, 1990).

Vaughan, Dai. *Odd Man Out* (London: British Film Institute, 1995).

Wapshott, Nicholas. *The Man Between: A Biography of Carol Reed* (London: Chatto & Windus, 1990).

Waugh, Thomas (ed). *"Show Us Life": Toward a History and Aesthetics of the Committed Documentary* (Metuchen, NJ; London: The Scarecrow Press, 1984).

Winston, Brian. *Claiming the Real: The Griersonian Documentary and Its Legitimations* (London: British Film Institute, 1995).

Index